MW00784609

MODERN HANDGUN FUNDAMENTALS:
From Beginner to Pro

Brad Engmann

I would like to dedicate this book to:

My wonderful, supportive wife, who has put up with my going to sleep at 3am on many occasions due to long writing sessions!

My parents and family who have always had my back in any situation, thick and thin, and who have helped me become the person I am.

The men and women of law enforcement and the US military who put their lives on the line every day so that we may live free.

Special thanks to:

Peter Palma, USMC, who has provided me with a great deal of advice and knowledge through the development of this book.

Design by Bruce Gardner
Photography by Pat Johnson Studios

CONTENTS

DISCLAIMER

Shooting a firearm is an inherently dangerous activity. Live ammunition can easily maim or kill someone. It can only take one small mistake or lapse of judgment for a serious accident to occur. It is YOUR responsibility to use proper range safety procedures and exercise extreme caution when handling a firearm at any time. It is YOUR responsibility to determine when something potentially unsafe is transpiring. Treat every gun as if it were loaded and be careful.

This book is designed as a guide for educational purposes only, and is not meant to cover the particulars of safety in every possible situation. The author of this book accepts no responsibility for any property damage, injury, or death that occurs either directly or indirectly from the training concepts or drills that are contained herein.

ABOUT THIS BOOK

ABOUT ME

I started off in the world of firearms knowing very little about anything. I do not come from a family of shooters, and growing up in San Francisco, California, my neighbors weren't exactly keen on them either.   For some reason or another when I was 13, I convinced my dad to take me shooting at the local static handgun range for my birthday (perhaps it was due to my first viewing of Bruce Willis in Die Hard). I had fired a gun exactly two times leading up to that point- a .22 at summer camp, and a scoped air rifle. Other than that, my sole exposure was through Duck Hunt and movies/TV.

I was immediately hooked.

Since that time throughout my teens, my dad and I frequented the range. Their facilities were decent and consisted of about 10 lanes going to a maximum distance of 50 feet. Rental guns were aplenty, but I quickly picked up a couple of favorites- a Sig P229 and a Beretta 92F. My dad hadn't had very much shooting experience at all prior to coming out with me, so the two of us stumbled along for awhile, but eventually picked up some things on our own. We were regulars, going about 2-3 times a month, and we eventually decided to buy our own gun, a .40 caliber Beretta 96F Brigadier Elite when I was 16. I took care of it like a first time mother with a newborn.

After some time on a static single lane range, my interest began to wane. I was pretty dialed with my pistol, but I wasn't really training for anything. Plus shooting at a single target became monotonous. I took a many year long hiatus and veered towards my other hobbies- baseball and auto racing. The latter was particularly interesting due to the emphasis on speed and consistency. Unfortunately it was also very time consuming and expensive. Fast forward a number of years again and I eventually rediscovered shooting, but this time sought out something that could get my heart rate a little bit higher. I found practical pistol shooting with the United States Practical Shooting Association entirely by accident by watching an episode of Mail Call on the History Channel featuring Dave Sevigny- who is one of the best in the world. (USPSA is the American version of IPSC- International Practical

Shooting Confederation.) This particular sport really appealed to me because it combined many different skill sets including engaging multiple targets, speed shooting, shooting on the move, and incredible accuracy. This seemed to me like racing with a handgun.

My first competition was an IDPA match (International Defensive Pistol Association) and I was so nervous I forgot my earplugs for the first stage! However, it was quite addictive and I kept going back once a month or so. Eventually I got really serious about my sport and became a Range Officer, which meant I had keys to the range (multiple bays, props, etc) and could practice whenever I wanted. Within six months I went from a B class to a Master class USPSA shooter. Within a year I became a Grandmaster. Since then I've pulled out all the stops. I now shoot regularly about 35,000 rounds a year and compete across the United States. Recently I placed 8th Overall in the USPSA Production Division National Championship, won the USPSA Production Area 2 Championship (California, Arizona, New Mexico, Colorado), won Stock Service Pistol in the Steel Challenge World Championship, finished 3rd Overall in the US IPSC Production Nationals, and came in 3rd in the USPSA Production Area 1 Championship (Oregon, Washington, Idaho, Nevada, Utah, Montana, Wyoming).

WHAT YOU WILL TAKE FROM THIS BOOK

One important thing to remember is that a great deal that I've learned about shooting I've had to learn on my own. While I have had some very good advice from some very considerate and helpful people at my home club, I've never had a coach or a mentor *per se*. Even then, I don't believe in just doing something because someone else told you to, and I don't believe that spending a few hours in a classroom to gain a certification automatically makes you an expert. I've learned through countless hours of practice and the continued observation of people who are better than me at gunhandling. I'm still learning, and have had the privilege of shooting with some of the best in the world. Technique can always be refined further, and often it is. This book represents some of the stuff I've had to learn the hard way, which I'm glad to share with you at a fraction of the cost.

If you're a brand new shooter picking up a gun for the first time, you'll be guided towards making a purchase decision that suits you. You'll learn what to look for in a handgun and why it makes sense. Then you can start with the basics of shooting technique. By going through this program, you'll be able to understand the rationale behind the fundamentals of modern shooting, and be able to critique your own technique to evolve your skills. If you're an experienced shooter that has been around guns for awhile, you can take away the advanced points in this book about correcting problems and bad habits, as well as learn how you can be faster and more accurate. Even if you've been to a lot of classes and think you have everything down pat, check out the basics on grip and stance anyway. What you're doing might look correct from outward appearances, but could still use some improvement. I've adjusted my technique countless times to arrive on something that makes sense to me and there's no harm to periodic self-evaluation. Also, be sure to read the equipment selection sections, as you might find that your current firearm or accessory isn't the best for you.

There are many different shooting "systems" out there, all of which have some degree of justification as to their effectiveness. What I recommend to anyone trying to become better at anything is to constantly experiment to figure out WHY something works and to improve upon it. I've taken great pains to explain why I currently practice my methods. If you disagree with me, then go experiment in a controlled atmosphere! Try your method, then try mine. If you find it works better for you one way, then do it. But avoid what I call the "golf swing dilemma." Inevitably when you try something new your ability will decrease in the short term. For example, if you're used to swinging a golf club incorrectly and someone fixes it, you're going to shoot a worse score until you adjust. Many people will immediately go back to their old technique to eliminate the performance dip and save themselves from possible embarrassment. This is the wrong way, and will inhibit your future potential. Give everything time and have patience.

One more thing: This book is primarily designed to teach you marksmanship, not gunfight tactics. There are more qualified people than me to tell you about large team based room clearing. (Although I have included some tips on defensive shooting, which should serve as a good foundation.) You can apply the fundamentals you develop here according to your needs. Once you know that you can hit whatever you put your sights on it's a lot easier to implement advanced offensive/defensive confrontation skills.

Above all else, be safe and good luck with your shooting!

CHAPTER 1

TYPES OF HANDGUNS

HOW A HANDGUN WORKS

A gun is a pretty simple thing really. The principle it operates on is expansion of gas during an explosion. Essentially it puts a projectile in a confined space and lights off a charge right behind it. Since the gas from the explosion has nowhere else to go, it will shoot out the front taking the path of least resistance and pushing the projectile along the way.

For centuries, guns were just based on pouring powder down the barrel then cramming a round ball wrapped in wadding (to seal the gaps) down there in front of it. Then the shooter would ignite the powder through a hole in the side of the gun, and BOOM! Today we have cartridges which do much of the same thing. *(See Figure 1)* The only difference is that everything is self contained. A brass casing is filled up with powder, and a primer (or rim ignition)

Handguns come in all types, shapes, sizes, mechanisms, and materials including:

- *Steel & polymer*

- *Hammer & Striker fired*

- *Semi-automatic & revolver*

is put in the rear. A bullet is then seated in the top of the case and crimped in so it can't shift position. The result is quite durable and does not go off easily except in controlled circumstances. When the primer is struck with a hard object with a good deal of force, it will direct an explosion towards the powder. The powder will turn to gas quickly creating a lot of pressure. This pressure will be enough to propel the bullet forward.

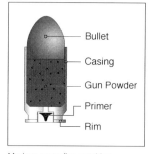

Modern centerfire cartridge

Ever see in a movie where ammo falls into a fire and shoots bullets everywhere in the room? It doesn't happen in real life. Why? Because to have pressure you need to have compression. This is what the chamber of the gun is for. When a cartridge sits in the chamber of a gun and is fired, a seal is created on all sides by the casing of the cartridge except pointing forwards. This directed blast is much more concentrated than a cartridge just going off in the environment.

In order for the gun to fire a number of things need to happen. First off, in the typical modern handgun there are multiple safeties which prevent the gun from firing unless the operator intends it to. Some are deactivated merely by pulling the trigger, while others must be switched off. (These are discussed in detail later) Once these are out of the way, the trigger's job is to cause the firing pin to be propelled towards the cartridge at a high rate of speed. This will cause the cartridge to detonate and the gun to fire. Now how this actually mechanically happens (and how the cartridge gets in the right position in the first place) varies drastically based on the type and manufacturer of the handgun. As you'll learn, there are a plethora of individual designs which are used to accomplish this relatively straightforward task in the most.

Point of note: Typically the words "bullet," "ammo," "round," and "cartridge" are used interchangeably when describing ammunition ready to be fired. However, a bullet in actuality just refers to just the projectile that is fired from the gun. A "shell case" or "casing" is the empty piece of brass remaining when a cartridge is fired.

HANDGUN DESIGNS

A note about this chapter: There are tons of different types of guns and firing mechanisms with a near infinite number of particularities. The objective of this chapter is not to go into detail about the nuances of each gun, but rather to give a general overview of the types of modern guns you'll encounter. If you want to learn more about gun history, there is plenty of literature out there discussing the evolution of the handgun, but it is beyond the scope here.

SEMI-AUTOMATIC

A semi-automatic handgun is now the most common type. When you picture a pistol that has a slide that moves back and forth and ejects spent shell casings when fired then you're probably thinking of a semi-auto. The reason it's called as such is because as the shooter you

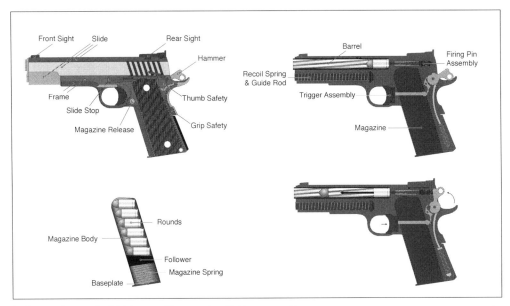

Basic parts diagram of a 1911- Frame, slide, magazine with trigger assembly

don't have to do anything other than pull the trigger. Once you fire a round, the slide will cycle and eject the spent shell casing you just used, and push another round into the chamber. Then you just have to release the trigger and pull it again to fire. The slide will also lock back on an empty chamber.

This type of pistol has three basic components:

- **Slide.** The top half of the gun. It is held in place on the frame by two rails that it slides (get it) on back and forth. The impact of the gun firing causes the slide to move rearward and cycle additional rounds from the magazine into the barrel's chamber to be fired. It contains:

  - **Barrel.** This is what the projectiles (bullets) actually come out of. The barrel contains rifling which adds a spin to the bullet to stabilize it in flight. The term "bore" also commonly refers to the barrel of a handgun. The barrel remains locked on in place against the frame for the most part while the slide cycles (after the gun fires). The chamber is visible just before the rifling in the photo of the Glock 35 barrel.

Rifling of a Glock 35

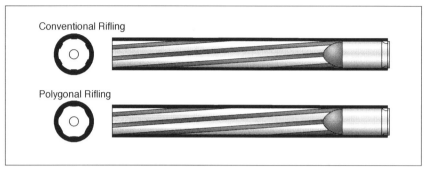

Conventional vs Polygonal rifling

- **Firing Pin (Striker) Assembly.** This is a steel pin that whacks into the primer of a bullet and usually is connected to a spring.

Extractor on a Glock 35

- **Extractor.** A hook that attaches to the extraction rim of the cartridge when the slide goes into battery (meaning that the slide is locked in the forward position and ready to be fired). This is either under mechanical tension or spring loaded. When the gun fires and the slide moves to the rear, the extractor pulls the empty shell case towards the rear. It will then be knocked out by the ejector (part of the frame).

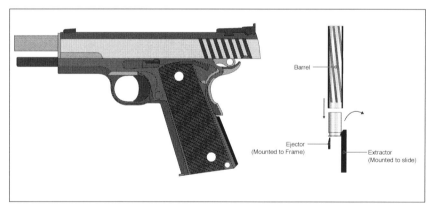

Basic operation of an extractor

- **Recoil Spring/Guide Rod Assembly.**
  This is wedged between the barrel and the slide. When the gun fires, the recoil spring compresses and acts as a shock absorber of the recoil to prevent the slide from slamming into the frame of the gun. Once the gun has

Recoil spring & guide rod

4

fired, the recoil spring then causes the gun to move forward and lock back into battery. The guide rod simply guides the path of the recoil spring.

- **Sights.** Used for aiming the gun (duh!).

- **Various Safeties.** These will be covered in detail later on in this chapter.

- *Frame (Receiver).* This is the "grip" portion of the handgun, and is also the part of the gun that's actually registered with the Department of Justice. One gun can have many different slides for it.

    - **Trigger Assembly.** When you pull the trigger in a semi-auto pistol, you're always causing some kind of spring loaded tension to be released. Once it is released, the firing pin either propels itself (striker fired handgun) or is whacked (via a hammer) towards the primer of the cartridge. Once the gun goes bang, the action of the slide moving back causes the trigger mechanism to decouple and spring loaded tension to be created again (how this happens depends on the manufacturer). In order to reset the mechanism, you must release the trigger to prepare for another shot.

    - **Hammer.** Found in certain types of semi-autos, the hammer is used for hitting the firing pin when it's released. It is held under spring tension from the mainspring (in the grip of the gun) and when the trigger is pulled, it drops on the exposed firing pin in the slide.

    - **Locking Block.** This is what the barrel sits on and is connected to when the gun is fully assembled. Typically when a semi-auto handgun fires, the barrel will tilt down towards the rear of the gun to allow the chamber to get lower and allow the next round to enter it more easily.

    - **Ejector.** A rod that whacks the shell case out of the gun as it's being pulled to the rear by the extractor after the gun is fired.

    - **Magazine Release.** A button that when pressed will drop the magazine.

    - **Slide Stop.** This will hold the slide back and allow you access to the chamber. epressing this will release the slide forward.

    - **Various Safeties.** These will be covered elsewhere in the book.

- *Magazine.* This is where the cartridges are stored under spring pressure. They feed the rounds into the chamber of the gun as the slide moves back and forth. It is held in place by a latch connected to the magazine release. Also, once the magazine is empty, the follower (that thing that pushes up on the bullets) will contact your slide stop lever and hold the slide back after the last round fired. Upon inserting a new magazine, you can drop this lever and be ready to fire without having to manually pull back on and cycle the slide.

Striker-Fired

A striker-fired handgun is a popular version of the semi-auto. It utilizes a simple concept of releasing spring pressure to catapult the striker (firing pin) towards the primer. There are variations in firing mechanisms between manufacturers, but the basic principle is that the striker is attached to a spring within the slide. When you drop the slide forward, the recoil spring pressure allows the slide to lock into place, and the chamber to be sealed. As the slide moves forward, the part of the striker which extends below the slide will catch onto a piece of metal connected to the trigger assembly called the sear. This causes the striker to be held under tension because the striker spring wants to push the striker forward, but cannot because the striker is being held in place by the sear. When you pull the trigger, you effectively are moving the sear out of the way (typically downwards) so that the striker is released and propelled towards the primer of the bullet.

Basic striker-fired pistol mechanism

Common models of striker fired handguns are the Glock series, the Smith & Wesson M&P Series, and the Springfield XD Series. These usually come with polymer frames instead of steel which makes them lighter. They also typically come with a wide swath of internal safeties which prevent the gun from accidentally firing if dropped. They usually do not have any external manually operated safeties, which means that if you pick up the gun in your hand and pull the trigger, it will fire. There is no external hammer, and since there is only one firing mechanism, each pull will feel exactly the same, unlike DA/SA which is covered next.

DA/SA

DA/SA stands for Double Action/Single Action. Unlike striker fired handguns, these models come with an external hammer to activate the firing pin. In this type of handgun, the firing pin also rests in its channel with a spring attached. However, the spring actually pushes the firing pin away from the primer. This is because when the hammer falls, it will have enough force to overcome that spring pressure and cause the pin to move forward for a split second to set off the cartridge.

Double action is the term for when the trigger is pulled and the hammer moves back to cock itself, then drops in one motion. Single Action is when the hammer is already back and the trigger pull releases the hammer. Obviously a DA/SA gun incorporates both features so that on the first shot the hammer will go back then forward. When the slide cycles over it, the hammer stays back for single action shots. Typically a double action pull is considerably heavier and longer than one in a single action or striker fired handgun. The single action is usually much lighter and crisper.

Hammer of a DA/SA Sig P226

DA/SA handguns may or may not incorporate external safeties or decocking levers (which safely drop the hammer from single action without firing the round). They also contain multiple internal safeties to prevent the gun from firing if dropped. DA/SA examples include the Sig P226 and Beretta 92F.

Single-Action Only

The single action only handgun shares the similarity with the DA/SA in that it has an external hammer. However, if the hammer is not manually cocked first then the gun will not fire. A typical example of this type of handgun is the famous 1911. Single action handguns can have some of the best triggers imaginable due to the fact that the entire mechanism simply drops the hammer, which is held in place by the sear.

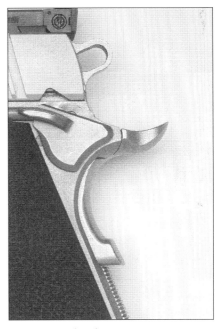

Since one would obviously not want to drop a safety-less cocked single action handgun, there are typically a number of associated safeties which come with this type of pistol. Two of the most common are the grip safety which is at the top of the handle under the beavertail, (which will not allow the gun to fire if not depressed) and the thumb safety (which if clicked up will not allow the gun to fire). Additionally a "half-cock" notch might be present where if one slips before cocking the hammer all the way, it won't fall on the primer.

Beavertail grip safety of a 1911

Double-Action Only

The Sig P226 DAO is an example of this type of handgun. A double action only is quite simple. The hammer always stays down and pulling the trigger will cause the hammer to go all the way back then all the way forward again. Typically this type involves a heavy and long pull.

Polymer or Steel?

Semi-Auto handguns come in two main frame types- polymer or steel. The frame rails and slides are always made from metal however. (No a Glock can't pass through an x-ray machine undetected!) Polymer is lighter but incredibly durable, and also typically has some stippling cast into the plastic to provide enhanced grip. Steel is heavier and can provide some advantage in recoil control due to the mass of the gun (depending on where that mass is centered in the hand). Ultimately it comes down to preference, as the polymer vs. steel debate will continue to rage well into the Johnny Quest ray-gun era. Don't worry too much about it and just pick something you like.

REVOLVER

A revolver is another type of handgun which incorporates a rotating cylinder that contains the ammunition as opposed to a spring loaded magazine found in semi-automatics. The concept is quite simple. When the hammer is pulled back either manually (single action revolvers) or by using the trigger (double action revolvers) the cylinder rotates to align the next cartridge with the barrel and hammer. This must occur in perfect synchronization because unlike the semi-auto which locks the cartridge into place within the chamber, a revolver has gaps around the cylinder and everything must line up perfectly. Then the hammer is dropped which will fall on the primer, and the gun will fire.

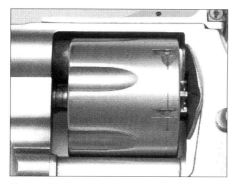
Close up of a revolver cylinder

The most common revolver design incorporates a swing-out cylinder which usually goes to the left of the gun. However, there are a number of different ways that a revolver can accept new rounds, including having the top of the gun break open (the front of the barrel and back of the gun point towards the ground), to allowing the cylinder to be removed entirely. Having access to a complete cylinder facilitates quicker reloading. Some older design revolvers such as the Colt .45 (Single Action Army or Peacemaker) require shells to be ejected and loaded one at a time.

A revolver contains the following components:

- **Barrel.** This is mounted within the frame of the pistol and cannot be removed easily like the semi-auto barrel.

- **Cylinder.** This rotates either clockwise or counterclockwise and contains a number of slots for cartridges.

- **Cylinder Release Mechanism.** This tab or lever opens the cylinder for reloading.

- **Ejection Rod.** Revolvers all come equipped with an ejection rod. For modern revolvers, when the cylinder is open, pushing on this rod will whack all of the spent cases out of the gun to prepare it for fresh ammo. Older revolvers such as the aforementioned Peacemaker required this rod to be pushed each time to knock out the shell for each cylinder. Also, top break away revolvers typically activated this rod automatically when the gun was opened.

Revolver ejection rod

- **Hammer.** This is found on the top rear of the gun. When this is released under spring tension, the hammer falls through a hole in the frame to contact and ignite a primer.

- **Transfer Bar.** Rather than having the hammer contain the firing pin (attached using a rivet), instead the hammer face is more or less flat. When it's released it strikes the transfer bar which strikes the primer. (Like a firing pin in an external hammer semi-auto.)

- **Trigger Mechanism.** Typically much more complicated than those found on semi-autos, the trigger on a revolver can be responsible for anything from simply dropping the hammer to even rotating the entire cylinder AND firing the gun in sequence.

- **Sights.** Used for aiming! Also, occasionally the rear sight serves as the cylinder release mechanism as well.

- **Half-Cock Safety.** This is designed to prevent the hammer from accidentally falling from single action if the hammer is cocked and the trigger is not pulled. Revolvers don't typically have external safeties.

- **Moon Clip.** This holds the revolver's capacity of rounds together in a metal binding so that they can all be thrown into the cylinder at once to make reloading easier. It's similar to a magazine on a semi-auto, but is not required to reload.

DA/SA

The double action/single action revolver is one of the most common designs. With this type you pick up the gun and pull the trigger each time to fire from double action (hammer travels back then falls). If you prefer a lighter, crisper trigger pull, then you can cock the gun manually to fire it from single action. However, unlike semi-autos, revolvers will not cock themselves and require the hammer to be manually pulled back before ANY single action shot. While double action shots can be heavy, the single action shot can be made ridiculously light if so desired.

Double Action Only

With this type, there is no single action option. Many double action only revolvers can be identified by the absence of a flat platform on the hammer which would be used for your thumb to cock a gun with a single action option. In some cases the hammer is even flush with or embedded into the frame. Naturally each time you pull the trigger, the cylinder also is rotated to expose the next round.

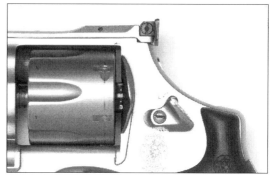
Smith & Wesson 625 hammer without spur

Single Action Only

This is one of the earliest revolver designs, and was made famous by the Colt Peacemaker. With it, you have to manually cock the gun prior to each shot, as there's no way to fire the gun with the hammer down. These typically come with a loading/unloading gate and do not feature a swing-out or breakaway cylinder. In order to load the gun, you must open the gate and drop in one round at a time, rotating the cylinder by hand as you do it. To unload the gun, you must reopen the gate and use the ejector rod to knock out each spent shell case. It's quite a time consuming process and is done today more out of nostalgia than practicality.

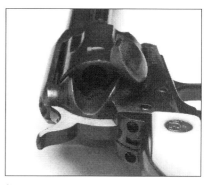
Single Action Army (Peacemaker) loading gate

There are many people who currently shoot single action replicas of historical firearms. This organization is called SASS (Single Action Shooting Society). If you're ever wondering just how fast these guns can be driven, I suggest you check it out. There are some absolutely amazing marksmen such as Spencer Hoglund (aka the Lead Dispenser), who will shoot a 150 year old design faster and more accurately than a large amount of experienced shooters with modern guns. It's pretty darn cool.

Derringer

A derringer (based on the original designer's name Henry Deringer) is a catch-all moniker for a small pistol which typically holds one to four small caliber shots (usually two). These tend to have breakaway barrels (where the top of the gun pivots and opens to expose the inside of the barrel's chamber) for top loading. Derringers are designed for concealment and as extreme close range backup weapons.

CALIBERS

The caliber of the handgun refers to the diameter of the bullet which it shoots. There are an absolute ton of different calibers which are available, both in standard and metric measurements. Sometimes a gun can shoot multiple calibers either by accommodating different cartridge lengths (such as the .357 Magnum and .38 Special- which actually have the same bullet diameter!) or by allowing for caliber conversions (by switching the barrel and a few other components).

For handguns the following represent the most commonly available.

- .22 Long Rifle
- .32 ACP
- .380 ACP
- 9mm Parabellum
- .38 Special (bullet diameter is .357")
- .357 Magnum (bullet diameter is .357")
- .38 Super (bullet diameter is 9.02mm)
- .357 SIG (bullet diameter is 9.02mm)
- .40 S&W
- .44 Magnum
- .45 ACP

(No, I'm not going to include the .500 S&W or the .50 AE in that list because those are pretty much novelty guns and are not found in common use in spite of what you might see in Hollywood.)

Point of note: Yes I know that cartridges that might appear bigger or smaller are actually the same diameter. For example, when the .38 Long Colt (the original .38) was introduced, it was a heeled bullet which had a narrower taper at the back that sat inside the case. The bullet diameter was actually the same as the case diameter- approximately .38". Later on someone developed the .38 Special which sat entirely inside the same size case, it just kept the same name in spite of the narrower actual bullet. Much like many other disciplines, the firearms world will sometimes come with older or confusing nomenclature. It's just something that you'll have to get used to, although the history is sometimes interesting.

Generally the rule of thumb is that a higher caliber usually means more recoil. The exceptions to the rule are usually as a result of more powder (which produces more velocity) in a longer case. A .357 Magnum, while narrower than a .40 S&W, will generally produce more felt recoil due to higher muzzle velocities. Also, a .44 Magnum will produce more recoil than a .45 ACP. Also, depending on the load (weight of the bullet and amount of powder in the cartridge), two different rounds of the same caliber can have dramatically different recoil.

This can be explained through the formula for kinetic energy: One half of mass multiplied by velocity squared. If the bullet weights the same but is shot with more powder (therefore resulting in a higher velocity) then it will have more power. This additional power will be directed back at you when the bullet leaves the barrel of the gun. It's simple physics.

One key misconception is that if the gun itself is smaller then it necessarily produces less recoil. This is usually the case, but only because smaller guns tend to use smaller, less powerful calibers. If you take a smaller gun versus a larger gun shooting the same round, the smaller gun will tend to have more felt recoil. This is because the mass of the pistol is lower and therefore the object tends to react more to the force exerted on it.

The two main types of ammunition for handguns are:

- **Centerfire**. In this case there is a primer seated in the back of the loaded round. A direct hit to this small explosive will cause the gun to fire. These tend to come in both rimmed and rimless varieties.

- **Rimfire.** Typically found in smaller cartridges such as the .22LR, instead of striking the primer, the firing pin or hammer will fall onto the edge of the case which will ignite a circular rim of explosive INSIDE the case.

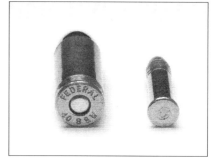

Rimless centerfire vs rimmed rimfire

Point of note: Just because the bullet fits in the gun doesn't mean it was intended to be shot in it. While a gun chambered for a .357 Magnum can shoot .38 Special rounds (lower pressure), a gun chambered for a .38 Special cannot fire .357 Magnum rounds (pressures are too high). Trying to shoot a round that's too powerful for your gun can be very dangerous. Be certain you use the right caliber too! Putting the wrong caliber of ammunition in your gun can spell disaster. Make sure you read your gun's manual to determine which loads are acceptable for it.

Here's a tip: Pick a gun with commonly available ammo. Don't go buy something in some bizarre caliber that costs $1 per round. Guess why? You'll never shoot it and it will become a very expensive paperweight.

Once you've decided on a caliber, for more information on Ammunition Selection check out the relevant section near the end of the book.

FEATURES

Each handgun, depending on the manufacturer contains a variety of features that you should keep an eye out for. Below I will explain the most common ones and go into detail about what they do. As you get more experienced, you can modify the gun to suit your needs, but this explains the generalities of a stock handgun.

- **Sights.** Pretty much all handguns have sights. On defense models and older revolvers you might just see one single front sight and a small channel in place of a rear sight. However, most handguns contain a standard notch and post sight. The principle here is to alight the front sight directly between the posts of the rear in order to aim properly (more about this is covered in the technique section of the book). These notch and post sights come in many different combinations:

– **Flat Black.** There are no markings on the sights. You're just looking at a rear matte black notch and a front matte black post. These are useful for target shooting, but are difficult to pick up in low light conditions and against dark backgrounds.

– **Three Dot.** The rear will have two dots and the front one- typically white. These white dots are easy to pick up and align, but the rear dots sometimes distract focus from the front dot.

Flat black notch & post sight

– **U Rear, Front Dot.** In this case, the rear sight is U shaped white line. The front white dot goes in the center. These are easy to line up and you won't confuse the front white dot with the U.

– **Single Dot Rear, Single Dot Front.** In this case you're supposed to put the front white dot directly above the rear dot. Sometimes your eyes have a tendency to pick up the rear dot first.

– **Front Dot Only.** For more experienced shooters that require less of a visual aid to line up the rear sights, this variation allows you to quickly pick up the front sight of the handgun which should be the main point of focus.

– **Fiber Optic.** Fiber optic channels take the place of the dots and pick up sunlight really well.

Fiber optic front sight

– **Night Sights.** Instead of a white dot, night sights contain Tritium, which glows in the dark. These can be used to great effect in dark conditions, but are typically wider (aiming is more difficult) than other sights, and are more expensive. They sometimes come standard on a pistol.

Night sights

■ *Safeties.* These are either manually activated or automatic, and all are designed to prevent the gun from firing unintentionally.

– **Gun Lock.** This device prevents anyone who does not have the specific key from using the firearm. Typically the lock is built into the back of the gun and interacts with the firing mechanism. The key does not have to be inserted in order to fire the gun, but rather the lock simply turned to a certain position (it'll stay there unless locked again).

– **Thumb Safety.** This is found on the exterior of the gun, and when activated either does not allow the shooter to pull the trigger, or will completely disengage the firing mechanism on the gun altogether. A good thumb safety (such as those found on 1911s) will allow you to easily disengage it while forming your grip (strong hand thumb pushes the safety down). Some of these only work while the gun is in single action, others are combination decockers, and will put the gun on safe and double action when used (such as on the Beretta 92F).

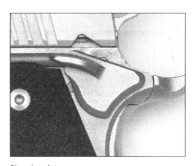

Thumb safety

– **Decocker.** This simply is a lever that when pressed will decock your gun from single to double action (drop the hammer safely). These are found on the SIG P226 for example.

– **Grip Safety.** Typically found on the 1911, 2011, and Springfield XD series, the grip safety is a lever at the back of the gun that must be depressed for the gun to fire. When it is pushed in such as while grasping the handgun, it disengages.

Decocker

– **Trigger Safety.** This is typically found on striker fired handguns such as the Glock, S&W M&P, and Springfield XD. In order for the trigger to move to the rear, you must depress a spring loaded lever on the front of the trigger face. This lever, if not depressed, will contact the frame, stopping the trigger from moving.

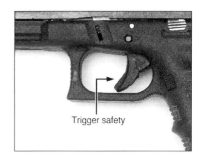

Trigger safety

– **Firing Pin Block.** In order to prevent the gun from firing when dropped, there is a spring loaded firing pin block in the firing pin channel. While this is in its normal position, it contacts the firing pin, preventing it from moving forward into the primer. When the trigger is pulled, a lever will push this block in, moving it out of the way so the gun can fire. For guns with external hammers that don't have these, the firing pin spring tension is usually good enough to prevent the gun from firing if dropped.

Firing pin block

- **Drop Safety.** This is either integral to the design of the trigger, or is included as part of a half cock notch. In a striker fired handgun, this is designed to prevent the striker from dropping off the sear if the gun falls.

- **Magazine Disconnect**. This feature prevents the gun from firing if there is no magazine in it.

- **Chamber Loaded Indicator.** This indicator will allow the user to tell either by sight or feel that the chamber is loaded. Sometimes this is as simple as seeing the extractor raised on a loaded round, which is fairly common.

- **Striker Cocked Indicator.** Found on striker fired handguns, this signifies that the gun is cocked and ready to fire.

- **Hammer Block Safety.** This is a little piece of metal in the back of a revolver which prevents a hammer mounted firing pin from going through the frame to contact a primer unless the trigger is pulled (then it's pushed out of the way).

- **Transfer Bar Safety.** This is a piece of metal also found on revolvers which prevents the revolver's hammer from hitting the transfer bar (firing pin) unless the trigger is pulled, whereupon it moves out of the way.

- *Miscellaneous.*

  - **Magazine Releases.** These come in standard, reversible, and ambidextrous forms. If you're a righty, then the gun was likely designed for you to reload using your thumb. However, many manufacturers allow these to be changed around according to user preference. Keep an eye out for stupid magazine releases (I've seen quite a few on guns, such as the "push down on the triangle" type... ugh). It should just be a button that you press, and can press easily. It should be comfortable to hold, and the magazine should not fall out while you grip the gun.

  - **Slide Catch Levers.** These will stop the slide when pushed up either manually by you, or automatically by an empty magazine. These also sometimes come in ambidextrous configurations.

  - **Lanyard Loop.** This is a little hole on the bottom part of the grip to attach things to.

  - **Accessory Rail.** This rail on the front of the gun below the slide allows mounting of accessories such as flashlights and lasers. This is a Picatinny rail, sometimes called a "tactical rail."

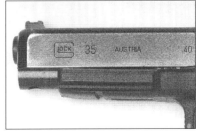
Accessory rail

– **Interchangeable Grips.** These are found on lots of handguns and can either include just the left and right sides of the gun through the grip panels, or can even include the entire backstrap of the gun (where your strong hand palm grips the handle). These are particularly useful for accommodating various hand sizes.

CHAPTER 2

WHICH ONE SHOULD I PICK?

Buying a gun for the first time can be daunting. I know this for sure because when I first picked one up I didn't know anything about it either. Fortunately when I bought my first handgun I knew how to shoot it, but I still had no clue about what features to look for. Many new buyers have little or no experience with handguns whatsoever, and intend to learn after they buy. My advice to you is to first understand why you're buying the handgun and what specific characteristics you're interested in having with your purchase.

I was recently at a gun store when I overheard the following conversation:

> *New buyer:* "Those are Glocks right?"
> *Salesperson:* "Yup"
> *New buyer:* "Those don't look that expensive. Hmmm. I know that HK over there is also a .40 but is about $200 more. Aren't those like a higher echelon of gun?"
> *Salesperson:* *(Senses the commission)* "Yeah, they certainly are. Let me show one to you!"

Pick a gun that's right for you!

- *Decide what you're going to use it for primarily*

- *More expensive doesn't necessarily mean better*

- *Try before you buy if you can*

Many new buyers make a purchasing decision based four factors. (Aside from "cool factor.")

- Name Recognition (especially through movies, TV, and music). And by this I don't mean people will buy for this reason alone, but rather those guns will be the first things new buyers ask for. This is why the Beretta was so popular in the 80s (Die Hard, Lethal Weapon, etc), the Desert Eagle in the late 90s (The Matrix), and the Glock still remains popular in music (what rhymes with Česká Zbrojovka?).

- Cost.

- How it feels in their hand.

- Perceived safety of the gun.

Additionally, they will tend to ask the salesperson questions about impossible to quantify generalities such as the gun's "stopping power." However, this ultimately makes buyers susceptible to what I call "stupid guns". In other words, I believe that there are guns out there (as well as many other products) so stupid that nobody should ever buy them. They either are way too expensive in comparison to perfectly good substitutes, very unreliable, or have inherent design flaws which make the rationally minded cringe. Unfortunately the new buyer doesn't know any better, so these guns eventually get sold. So, rather than ranting about which guns you SHOULD and SHOULDN'T buy (which will obviously reveal my bias) I will lay out the characteristics I recommend you look for in a pistol.

And don't be intimidated! Just because you don't know the nomenclature or the abbreviation for some doo-hickey on the gun, or the name of every part, doesn't mean you should let some salesman push a pricier gun on you. Every sport, every profession, and every hobby has its own vernacular. If the guy behind the counter has an attitude because you're a new shooter, screw him- give your money to somebody else who will listen to your concerns.

I strongly encourage you to try out a new gun on the range before buying!!! Gun rentals are cheap!!!

WHAT ARE YOU GOING TO USE IT FOR?

The first question which you must ask yourself prior to purchasing a handgun is "What do I need this for?" Whether it's for personal defense, target shooting, or to prepare for the impending zombie invasion, you need to decide specifically what you're looking to accomplish with it. As I've recommended earlier, you should first try out a variety of handguns either by borrowing them from a friend or renting them, because at a few hundred dollars, they can be expensive to buy. Additionally, you should learn to shoot first. To use another golf analogy, if you don't know how to play golf, then what business do you have selecting your first set of clubs? You could have a fast swing and need stiffer shafts, you could be taller and need longer clubs, but you wouldn't know that without any background. The more experience you have will allow you to more intuitively know what to seek out.

Generally speaking, there are three main types of purposes that people tend to buy handguns for: Defense, Target Shooting, and Competition, or a combination of any of the three. (Yes I know hunting is one of them, but that's a specialty field and beyond the scope of this book). The point is that you should decide what the primary purpose of the handgun is, and select accordingly even if it's for multiple uses.

Also, make sure you read the next section on **Things to Look For** in a handgun, as once you've decided on its primary purpose you'll then begin to search for features that appeal to you.

DEFENSE

This can either be concealed carry, a gun for your vehicle, or a home defense gun. (One major consideration for home defense is whether to even buy a handgun at all. A shotgun is much easier to pick up and shoot, will cause more damage on the target, and buckshot is less likely to penetrate walls to hit bystanders.) A concealed carry gun, for example, will be somewhat smaller and more streamlined to allow for comfort and ease of carrying/stowing. After all, you're going to be sitting on it 99.999% of the time and defending yourself with it only if you're in a really really bad situation, so there are some compromises to be made. If the gun is intended for your glove compartment or under your bed, then size obviously isn't going to be as big of a factor.

Smaller size guns naturally tend to be of a smaller caliber due to the fact that the slide & grip have to accommodate the rounds. If the round is wider, then so is the gun. Additionally, the smaller the gun in a given caliber, the harder the recoil, so shooting a .45 ACP out of a tiny gun will not feel very comfortable. Smaller guns tend to have shorter barrels, smaller magazine capacities, and aren't as accurate. (Accuracy in my opinion isn't really a huge factor because unless you're an expert, you won't be able to shoot to the accuracy potential of the gun anyway, and if you do have to draw it, then your target will likely be at a distance of a few yards at most.) The natural advantage is that these guns are easily concealable, and can be placed in your pocket or in an inside the waistband holster. Keep in mind that the easier it is to carry, the more likely you'll actually carry it. If it's a huge pain to take on and off, then you'll find you won't take it with you as often.

Larger size guns are easier to shoot generally, and more accurate as well. When larger calibers are fired from a larger pistol less felt recoil is produced in comparison to a smaller gun due to the gun's increased mass (see Newton's 3rd Law). Larger calibers also tend to produce more damage to the target (stopping power). They typically come with larger magazine capacities, and depending on the model can be considered more reliable. These tend to be better home defense handguns.

My recommendations (and there are reviews elsewhere in the book) for when you're looking for a defense pistol are:

- Figure out if, where, and how you're going to be carrying it. If you're wearing it, then determine how much comfort and conceal-ability you want to have.

- Seek out a caliber that suits your needs. Bigger bullets will be more effective on target, but will be more difficult to shoot and could make a conceal-carry gun wider and less comfortable.

- Find a set of sights that will be visible in low-light and are easy for your eye to pick up.

- Look at various safety options and decide which you're the most comfortable with. If it's in your pocket with a bunch of keys and a knife, then maybe you want a heavy trigger for the first shot or an external safety so the trigger doesn't catch something and accidentally discharge. If it's in a holster (especially one on your back), then figure out how easy it's going to be to disengage that safety and put your first shot on target. If it's in a box in your house in a locked container, then do you really need to worry about multiple safeties on the gun once you remove it with the intent to fire?

- Practice!!! Too many people don't like shooting their defense guns because they're not fun to shoot due to a heavy trigger or heavy recoil. If you're going to draw it, practice your draws a few hundred times so that you can do them automatically and without fumbling if needed.

- Test It!!! Shoot whichever combination of gun and ammo you're going to be carrying for a few hundred rounds. Why? Because you want to know if it's going to work. Don't go to the range with round nose bullets (see Ammunition Selection elsewhere in the book) then load "super duper defense expanding mushroom loads" that you've never shot before in your carry magazine. You don't want a failure to feed (see Common Malfunctions elsewhere in the book) or a light primer strike when you need the gun to function the most. Put the gun through its paces.

Keep in mind that in spite of the lengthy debates you will doubtlessly encounter about the "stopping power" of a given round, shot placement is much more important. Shooters are trained to aim center mass not only because it's the largest target, but because a direct impact to the centerline of the body will cause the fastest possible threat neutralization. Your ability to shoot quickly and under pressure will dramatically improve your chances of surviving a hostile situation than the ballistics of any round. I cannot stress enough the importance of practice. People tend to fall back on their training when their adrenaline is high as muscle memory takes over and focus narrows. Just having a gun doesn't make you safe. The late, great Jeff Cooper once was quoted as saying "Owning a handgun doesn't make you armed any more than owning a guitar makes you a musician."

If you're going to buy a gun for defense, train with it and train hard.

TARGET SHOOTING

Many people enjoy simply going to the local range and dropping a few rounds at targets. It's pretty darn fun! For this pursuit, you're most likely going to be interested in shooting a gun that's comfortable, accurate, and doesn't beat you up every time you fire it. If you're learning on your first gun, then typically a smaller caliber, large frame pistol is the way to go. This emphasizes proper shooting technique without introducing a flinch caused by excessive amounts of recoil.

The goal of target shooting is to be able to develop proper fundamentals along with speed and accuracy. You could, for example, build these skills with a pistol devoted to target shooting, while simultaneously owning a defensive pistol which you don't shoot as much. For example, a 9mm handgun might be good to just go out and practice or plink with, while you might keep a .45 stowed in case of emergency.

For newer shooters who intend to learn, it's typically best to minimize recoil as much as possible. A highly accurate .22LR pistol can be had for cheap. It will give instant feedback on your technique without a huge explosion going off in front of your face, and these skills will serve as a good foundation once you start working on recoil management with larger caliber guns. Accuracy is your first priority and getting distracted with huge booms every time the gun fires won't help you. 9mm guns work here too.

DUAL USE

The vast majority of first time buyers are purchasing just one gun for the ambiguous purpose of "dual-use." In other words they want to own a gun that they intend to shoot sometimes at the range for fun, but also want it to be practical. In this case, I can only make the following recommendation: Buy something that you're going to go practice with. If your gun has a lot of recoil that you're not used to managing, or is in some way uncomfortable to shoot, or the ammunition is expensive, then you will not want to go shoot it anymore because it won't be fun. It will end up sitting under your bed collecting dust right next to your VHS copy of 8-Minute Abs. Hopefully it will stay there, because if you run into a situation that requires you to defend yourself with it, then a completely inexperienced shooter with a high recoil gun could be a danger to him/herself or others.

In short, buy something that you're going to want to learn with that will not induce bad habits from really heavy recoil. Don't spend too much money on the gun either. Instead of putting $1000 towards something you may or may not want to use, buy one for $500 in a reasonable caliber (9mm or maybe .40 S&W) and spend the other $500 on ammo and range time.

Another thing is that you should never say never when it comes to applications for your guns. Some people buy a gun for just one reason, and exclude all other possibilities. For example "I'm never going to shoot competition!" Keep an open mind and select something that can be versatile for multiple uses. Don't limit yourself to one thing only at the time of purchase because who knows what you might be doing a little down the line.

COMPETITION SELECTION

If you are a first time buyer and have limited experience with firearms, don't worry about jumping directly into competition. Simply go the target shooting route until you've built your skills up to par. While there is a great deal new shooters can learn from being in a competitive environment, and I recommend starting as early as possible, you need to figure out the proper mechanics first. If you're not a first time buyer, and you've been shooting for awhile and are interested in getting into the world of firearms competition, then there are many possible considerations.

When I first started shooting matches, I had no idea what gun I should have. As a matter of fact, I shot my first year of competition (only a few matches) with a SIG P226 which is relatively uncommon in my division of the sport. Usually there are certain guns which dominate different shooting sports, or different segments of each shooting sport. This is simply because these guns are well engineered, people know how to work on them, and they've been proven multiple times by top competitors. I'm not saying that you should simply buy something because someone else is using it or because you've heard that it's good. I'm simply stating that within competition circles it's pretty well established which guns work best and which don't. Make sure that you do the research on the prevalence of the pistol you're using for a given sport.

I would recommend buying a pistol that first follows the advice in the next chapter, **Things to Look For**, then once you gain a certain amount of experience you can start to customize or swap out your gear. "Competition shooting" includes a variety of different disciplines, USPSA/IPSC/IDPA obviously being mine. There are different guns for different sports. However, each person is unique, and what works well for somebody else, even a top ranked shooter, might not work well you. This could be due to body mechanics or even state law preventing you from making the purchase. This is why there are certain traits in a pistol that you should seek out for yourself.

Also, keep in mind that you don't want to spend too much money on something for competition if you've never done it before. Go buy some cheap, functional stuff. That way your cost investment isn't prohibitive and you won't lose too much if you decide you don't like it. The equipment only provides an edge of a couple of percentage points anyways.

CHOOSING BETWEEN SEMI-AUTOMATICS & REVOLVERS

There are a great deal of misconceptions surrounding the semi-auto vs. revolver debate. I'll list below some advantages and disadvantages of each one. Keep in mind that a well designed gun that's cleaned and maintained properly is highly unlikely to have any problems with it at all. (I cleaned my first gun, a semi-auto, every time I went to the range. I didn't have a single jam for 35,000 rounds over 5 years in spite of the fact that my model was notorious for having malfunctions both in online communities and the press.)

Reasons to Purchase a Semi-Automatic Handgun:

- *Magazine Capacity.* Revolvers tend to hold anywhere from 5-8 shots. Out of the box semi-autos can hold anywhere from 8 to 19 rounds. (More with extended mags)

- *Reload Speed.* Unless you're Jerry Miculek (probably the best revolver shooter in history and a heckuva nice guy) then chances are you will be much, much slower reloading a revolver than a semi-auto. Also, the gun will let you know when you're out of ammunition by locking the slide back.

- *Cost.* Semi autos are generally several hundred dollars less expensive from brand name manufacturers than revolvers. For example a Smith and Wesson M&P .40 costs about $700 while a 625 is well over $1100. Obviously this differs by manufacturer and the gap isn't always as wide, but is typically the case.

- *Reliability.* Semi-automatics are not as susceptible to carbon buildup as revolvers and have fewer moving parts. (Although this is debatable with single action only revolvers)

Carbon can build up on both the ejector star and within the cylinder itself. This may cause revolvers to jam, have out of alignment hammer strikes, or have light primer strikes. However, in spite of modern semi-auto engineering, they will always be more ammunition sensitive than revolvers. If your semi-auto doesn't like what you're feeding it then you will have a headache.

- **Simplicity of Maintenance/Modification.** Semi-automatics can be cleaned quite easily and typically parts are easier to swap than on a revolver. This includes sights, barrels, recoil springs, triggers, even entire slides, etc.

- **Reduced Recoil.** A semi-automatic has a recoil spring which absorbs the recoil as the slide moves to the rear. This spring can even be changed to accommodate different acceptable levels of recoil depending on the load. Also, very importantly, the design of the grip on semi-autos allows your strong and support hands to get higher up on the gun therefore giving the gun less leverage over the grip in recoil.

- **Easier First Shot.** Striker fired semi-autos can have an extremely light first shot. DA/SA or even Double Action Only semi-autos can have a lighter first shot due to the fact that the only action being performed by the trigger is moving the hammer (and possibly disengaging a safety). A revolver must perform a great deal of mechanical action to rotate the cylinder (not necessary on single action only revolvers).

- **Superior Trigger Reset.** It's easier to fire a gun more quickly when you don't have to pull the trigger very far. Revolvers have a considerably longer reset than semi-autos because their pulls have to revolve the cylinder. This makes them a lot more difficult to shoot quickly.

- **Accessory Rails.** Many semi-automatics these days are being offered with rails under the slide to mount various accessories. Very few revolvers have these.

- **Safeties.** Semi-autos usually have a wider variety of safeties available including many that can be deactivated by doing nothing other than gripping the gun, such as the grip safety and the thumb safety.

- **Wrist Cant.** The design and the angle of the grips on many semi-automatic handguns allow the shooter to achieve a more angled support wrist cant, thereby allowing them to reduce recoil more effectively.

Reasons to Purchase a Revolver:

- **Reliability.** Semi-automatics depend on the force of the fired round to send the slide all the way back to the rear thereby cycling the gun (cocking the hammer/striker, and loading another round into the chamber and locking closed). If the round doesn't have enough force to do this then you will have a jam, either a stovepipe (where the ejected shell case gets stuck between the slide and the barrel) or a failure to feed (where there isn't enough force to push the next round into the chamber). Revolvers do not depend on their ammunition at all to perform a mechanical action thereby allowing them to shoot pretty much anything that fits in the gun. Also, "limp wristing" can cause a jam in semi-autos not seen in revolvers. In this case a new shooter with low grip strength and a bad, low

A low, limp wristed grip

grip on the gun might cause it to jam because instead of the gun recoiling in a linear fashion after firing, it will tend to react in more of an arc. This can cause the next round in the magazine to nosedive, and fail to feed.

- *Loading.* New shooters that do not possess a great deal of strength may have trouble racking the slide (pulling it back and releasing it on a full magazine to load the gun). A revolver doesn't require much strength to load/unload.

- *Training for Novices.* New shooters will have no trouble figuring out a revolver due to its relatively easier operation, but will have to be taught how to clear jams in a semi-automatic.

- *Ammunition Versatility.* It's easier to switch between practice loads and defense loads without worrying about causing a jam in a revolver. You would have to test a number of rounds through a semi-auto for function to be sure first. (Although as mentioned above, modern semi-autos can handle vast differences in ammunition without any issue)

- *Crisp Single Action Trigger.* When the hammer is cocked manually, firing the gun can be smoother and crisper than shooting a factory striker fired pistol. There's no advantage here when you compare them to DA/SA and single action only semi-autos though.

For most shooters, new and otherwise, I tend to recommend semi-automatics. In my opinion their advantages, especially in terms of magazine capacity and reduced recoil, far outweigh their drawbacks. Revolvers have their place and are durable, reliable handguns that function well in many various conditions. Semi-autos do require a little bit more knowledge to work with (including knowing your ammo), but everything is pretty easy to learn. I must point out that the notion of a semi-auto pistol being inherently less reliable is very far from the truth. (I've seen some perform flawlessly under horrible conditions.) Let me reiterate that when you're making your decision on which handgun to own, know what you're purchasing it for.

One more point of note: Revolvers typically take rimmed ammunition. This is because the rim of the bullet is what holds it in place in the cylinder. However, when used with moon clips (speed loaders holding all the bullets so that they can be dropped into the cylinder together) rimless ammunition can be used as well. Semi-autos pretty much always take rimless ammunition because it's held in the chamber by spring pressure instead of resting on the rim (.22LR tends to be the most common rimmed ammo in semi-autos).

THINGS TO LOOK FOR

When selecting a handgun, don't just buy something because it's expensive or it comes from a big name company. These have literally nothing to do with the quality for that particular model. Picking out the perfect handgun for you depends on how it works for you. There are some objectively better than others, but you should be able to figure that out pretty quickly. Once you've decided on what you want to use the gun for, you should select a variety of them and give them rankings on a scale from 1 to 10. Below I've listed an assortment of characteristics that set guns apart from one another in rough order of importance.

One point of note: When shooting two guns of the same caliber and same approximate size, don't worry too much about figuring out which of them has more felt recoil or accuracy. Chances are that you aren't using proper technique yet, and many of those forces can be greatly reduced with practice. Furthermore, there are simple modifications that can be made to the gun which will dramatically lower the recoil while avoiding a reduction in reliability.

RELIABILITY & SAFETY

Naturally if you're buying a gun for any purpose a major concern is going to be reliability. Some guns are more finicky than others. In other words, certain guns will work flawlessly with only certain types of ammunition, or will have to be cleaned all the time, while others will be able to function without fail shooting pretty much anything in the worst possible conditions.

Unfortunately it's pretty difficult to determine how reliable a given gun is just by picking one up and looking at it. This is the point of the evaluation process. Just because a gun doesn't like one particular brand of ammunition doesn't mean it's a bad gun. As an owner, it's your responsibility to find a configuration that works really well for you by experimentation and to stick with it. Furthermore, it's your responsibility to understand why something works or doesn't (some of this will be covered under the **Common Malfunctions** section elsewhere in the book). For example, if you buy really light target shooting ammo and Gun X jams with it occasionally while Gun Y works okay that doesn't mean Gun Y is automatically better. Keep in mind that not all ammunition problems are gun problems.

There is also a misconception that revolvers are much more reliable than semi-automatics because they appear to have fewer moving parts. This is not the case. As a matter of fact revolvers are actually more complicated internally because they have to perform more mechanical action such as rotating the cylinder. Don't limit yourself to a certain type of handgun because someone told you that they think that it's less reliable. For example, a certain type of gun can fire perfectly fine after a week long sandy salt water bath but not after you put the wrong kind of flashlight on it. (True story) Do your research to figure out if a particular gun you're interested in is having certain issues. Not only will common complaints be found by speaking to those in the know, but also common solutions to those problems. Some manufacturers have produced both really awesome guns, and really horrible guns. Be inquisitive and don't dismiss something based off an anecdote.

There are a couple of other points I wanted to make here as well. First, as I recommended earlier, you should test out a gun first prior to buying it. However, you should be cautioned that most shooting range rental guns are in very poor condition. This is because the staff rents them out for long periods without any sort of cleaning or lubrication. So if the gun has a problem don't judge the entire brand line based on it. Second, in a lot of gun magazine reviews the author will spend a few hundred rounds with the gun and "test it for jams." One issue of reliability is how quickly little parts on the gun such as springs will break. This is impossible to determine in a few hours and can only be seen over the life of the pistol.

As per safety, most modern handguns are built with internal safety mechanisms preventing them from firing when not intended to. However, you should verify this as well. If the gun costs $120 and comes from some manufacturer that you've never heard of, do your diligence and see what these internal safeties are and if anyone has ever had an accident with one. Usually a quick search will reveal some potential pitfalls.

ERGONOMICS

Fitting Your Hand

It's vitally important that the gun fits in your hand properly while you are using the proper grip. (Just because it feels good now doesn't mean that it will when you use correct technique). While the **Grip** is covered extensively elsewhere in the book, I'll give a brief overview of what

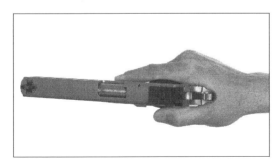

1911 centered in the web of the hand

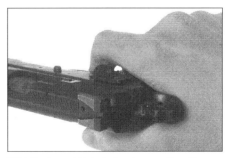

SP01 Shadow as high in the hand as possible, with daylight between trigger finger and frame

to look for here. The foundation of a good grip is making sure that the gun sits squarely in your hand while allowing you to pull the trigger comfortably. The first point of contact with the gun is to fit the backstrap of the gun squarely in the web of your hand as low as possible. Or in other words, try to wedge your strong hand as high on the back of the gun as possible. The next point of contact is ensuring that the gun is centered between your thumb and index finger. The last point of contact you're looking for here on your strong hand is whether the last pad of your index finger can easily reach the trigger. Check to see if your index finger makes contact with the grip/frame while reaching for the trigger. You should be able to see a decent amount of light between the center joint of your index finger and the frame.

People with small hands are at a natural disadvantage in gun selection. This is because a great deal of handguns have large grip sizes which means that the gun must sit off-center in the hand in order for you to pull the trigger. This causes the gun to track improperly under recoil, therefore making it harder to connect with multiple shots accurately.

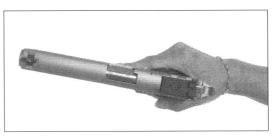
Large frame 1911 sits off-center in a small hand

The next feature that you're looking for ergonomically is the distance to the controls on the handgun. Optimally you should not have to move your hand much in order for your thumb to hit the magazine (or cylinder) release button. The reason this becomes important is if you want to perform a reload of the pistol (this technique is covered elsewhere in the book) you don't want to have to shift then reform your grip too much.

Doing so causes you to be slower on your next shot after the reload, and possibly less accurate. The slide release is supposed to be far enough away from your strong hand thumb so as not to be in contact with it while firing. This could cause the slide to inadvertently lock back while firing. Another thing to check for is if your gun has a thumb safety, make sure that you can easily rest your strong hand thumb on top of it while forming your grip.

One handed grip of an M&P

One key point of a good grip is contact with your hands all the way around the gun. This is vital because it enhances control by increasing the overall amount of surface friction, and evenly distributes grip pressure. A gap between your hand and the gun can result in more difficult sequential shots because the gun is being pushed more one way than the other. One of the problems that people with very large hands have is that their palms tend to bunch-up when gripping a gun with a really small grip. This can create gaps between

Shift of hand to hit the magazine release

the gun and the hands. Ideally you want your strong hand to make comfortable contact with the entire side of the gun (on the grip's palm swells), and wrap all the way around so that the last joints on your finger at least overlap on the other side of the gun. This will produce a natural feel to the handgun.

Finally the last ergonomic thing to look for in a handgun is the ease of placing your support hand on it. The correct semi-automatic pistol grip uses a thumbs-forward technique with the support hand index finger wedged into the bottom of the triggerguard. You don't want your support hand rubbing into any of the controls such as the take-down lever (used for disassembling the gun) as it both doesn't feel good and could even cause a malfunction.

Two handed grip

Bear in mind that many handguns these days are offering multiple interchangeable grips either from the factory (OEM) or from aftermarket sources. Some of these come with new backstraps as well such as the Smith & Wesson M&P, Springfield Armory XDm, and Glock Gen4, among many others. Also, for the 1911/2011 series of handguns and many SA/DA models, new side panel grips (but not the backstrap) can simply be screwed on. Make sure you check out the options available to you.

Low Bore Axis

A low bore axis handgun is very important to recoil management. This is due to simple physics of leverage. The longer the lever and the farther away the pivot point the more force is exerted. The same is true with a handgun. The lower the bore of the gun is in your hand the less leverage the gun has over you under the force of recoil. This is why you must get your strong hand as high up on the gun as possible.

A feature you're going to be looking for here is a nice contoured beavertail /backstrap with the barrel not sitting too high above it. You want your hand to rest high on the gun but not to interfere with the slide. This is a problem for some large handed shooters who have the cuts in their hands to prove it!

Key Points to Remember:

- Put the gun as low as possible in the center of the web of your strong hand. Can you easily reach the trigger? Do the last joints of your hand reach around to the other side of the grip?

- Are there gaps between your hand and the gun when gripping it?

- Can you easily reach the controls you need to?

- Will you accidentally use controls when you don't want to?

- Does the gun have a low bore axis against your hand?

As part of the low bore axis, slide weight is also a consideration. The idea is accounting for the amount of mass that resides above your hand. Increased mass up there will mean increased inertia when the slide cycles, which may induce more recoil. Lighter, faster slides tend to kick back less.

TRIGGER

The factory trigger on a handgun is very important to those who don't wish to modify it at all. It's also somewhat important to tinkerers because one that's good from the factory can be excellent when modified. The actual mechanism differs greatly from manufacturer to manufacturer, and some are capable of producing considerably better results than others.

Ease of Pull

How easy a trigger is to pull depends on two things:

- **Weight.** The pull weight is determined by figuring out how much overall pressure needs to be placed on the center of the face of the trigger in order to get the gun to fire. Some Double Action/Single Action guns require a substantially heavier first shot from double action than the successive single action pulls. About 9lbs for double action and 4.5lbs for single action is about average. Lighter triggers mean the gun will fire more easily.

- **Smoothness.** The smoothness of the trigger reflects how much consistent pressure must be applied for the gun to fire. In my opinion this is very important because a gritty feel will cause people to jerk the gun when firing. Some guns will have a "sticky point" at the beginning or end of the pull. You ideally want a pull that's as smooth as possible all the way through. The way to test this is by just applying a slow increase of pressure on the trigger and feeling the action work.

Break Point

When many triggers are pulled you can feel the "break point" at which if only a very slight amount of additional pressure is applied the gun will fire. Ideally the break point will be very crisp. One that is less precise will be described as "mushy". This is important because it allows the operator of the handgun to know exactly when the gun will fire both for shooting quickly and accurately.

Reset

Trigger reset is one of the most consistently overlooked features of any handgun, just as it's one of the most overlooked techniques of shooting. The reset means the distance you must release the trigger once the gun fires to be able to shoot the gun again. (Having no reset needed to fire another shot = an automatic gun!) As explored in detail later in the book, the faster you can get it to reset and the less distance it has to travel means the quicker and more accurately you can get follow-up shots on target. The way to test the reset on a semi-automatic is to dry-fire the gun (no bullets inside) then keep your finger depressed on the trigger while you cycle the slide manually by pulling it to the rear and releasing it. Next slowly let the trigger out, and eventually you will feel/hear a click. Once it clicks you can pull it again to fire the gun.

Overtravel

This is another heavily overlooked facet of guns. When you pull the trigger and the gun fires (try this dry-firing without any bullets in the gun), it will travel further towards the rear past the break point. This is called overtravel because it identifies the additional distance the trigger moves back after the gun is fired. It relates closely to the reset because the less amount of overtravel there is, the shorter the reset, and the quicker you can shoot the gun.

Key Points to Remember:

- Is the trigger easy to pull?

- Does it break cleanly?

- Does it reset quickly?

ACCURACY

The truth is that most handguns are pretty darn accurate, especially if they come from a well known manufacturer. For example I can easily shoot 8 inch steel plates at 65 yards with an out of the box Glock. Guns with shorter barrels tend to have wider groups (the distribution of shots on a target), especially subcompact handguns which are used for concealed carry. However, most shooters will not be able to perform up to the level of accuracy of the handgun without considerable practice anyways. This makes accuracy one of the most unnecessarily debated considerations of a handgun purchase- especially for new buyers.

As mentioned earlier, you must first decide what you want to use the handgun for. Generally a full size handgun should be capable of producing a group of a couple inches or so at 25 yards. Unless you're shooting a specialized event such as NRA Bullseye or the Bianchi Cup which requires extreme accuracy in some cases, then you shouldn't worry too much about the complete accuracy potential of the gun (especially when it requires an additional couple hundred bucks for a "match grade barrel"). If the gun is known to produce groups of larger than 3-4 inches at 25 yards, then we're getting into the realm of inaccurate. Of course you want to be able to hit what you're aiming at. What you should set is an accuracy ceiling that's right for you (I would say 3" groups at 25 yards). Anything under it is fine. Just don't nitpick about which handgun can shoot ¼" more accurately than the other. Ammunition selection plays a large factor here too.

There are naturally issues with a gun that could cause it to be wildly inaccurate such as a barrel that's not sized properly. However, these types of problems tend to be endemic of low budget cheap guns which you should be able to recognize at first glance on your own. The other alternative is that a gun has been so highly customized (we're talking compensators, slide lightening, custom barrels) that it sometimes causes bullets to tumble, which is a very rare case, and virtually never occurs with factory guns.

By far the largest complaint about any gun on the market is "perceived inaccuracy." Guns aplenty have been returned to gun stores or taken to armorers because "the darn thing won't stop shooting 10 inch groups low left!" Often the myopia of some shooters will inevitably make its way to the online gun forums where certain entire brands will be trashed because a certain gun supposedly can't hit the broad side of a barn. Almost all of these cases are due to shooter induced error. Most handguns are absolutely fine, and just because you're more accurate with one doesn't mean that it's superior. Chances are that particular gun just compensates for some of your bad habits a little better right now. If you think a gun is inaccurate, have someone with a lot of experience shoot it to verify your claims.

POINTABILITY

Certain handguns have a different "grip angle" (yes Top Shot fans) to them relative to the bore axis. When you pick up the handgun your strong hand wrist will have to sit at a different angle in order to point the sights at the target. The two most commonly compared examples of this are the Glock and the 1911. The former tends to have a more oblique grip angle while the latter is closer to a right angle.

1911 vs Glock grip angle

The effects of a different grip angle are referred to as the "pointability" or "natural point of aim" for the handgun. If you're used to shooting a 1911 and someone hands you a Glock then you'll likely have the gun point much higher when you first aim it and vice-versa. Either grip angle can be trained for and practiced; it's just a matter of what you're comfortable with. Some people prefer having to set their wrists a little bit more (proponents claim recoil reduction) while others believe that the 1911 style angle feels much more natural (faster target acquisition). At the end of the day, each one works just as well as the other in my opinion. There are lots of variations of those angles depending on the manufacturers. When buying a new handgun, this factor can be taken into account.

The way you can test which grip angle you prefer out of the gate is to hold the handgun in your natural grip at your chest in a "low-ready" position. Then look at a fairly small target in the distance and mount the gun to it and acquire a sight picture on the target. Do this a few times. If your front sight tends to start lower than your rear, you might want a more oblique grip angle. If your front sight tends to start higher than your rear, you might want a grip angle closer to 90 degrees. Again, this should not be a major consideration for you, nor should it outweigh more significant factors in your selection process such as the ergonomics of the gun. Training yourself to draw and mount to the correct grip angle for your gun doesn't take that much time. However, some people complain that they're always trying to find their sights when acquiring a target, which might be contributed to by this.

MAGAZINE CAPACITY

The magazine capacity simply means how many rounds you can fit in the gun. Usually you'll hear a number such as 15+1, which means that 15 rounds will go in the magazine along with one in the chamber. (This is called topping off the handgun, where you are ready to shoot with a full magazine inserted). Usually larger caliber handguns have lower magazine capacities in comparison to smaller caliber handguns of the same model (a .40 version of the gun vs. a 9mm, etc).

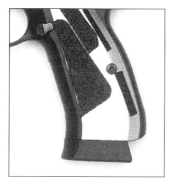

Extended magazine baseplate

This is an important concern because it stipulates how much you can shoot the gun without reloading- which plays a role in both defensive and competition environments. The higher this number is the more ammo you can carry on your person and the more you can fire without stopping. Usually the capacity of a handgun is proportionate to its size as smaller guns tend to have lower ones. There are exceptions however with many models of handgun capable of taking longer magazines or offering additional capacity baseplates. For example, the Glock compact guns can take full size magazines even though the bottom of the magazine will protrude past the grip. Also, the CZ SP-01 naturally has a thick baseplate which raises its capacity.

In certain states, such as California, magazine capacity in both handguns and rifles is limited to 10 rounds total. In this situation, all magazines from the factory will be permanently altered to prevent them from taking in more than 10 rounds. Sometimes these can be less reliable than standard capacity factory magazines. More on this is found in the **Common Malfunctions** section.

AFTERMARKET SUPPORT

One of the big kickers for firearm selection is aftermarket support. This can include everything from the number of gunsmiths that are familiar with and competent at working on the gun to the availability of aftermarket parts such as trigger kits and additional magazines. Furthermore, generally the more prevalent a given gun is the larger the support community is (especially online). For example, if you buy a 1911, then you will have access to ideas and tips from essentially 100 years of built up knowledge. If you buy a gun manufactured in quantities of 10 in someone's basement in Mississippi then you're pretty much on your own.

If this is your first handgun, buy something that everyone knows about so they can help you if your gun breaks or give you advice on how to make it better. This also relates to spare parts and accessories available. The best example of this is actually not a handgun, it's the venerable AR-15, America's most produced and well-known rifle. Everybody makes AR parts and accessories. Everyone knows how to build them, how to fix them, and how to clean them. There are about 1500 different varieties of optics you can put on them. This is an easy gun for a new shooter because you can easily see what works and what doesn't.

However, I must insert a caveat here as well. Just because you see the military or some law enforcement departments buying a certain gun does NOT mean it's a great gun. There are a multitude of elements that go into the acquisition process for government agencies that have nothing to do with how well the gun shoots. Remember that you're buying the gun for you, and that you should figure out what works well for you and what doesn't

PRICE

Prices per gun vary greatly. You can buy them used for only a couple hundred dollars (that's decent guns, mind you) or purchase a new one for up to and over a thousand. As I've stated earlier, just because something is more expensive doesn't mean that it's better. That should be a well understood principle in any consumer sector. While cost and quality tend to have a somewhat linear relationship, with handguns there are many peaks and valleys. What you should do when seeking a handgun is to determine your budget range, then analyze all available models within it. Compare and contrast them based on the above characteristics in order to make your decision.

CALIBER

The type of ammunition that your gun shoots is a major consideration. It affects a number of things including the recoil of the pistol, the magazine capacity, and possibly the gun's potential for defensive applications. Furthermore, it also determines how much it will cost to actually shoot! Much like every other aspect that you're looking at for your purchase, caliber selection will ultimately depend on what you want to do with the gun.

.22LRs are ridiculously cheap in comparison to any other type of ammo at about $3.50 for 50 rounds. However, they're pretty much for target shooting only. 9mm is also pretty cheap at around $10-15 for a new box of 50 rounds (depending on brand). 40 S&W ranges from $15 to $20 and is a good intermediate cartridge. .45ACP typically is a little more expensive than the .40s and usually start around $17.50 for a box. Of course there are a ton other calibers to choose from, but you might as well stick to the most common if you're just getting started. For more information on ammunition selection, check out Chapter 17.

THINGS TO AVOID

Here are a couple of tips on what not to look for in a pistol:

- The "cool factor" should not play a role here. Unless you're a legitimate collector that's seeking rare pistols, then you should not be looking into high priced guns just because they look slick.

- Video games and movies are not good selection tools. Just because a gun was part of your favorite kit in Call of Duty doesn't mean that it will work the same in the real world or fit you as well as some other models. I've never seen a gun jam in a video game.

I know that image is important for some people when buying guns, it's natural. Something looks really nifty on film or in some other form of media, and you think to yourself that you have to have it. People do it all the time, from fashion to cars. That's why Omega sponsors James Bond (and

I know a bunch of people that own Omegas). However, one of the purposes of this book is to dispel misconceptions about firearms and steer you towards something that you'll enjoy shooting and will last you a long time. If you're buying on image, then you're placing way too much emphasis on form over function and ignoring other models that could better suit you. Also, you're running the risk of spending a good chunk of change on something that you might not use when that cash could be put to better use elsewhere.

EXAMPLES OF DIFFERENT GUNS

Now that you have an idea of what criteria you should use to determine if a handgun is right for you, I'll go into detail about some of the commonly available ones on the market. I do not intend to follow a point or star system because most people would just simply look at what gun has my highest rating and start with that one. It's more important that you understand the advantages and disadvantages of a particular gun so that you can apply that knowledge to your purchase. All of the guns I've cited below I own personally, and have had lots of time to try out on the range. I'm not a gun collector and don't just go buy something because it's novel. Each one of these guns I've acquired because it serves a purpose for me and will hopefully guide your decision-making.

Reading below, you'll see kind of a "rock – paper – scissors" effect taking place. I've listed three striker fired pistols, two DA/SAs, one single action only, and one revolver. Take note that some offer better ergonomics, some better magazine capacity, some better recoil control, some better reliability/aftermarket support. No single gun is the best in everything, which is a vital thing to remember. You need to decide what your criteria for evaluating a pistol are then figure out what's more important to you. For your reference, I have not included any "stupid guns" in this list because that could literally be the subject of another book and I'd rather guide you to the good stuff. I also have omitted several excellent guns for space considerations. Keep that in mind as you shop- are there other pistols that are better than this one, and if so, how?

Point of Note: I'm listing MSRP prices. You can often get guns for cheaper than listed. (Too bad it's not that way with cars!)

Another Point of Note: Just because a gun doesn't come the way you want it out of the box doesn't mean that it can't be configured to meet your needs. Make sure that you factor in the ease of customization. Triggers and sights are easy to modify, frames are not.

GLOCK MODELS

Glock produces an assortment of models which are all built around the same central design principles. It is a striker fired pistol (one of the first major adaptations of the design by a company) featuring a polymer frame and hardened steel slide. They come in various calibers ranging from .380 to .45 ACP and various sizes ranging from subcompact to extended-length slide competition models. Additionally, this pistol features polygonal rifling (shaped like a hexagon) instead of the traditional land & groove rifling (which has platforms and valleys).

Glock 35 with grip tape and Warren Tactical sights

Common Features:

- **No external safeties.** Glock has a patented three safety system which prevents the gun from being fired unless the trigger is pulled, including a trigger safety, a firing pin block, and a drop safety. Simple to understand and operate.

- **Finger Grooves.** The grip has a set of rough textured finger grooves to promote easy handling and a solid grip.

- **Oblique Grip Angle.** The handle of the gun is offset towards the rear more than the 1911 style which is closer to 90 degrees.

- **Accessory Rail.** Recent models of this gun come with an accessory rail on the front of the gun to mount things like flashlights.

- **Striker Fired.** Each trigger pull is the same every time. There are no hammers to cock.

Advantages:

- The factory trigger is relatively easy to pull for experienced and new shooters alike. It's light enough so that it's very easy to make your first shot accurate, and heavy enough to prevent you from pulling it accidentally (ranges from 4.5 to 5.5 lbs). The reset is also short for quick follow-up shots. It can also be modified to your preference at a low cost.

- The various internal safeties make the pistol extremely safe, even when dropped from a considerable height, or while bouncing around in your glove box.

- The design of the grip adds considerable tack to the plastic and allows even people with slippery, wet hands to pick it up and fire it easily.

- Compact models have a high magazine capacity, are accurate for their size, and have easy to pick up factory sights- even in low light conditions. Their dimensions are also very slim, enabling good, comfortable concealment.

- Standard length models are also very accurate out of the box.

- Long slide versions such as the Glock 34 & 35 are perfect for competition and allow extreme accuracy and a longer sight radius (helpful for aiming more effectively). These are some of the most popular USPSA pistols in Production Division. (See the Competition section elsewhere in the book)

- The low bore axis and high beavertail of the Glock allows the shooter to get his/her hands up high on the gun to counter the forces of recoil.

- Glocks tend to have good magazine capacities and affordable mags. A Glock 17 for example can hold 17+1 rounds of 9mm ammunition. The compact version can hold 10+1. Optional extended magazines increase this capacity to 19+ or even 33+1!

- This pistol is one of the most reliable that you'll ever find. There have been various tests conducted (by enthusiasts) including dropping the pistol from a moving airplane after which it still fires. It will work in pretty much all conditions without much cleaning. It is also ridiculously easy to completely disassemble. Any part on the gun can be replaced in about 2 minutes or less.

- Aftermarket support is simply spectacular, and parts for most Glock models are interchangeable. This allows for incredibly simple maintenance, as well as drop in upgrades for the gun such as trigger kits and a wide selection of sights. There is a guide for literally anything you want to do to this gun online, and most work can be performed by people with little gunsmithing experience.

- At about $500 for a G17, Glocks are pretty cheap compared to other guns.

Disadvantages:

- The grip size is pretty large for the full frame models, and might not fit well for small handed shooters. If you have small hands and try to shoot these guns then the backstrap will likely be offset towards your thumb. The reason is because you'll have to shift the gun in your hand in order for you to reach the trigger. This causes the forces of recoil to track less consistently. Additionally, the large size of the grip causes small handed shooters to have to rotate the gun in their hands in order to reach the magazine release, thereby causing slower follow-up shots.

- The beavertail at the top of the grip is pretty wide and exacerbates the above problem, causing the shooter to spread his/her fingers outward to accommodate it. However it is at a pretty short, flat angle as well. This combination causes large handed shooters to sometimes have skin overlapping the top of the grip and interfering with the slide which results in "Glock bite" and cuts sometimes. It also causes small handed shooters to have more trouble reaching the trigger.

- Some shooters find the factory Glock trigger to be mushy, and not crisp in comparison to an external hammer style pistol such as the 1911. While the trigger, if properly prepared, can get quite good, the 1911's trigger geometry allows it to have more potential for lightness, reset, and overtravel.

- The sides of the gun are flat and do not have much in the way of palm swells. This creates gaps between your hand and the gun.

- The extended magazine release in Gen3 models is pretty sharp and sometimes must be rounded off for comfort. This is completely replaced by a paddle style in Gen4s.

- The Glock barrel is known for lead buildup if shooting non-jacketed lead bullets.

In a nutshell, the Glock is a fantastic pistol. It's pretty cheap, highly accurate, and extremely reliable. It has a great deal of aftermarket support and performing maintenance or upgrades is also very cheap and easy. It will never have the absolute best trigger out there, but you can get it to be pretty good with very little work. However, if you have smaller hands it's not ideally suited for you due to its large grip size. Even the Gen4s do not completely solve the problem as their flat sides still do not allow for optimal contact for your hands around the gun.

In spite of the possible ergonomic issues for smaller handed shooters including me, this gun is a great choice. I've won many matches with it. It will practically never break, and if it does you'll know exactly what to do to fix it. Glocks run and run and run.

CZ 75

The CZ 75 and its finely tuned cousin the SP01, is a venerable DA/SA Czech pistol. One of the interesting features about this pistol is that unlike most modern semi-automatics, the slide on this gun actually sits on the inside of the frame rails rather than on the outside. (Usually the bottom of the slide is visible from the outside of the gun, but not here.) The gun is usually made of all steel, and the SP-01 is quite heavy for a 9mm, a factor which seems to nicely reduce the recoil. There are also many other models of the CZ 75 family ranging from single action only to polymer frame.

Point of Note: CZ offers compact versions that look and function very similarly to the CZ 75 series of pistols.

CZ SP01 Shadow with aluminum grips, tape, and a CZ-85 trigger with a fiber optic sight

Common Features:

- **_DA/SA._** Most versions of the CZ 75 allow the gun to be fired from both double and single action.

- **_External Single Action Safety._** This is a thumb safety which prevents the gun from firing when engaged in single action.

- **_Internal Firing Pin Block Safety._** These are included in most models, but are absent from some competition versions such as the SP01 Shadow.

- **_Steel Frame._** While polymer is available in the Phantom version of this gun, most CZ 75 variants come with an all steel frame.

- **_Internal Frame Rails._**

- **_Accessory Rail._**

Advantages:

- With an all steel frame and an 18+1 round magazine capacity, the gun is heavy respective to other ones in its class. This allows for good recoil reduction and a less "snappy feel" to the gun. The magazines are also metal.

- The CZ 75 SP01 is one of the most ergonomic guns on the market with its thin contoured profile at the top of the backstrap under the beavertail (where the web of your hand will rest just under the slide). This allows people to easily put their thumbs on top of the safety while holding the gun for a comfortable feel.

- The thin profile of the pistol allows small and large handed shooters alike to get a perfect hold, and to easily access the magazine release.

- The single action pull is very crisp with excellent feedback out of the box.

- The SP01 includes an extended beavertail and an extremely low bore axis which help produce a very positive grip.

- It's known for being highly accurate.

- The gun is very safe and comes with both an internal drop safety as well as a firing pin block.

- There is pretty good aftermarket support coming from a couple of sources in the United States such as CZ Custom with USPSA shooter Angus Hobdell out of Arizona. Matthew Mink is another well known CZ USPSA shooter/gunsmith. There is also plenty of information about maintenance, modifications, and accessories available online.

Disadvantages:

- There have been reports in the competition world of needing to carry some spare parts around with the gun as it can be finicky if modified. (Jams, etc)

- Sometimes the gun will have issues with the magazines falling free due to clearance on either the magazine brake or the slide lock lever.

- The factory trigger reset on the SP01 is less than desirable due to the long distance the trigger bar must travel in order to re-engage the firing pin block. This is corrected either by removing the safety or buying an SP01 Shadow.

- Modifications to the gun can be time consuming and expensive.

- Not a wide variety of sights are available for the pistol. There is only one rear sight available for the Shadow variant due to the unique cut of the dovetail. Keep that in mind if you're getting into competition shooting.

- The double action pull is quite long, heavy, and can be difficult to reach. A trigger job is preferred for this gun.

- While the factory rubber grips provide good tack for the shooter, they are quite thick and can counteract some of the benefits for small handed shooters. To fix this, thinner grips must be purchased.

- While popular in Europe, the gun is somewhat rarer in the United States than other guns from Glock, Smith and Wesson, Sig Sauer, etc.

- The gun can be somewhat expensive coming in at an MSRP of $700.

The major reason to buy a CZ 75 or an SP01 would be for the ergonomics. I've never shot a gun that feels as comfortable. If you have small hands, or really like the contours of a 1911 but are looking for something with a little larger capacity, then this might be the gun for you. If you do a little work to smooth out the factory double action trigger and can find the sights you want then this CZ will be a tack driver in your hands. However, issues might arise in terms of getting the options you want on the gun and you might be required to tweak it for reliability.

SMITH & WESSON M&P SERIES (SEMI-AUTO)

The Smith & Wesson M&P Semi-Automatic Pistols are a recently engineered and introduced series of handguns that feature a polymer frame, multiple internal safeties, and various ergonomic improvements such as interchangeable grips. They are striker fired handguns that shoot a wide range of calibers and come in compact, full-size, and long slide competition models (such as the factory tuned Pro). Like Glocks, the basic design of the pistol is consistent across multiple sizes/calibers.

Common Features:

- **Polymer Frame.** This frame comes exclusively in polymer with a hardened steel slide.

- **Accessory Rail.**

- **Striker Fired.** Each trigger pull is the same every time. There are no hammers to cock.

- **Replaceable Palm Swells.** These easily interchangeable backstraps allow the gun to fit any hand size. Three different pieces in sizes small, medium, large come standard with the pistol and can easily be swapped out.

Smith & Wesson M&P 9L with grip stippling, grip tape, and Warren Tactical sights

Advantages:

- The M&P was one of the pioneers for incorporating features into the handgun allowing both right and left handed shooters of various hand sizes to shoot comfortably.

- It includes an ambidextrous magazine release button and slide catch lever.

- The gun has a good magazine capacity with 17+1 available in the 9mm full size version. The compact version comes with 12+1. The magazines are metal.

- Various safety features are optional on the pistol including an internal gun lock (the gun won't fire unless an internal lock is set to fire with a key), a magazine disconnect, and an external thumb safety. Standard features include a trigger safety, a drop safety, and a firing pin block, as well as a view window to see if the chamber is loaded.

- The factory trigger is quite smooth and rates at about 6.5lbs. Also, if you decide to do a trigger job you can get it to be pretty much the best out of any of the striker fired pistols available (due to the unique design of the mechanism). There are some very capable gunsmiths that have done wonders with this gun such as Burwell Gunsmithing in Pennsylvania.

- Reloading the gun is easy due to a slightly beveled mag well, along with the grip removal lever which protrudes below the gun and guides the magazine in.

- Factory grips provide a good amount of tack.

- Extremely low bore axis helps in recoil reduction.

Disadvantages:

- Aftermarket support is acceptable with this gun, although magazines tend to be expensive and somewhat difficult to find for the 10 round versions. While sights are readily available from various manufacturers, and the factory produces a drop in sear for a reduced trigger weight, the Glock's parts availability far outweighs the M&P.

- Even though this is a striker fired pistol, you require some training before working on this gun. A correct trigger job requires cutting into and filing down the sear. Even though there are some guides available online I would recommend sending it to a professional even if you're acquainted with the tools.

- Competition long slide versions are somewhat rarer than the standard version

- At over $700 MSRP, this gun is moderately expensive.

- Upon the gun's release, there have been some reported reliability issues including a higher probability of limp wrist jams with the factory recoil spring, problems with debris entering through the view hole in the barrel, and firing pins giving light primer strikes. Also, the gun seems to be somewhat ammunition sensitive and does not like hard primers or truncated cone bullets. (Smith and Wesson has claimed to have fixed these since the gun was released. Mine has worked great.)

Overall I really enjoy shooting the M&P. The multiple grip profiles allow smaller handed shooters such as myself to reach the trigger easily, which feels pretty good right out of the box. The gun is light which makes for good target transitions. With some modification work done, this has the best trigger you can find on a striker fired gun. It's very safe and has incorporated a lot of smart features that make it appealing to a wide swath of shooters out there. The ergonomics are second on this list only to the SP01. It does seem to have some reliability issues though, so ensure that you properly T&E a particular load with this gun. I would recommend the M&P to any shooter that has smaller hands and is looking for a light, striker fired handgun.

SPRINGFIELD ARMORY XD SERIES

Like the Glock and M&P, Springfield offers a striker fired handgun in a polymer frame with the XD series. These come in various sizes ranging from compact to competition long slide versions of different calibers. XDs have their genesis in a Croatian pistol known as the HS2000. Since acquiring the licensing rights, Springfield has released a variety of versions of the gun including the most recent XDm. The XD series is known for its assemblage of 1911-esque external safeties.

Common Features:

- **Multiple Safeties.** XDs include a collection of external safeties. These include a grip safety, a chamber loaded indicator, a cocked striker indicator, a trigger safety, a drop safety, and a firing pin block.

- **Polymer Frame.** This frame comes exclusively in polymer with a hardened steel slide.

- **Accessory Rail.**

- **Striker Fired.** Each trigger pull is the same every time. There are no hammers to cock.

- **1911 Style Grip Angle.** The grip angle of this gun is designed to allow users familiar with the 1911 to pick up and shoot it.

- **Ambidextrous Magazine Release.**

Advantages:

- The assemblage of safeties makes the gun very difficult to accidentally fire, even for new users.

Springfield XD Service 4" with Dawson Precision sights

- The gun is known for being quite reliable and producing few jams even under adverse conditions.

- The gun fits small to large hands especially with the addition of the XDm series with replaceable backstraps. The XDm also has ribs adding extra tack to the grip.

- Accuracy with the handgun is pretty good, especially with the XDm.

- The gun is very easy to reload.

- Springfield markets the "pointability" of the firearm, which is designed around the traditional grip angle of 1911 handguns.

- Magazine capacity on the XDm is good with a 19+1 limit in 9mm.

- Multiple slide serrations allow for easy grip and racking of the slide.

- There is a decent amount of aftermarket support for the XD, probably in the same range as the Smith & Wesson M&P. Various drop in accessories are available, including trigger kits, and magazines are reasonably available. There are many sight options on the market as well. Disassembly is around the same level of complexity as the M&P.

- Cost is good, coming in around the high $600 range for the XDm.

Disadvantages:

- The XD trigger break is by far the "mushiest" of the four polymer framed handguns listed here. While the takeup is light, the actual trigger break does not feel crisp out of the box. However a good trigger job can be had here too making it nice and crisp.

- The bore axis on this gun is the highest out of any polymer frame handgun I've fired resulting in somewhat less recoil reduction.

- The rear grip safety feels somewhat clunky in comparison to the 1911.

- The standard XD does not possess enough checkering to allow a positive enough grip under slippery conditions.

- Controls get in the way sometimes. The disassembly lever rubs against your support hand thumb (if you're right handed) with the proper grip. Also, your strong hand thumb tends to interfere with the slide release lever, sometimes causing the gun's slide to not lock back after the last round of the magazine has been fired.

- The sub-compact version of this gun is quite large relative to the offerings of Glock, Smith & Wesson, and Kahr. However, it does offer a pretty good magazine capacity for its size at 13+1 rounds of 9mm.

- Dry firing the XD can cause issues with the gun. The roll pin in the slide can break if it's dry fired too extensively. This is a problem rarely encountered elsewhere.

The Springfield XD is an all around solid gun. The XDm version incorporates some of the latest advancements, and I would recommend it over the standard XD series, particularly when comparing it to the other handguns on this list. It offers respectable ergonomics, a high degree of accuracy, and can have a pretty good trigger. My main issue with the XD is that it doesn't seem to be the best at anything. I think the ergonomics are superior on the M&P (with the exception of the reload), and the recoil control is better on the Glock (though the XD fits your hand better). The XD is kind of between those two guns' advantages and disadvantages. It's very reliable and shoots pretty well, which leaves its selection up to personal preference.

1911/2011 SERIES

The 1911 series of handguns constitutes one of the most widely used and well known pistol designs ever with its familiar contours and steel frame. The 2011 is an upgrade of it, incorporating new design elements such as polymer frames, double stack (increased magazine capacity) grips, and various other improvements in accuracy, recoil control, and reliability. Historically the M1911 came in .45ACP, but newer versions of the gun can shoot a vast selection of calibers. The 2011 now serves as the foundation of many competition and high performance custom pistols.

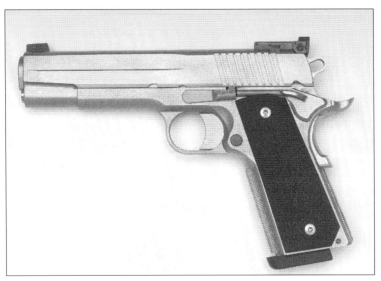

1911 with ErgoGrips

I must point out that there are substantial differences within this series depending on manufacturer, as a stock 1911 from a lower grade producer might run only about $500, while a high end version with a match barrel and a lightened slide might cost upwards of $2500. However, beware that cost doesn't always equal quality. I'll try to summarize the differences below as well as the possible applications for this fine pistol.

While most large scale manufacturers have a 1911 edition available for sale, 2011s are usually much more specialized. Some major frame manufacturers include STI and Strayer-Voigt, while builders include Limcat, and Brazos Custom.

Common Features:

- *Grip Safety.* Every pistol with this design has a grip safety under the beavertail at the rear.

- *Thumb Safety.* These, when clicked up, will prevent the pistol from firing.

- *Single Action Only.* With a few exceptions such as the Para-Ordinance Light Double Action handgun, all 1911s are designed to be cocked first then fired.

- *External Hammer.*

- *Flat Trigger Pull.* 1911 triggers are designed to move only from the front to the rear, not on an arc like many other guns.

- *Removable Grip Panels.*

Advantages:

- The vast array of different models, manufacturers, tinkerers, gunsmiths, enthusiasts, and so forth that support this pistol are mind boggling. You will not find a more worked on pistol in the United States than this one. This allows for a windfall of aftermarket support, parts, and accessories that enormously overshadow all other types of handguns.

- This is a very safe pistol with just the two safeties listed above. Certain producers also have included a firing pin block in their design as well.

- The trigger on this gun is usually pretty darn good out of the box, and has the most potential out of any trigger on the market. A competent gunsmith can get the pretravel, reset, overtravel, and lightness of this trigger to any level desired from competition to defense.

- Sizes of this gun range from large, long slide competition models down to tiny subcompact types.

- Lauded by many for easy "pointability" this grip angle is favored by many shooters.

- Magazine capacity can reach up to 17+1 rounds in a 2011 to even more with "big stick" magazines in competition.

- 1911/2011s can be incredibly accurate depending on the model.

- Aftermarket parts (as well as those from certain manufacturers) allow the gun to be tailored to various hand sizes through replacement grip panels, and dominant hands through ambidextrous slide and magazine releases.

- The heaviness of the gun allows for improved recoil control.

Disadvantages:

- Double stack models, especially with a thicker grip and top backstrap can be rather bulky for small handed shooters, allowing more difficult access to controls and a clean grip on the handgun.

- A single action only handgun must be cocked before firing. Therefore when it's carried on the person you must have the hammer back with the thumb safety on to allow a quick shot off the draw. Some people regard this as a possibly dangerous carry condition (although I feel that it's very safe with the proper training), and the exposed hammer can catch on articles of clothing.

- 1911/2011s tend to have a moderately high bore axis due to their slide resting on the outside of the frame rails and an external hammer, giving the forces of recoil somewhat more leverage.

- Some 1911s tend to jam more than modern designs at the same price.

- Magazine capacities on single stack 1911s are quite limited in comparison to other firearms out there.

- Reloads are difficult on out of the box single stack 1911s due to the small size of the magazine and narrow dimensions of the magwell.

- Some 1911s require extractor tuning to improve reliability. Internal extractors require maintenance and tensioning, while external extractors can cause problems for certain manufacturers.

- Quality differs drastically from manufacturer to manufacturer. I've had some that can digest a wide swath of ammunition types while another I couldn't get to run much at all with anything I threw at it. Magazine brands (Wilson Combat & Tripp Research are some of the best) and overall length/shape of bullets might be significant factors in the gun's reliability.

Since there are so many different types of guns built on this platform, it's difficult to discuss all of the positives and negatives of each particular model. The single stack 1911 series is most likely what you'll see in your average gun store as 2011s are usually specialty purchases not made by the average gun buyer. The question to ask yourself when purchasing a single stack 1911 is whether or not you can find a more comfortable gun with a higher magazine capacity elsewhere that is either striker fired or DA/SA. My overall opinion is that a lower end off the shelf 1911 has better alternatives elsewhere. However, if you're planning on working on the gun to get it the way you want, this gun can be customized to your exact preferences and exude awesomeness. Also the 1911/2011 is the standard bearer for many different types of shooting competitions, so that says something about its potential.

SIG SAUER P226

The Sig Sauer P226 is a very popular pistol with both law enforcement as well as some military units. It comes in 9mm, 40 S&W, and .357SIG, and is offered in a medley of different configurations. There are various trigger options and highly accessorized versions which include various grip profiles/sizes, and sights. The P226 frame is all steel, and most times offered in DA/SA. Sport versions of this gun are available as well.

Common Features:

- ***DA/SA.*** With the exception of the DAK double action only and the X-Five single action only versions, the Sig P226 pretty much always has a double action first pull with a single action follow up.

- ***Steel Frame Construction.***

- ***Wrap Around Grips.*** The backstrap of this gun is usually part of a screw on, wraparound grip.

Sig Sauer P226R with Meprolight sights

- **No External Safeties.** The P226 does not come with an externally activated safety and instead relies on its Double Action and internal safeties to prevent the pistol from firing accidentally.

- **Decocker Lever.** The rearmost lever on the gun is used to safely decock the hammer from the single action to the double action position.

- **Accessory Rail.** All new models of this gun come with one.

Advantages:

- The P226 is known for its reliability. Sturdy construction and high quality parts make for a gun that can function very well in less than desirable environments.

- A heavy frame reduces recoil and enables softer shots than lighter polymer guns.

- The backstrap of the grip shares some similarity with the SP01 in that it's nicely contoured to fit the web of the hand.

- The single action trigger of this gun is exceptionally crisp and comes in right under 4.5lbs from the factory with a good reset. When various options are added to the gun such as the Action Enhancement Package and SRT (Short Reset Trigger) from the factory, the single action works and feels exceptional.

- Controls are easy to reach even for smaller handed people.

- The double action on the pistol is very smooth, involves no rough spots, and is slightly easier to reach than the CZ SP01.

- Sigs are known for their incredible accuracy.

- The P226 Standard polymer grips have good tack and can be replaced easily. The E2 (Ergonomic grip) offers improvement over the P226 standard grip through shorter distance to the trigger and better traction.

- Large handed shooters will find this gun to be extremely comfortable to shoot and hold.

- Some aftermarket parts such as springs, sights, and magazines are readily available.

Disadvantages:

- A high bore axis contributes to additional recoil in the pistol as shooters cannot get their hands up as high on the gun as possible.

- The double action trigger pull is still pretty hard to reach for small handed shooters.

- The control mechanisms under the grip on the left side of the gun cause it to bulge outwards at the top. This makes the gun unnecessarily wide.

- The factory recoil spring is way too stiff and causes some light practice loads to jam the gun, as well as makes it difficult for weaker shooters to rack the slide. Furthermore, it induces additional recoil by absorbing less of the impact from the gun firing (more on this in the Gun Modifications section). This can fortunately be replaced easily.

- The P226 frame isn't that hard to completely strip, but replacing anything on the slide is a huge pain. The firing pin retaining pin is informally known as the "pin of death" because it's nearly impossible to get out and put back in. I've broken a couple of pin punches on it resetting it, and will never try to remove it again.

- The magazine capacity leaves a lot to be desired with a 15+1 standard in the 9mm version. Additionally, the mag well is rather narrow, leading to more difficult reloads.

- While there is somewhat of an enthusiast community devoted to Sig, there aren't a great deal of people out there customizing their guns or tearing them apart. So chances are if you want to really do something special to the gun, you'll have to send it to a professional or to the factory.

- Sigs are expensive. The base P226 comes in at $950 with the Elite at $1200, and more advanced sporting versions such as the X-Five at $3000.

Holding the Sig Sauer P226, you get the impression that you'll never break it. And you probably won't. The gun is very well crafted and very accurate. It has decent ergonomics in terms of the rounded edges of the gun and curve of the backstrap and larger handed shooters will adore it. However, for a gun this big, there's no reason why the magazine well/capacity is so small. Also, you get the distinct impression that most of the weight of the gun is above your hands when you lift it up to aim it.

For the price for one of these you could essentially buy a pair of Glocks, which will last just as long and be almost just as accurate. They will also hold more bullets and require less money to work on. Owning a Sig is kind of like owning a Mercedes. When you drive one you feel the quality of engineering and you're glad you paid for it. However all of the leather seat warmers and Bose stereo systems in the world won't prevent you from getting beat by a better driver in a Subaru.

SMITH & WESSON MODEL 625

Smith & Wesson is known for their long and adulated revolver history. They are perhaps best recognized for Dirty Harry's Model 29 (which catapulted sales after the movie came out- go figure) and the multiple .38 Specials carried by police for most of the 20th Century. The .45 ACP caliber 625 represents one of the pinnacles of S&W revolver engineering by serving as a popular defense gun and joins its cousin (the eight shot 627 in .38 or .357 Magnum) as one of the top performers on the competition revolver circuit. This gun comes in various barrel lengths, and a special Jerry Miculek edition is offered.

Advantages:

- The factory single action trigger is pretty crisp and easy to fire.

- Aftermarket support through the Smith and Wesson Performance Center is good. There are also a number of retailers offering parts for this gun including sights, hammers, and grips, so replacements are relatively easy to find.

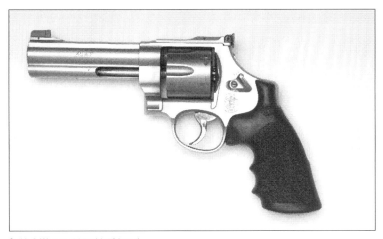

Smith & Wesson 625 with 5" barrel

- This gun is known for its accuracy and reliability.

- Being based off a long standing Smith & Wesson revolver tradition, there are plenty of competent gunsmiths capable of working on and enhancing this pistol.

- The heavy frame acts well to absorb recoil.

- Both rimmed and rimless cases can be used.

- Assuming that the trigger job (if performed) is not too light, then this pistol is capable of digesting wide varieties of ammo without fail.

- Reload times in comparison to other revolvers is quite good. To improve these, one can bevel the holes in the cylinder.

Disadvantages:

- These are quite expensive with an MSRP of over $1000 (as mentioned above, guns can often be found for under MSRP).

- In comparison to a semi-auto pistol, recoil is heavier on this gun as there are no springs to cushion the force, and by design any revolver has a higher relative bore axis.

- Moon clips will have to be purchased in order to operate this gun effectively with rimless cases. Rimmed cases can be used, but they're harder to find, and occasionally have extraction issues.

- The double action out of the box is very heavy and difficult to pull.

As far as revolvers go, this one is at the top of the line both in quality of engineering and performance. It's extremely reliable, very accurate, and easy to hold in the hand. However, as covered in the above section on choosing a firearm there are some inherent characteristics in the gun that render both advantages and disadvantages in comparison to semi-auto pistols. However, if one has the cash and the desire to pick up a revolver, the 625 should certainly be considered.

RECOMMENDED SAFETY EQUIPMENT
EAR PROTECTION

As someone who shoots a lot and has had his bell rung a couple of times by not being protected properly (usually not paying attention then having someone fire a gun right behind me), I tend to endorse lots of attention given to hearing protection. Why is this? Because your hearing doesn't come back; when it's gone, it's gone. Firearms are very loud devices, ranging from about 125 decibels for .22LR cartridges, all the way up into the 170 range for compensated rifles. Compare these to 140 decibels for a jet engine at 100 feet. Keep in mind that the scale is exponential, and for every 10 decibel increase the sound is *twice as loud!* A sudden impact in your unprotected ear can cause instant permanent damage through no more than one exposure. Yes, you read that right: one exposure!

Ever been to a rock concert? When you walk out your ears feel muffled and everyone around you appears to be mumbling. This is called a temporary threshold shift, where you ears have diminished your capacity for hearing in order to protect themselves from further damage. If you're lucky your hearing will return to normal, but there's a risk that you will experience a permanent threshold shift where some of your hearing is lost for good. Your inner ear is a sensitive configuration of small oscillating bones and auditory hair cells which reverberate to translate sound pressure waves into electrical signals that your brain can interpret. These organs are extremely delicate, and you cannot "toughen them up" by increased exposure.

Noise induced hearing loss (NIHL) is gradual, and OSHA has established industrial guidelines for noise exposure. Every shot you fire with an unsuppressed 9mm handgun well exceeds your daily recommended limit. That ringing in your ear? That's injury already occurring. Usually people with NIHL will not notice any changes until a lot of damage has been done already. You'll start having to lean in to hear things more frequently, your significant other will tell you that the TV is on too loud, you will start misunderstanding what people are saying because you can't pick up on the syllables. There's no reason to throw your hearing away either by being stubborn and refusing to wear protection or by under-protecting yourself. It's just dumb.

Here are some tips to safeguard your ears:

- Always wear ear protection when on a shooting range.

- Keep an eye out for the Noise Reduction Rating (NRR) of your protection. 33 decibels is about the highest you can get.

- Buy a good set of earplugs.

  - Disposable options are cheap, such as the very comfortable Howard Leight MAX and the EAR Superfit (good for determining proper insert depth).

  - Custom solid earplugs are available which are molded just for you to wear. E.A.R. offers a good solution. You can find these at pretty much all gunshows for about $60 a pair.

  - Custom electronic earplugs are available as well, which have a sound circuit through an electronic filter which allows you to hear normally but block out sounds louder than 70 decibels. These are incredibly expensive, but incredibly effective. (ESP makes them). If you're going electronic though, muffs are probably a better choice for the price (see below).

– Custom filtered earplugs are offered too which are marketed to not block out as much as solid earlugs and still allow the wearer to hear at a reasonable volume (many of these are used for musicians). Alpine makes an excellent filter and Westone an excellent custom plug. Less effective models are the Hocks Noise Breaker (which doesn't work as well in shooting environments) and Sonic Valve (which is okay for shooting a few shots, but not rapid handgun practice).

– Learn how to insert them properly. Roll them up between your fingers to the smallest possible size, then reach the hand opposite your ear over your head and pull up on the top of your ear to straighten your ear canal. Insert as deeply as possible.

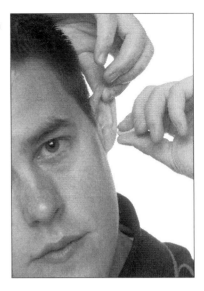

The proper way to lift your ear to insert plugs

■ Buy a good set of earmuffs.

– Peltor/AO Safety make excellent muffs from the passive 33NRR Optime 105s to the Tactical Pro/Tactical Sport electronic muffs (hear normal conversation and the circuit automatically blocks out loud noise).

– Pro Ears also offers some high protection electronic muffs.

■ For outdoor ranges, I wouldn't recommend using anything less than a 26 NRR for a handgun, but 33NRR is preferred either in a muff or a plug.

■ In indoor ranges, the echo of the firing makes things even louder. Make sure that you double-up on your ears. That's using earplugs and earmuffs over them.

■ What I use is a filtered custom earplug along with an electronic muff. This way I can hear everything that's going on perfectly fine, but am given maximum protection.

EYE PROTECTION

Eye protection is vitally important for shooters, particularly those shooting at steel objects (such as plates or pepper poppers). Even shooting indoors, safety glasses are always required since you never know what objects are going to come back uprange. I've been hit countless times with fragments of what I or people around me were shooting at. If you get one of those in your eye, it's going to be a trip to the hospital. Be careful.

Here are some recommendations for good eye protection:

- Buy correctly fitting glasses. By this I mean watch out for a gap in between the top of your glasses and your forehead. Hot shell casings might get ejected and land in here, which isn't fun.

- Buy glasses that wrap around somewhat to protect your eyes from the side. In many cases eyeglasses or sunglasses might look really stylish, but won't give you ideal protection. Plus you don't want to spend $200 on Gucci glasses just to scratch them at the range.

- Clear lenses are perfect for low light or cloudy conditions. Dark lenses are good for sunlight. I don't tend to like yellow shooting glasses as I don't find that they help my perception of the target or my sights at all. (This is my personal preference, and you should try them out if you're having trouble seeing in low light with clears).

Rudy Project photochromic lenses in the sun

- Photochromic lenses are the best all around lenses you can buy for shooting. These get darker automatically with exposure to UV light, and can be worn in all conditions.

- For rainy or indoor shooting I personally use Smith & Wesson fog free clear lens glasses. They cost about $5 a pair and are great with minimal distortion.

- For outdoor shooting in all other conditions I use Rudy Project clear photochromic sunglasses. I find that they let in a ton of light, allowing me to see my sights easily but still reduce glare.

- For prescription lens wearers like myself, my first recommendation is to buy contacts. It makes things a lot easier. Try out a bunch of different types from your optometrist to find the ideal clarity and comfort. Make sure that they don't dry out easily, as you'll have your eyes open for a long time while shooting. Additionally, try to ensure that your dominant eye (more on this later on in the book) can see equal to or better than your other eye. This will help you focus more quickly when mounting the handgun because your brain naturally causes you to see the image coming from the clearest eye. You want the clearer image out of the eye you're aiming with. If it's the other way around, and you're better corrected on your non-dominant eye, then when you're looking off into the distance at a target (for near sighted people) your brain will cause your perception of the target to come from your non-dominant eye. Then when you bring the gun up, you will have to focus on the sights with your dominant eye. This can cause you to pick up your sights slower.

- For glasses wearers, the one main issue is distortion. If you have glasses with a narrow profile, there will be some distortion around the edges. To see for yourself, put on your glasses and focus on an object in your periphery that's near the rim of your frame. Then while maintaining focus on it, turn your head. You don't want that distortion to affect your sight picture while shooting.. It's not a major problem, just something to be aware of.

CHAPTER 3

Your Shooting Foundation

When you're picking up a gun for the first time remember that it's supposed to be respected, not feared. A gun is a projectile shooting machine that has multiple functions from going out to plink bowling pins to defending your family. If you're reading this book, you're interested in finding out how operate this machine correctly and safely. Fearing something is usually based on uncertainty about what it can/will do. Respecting something is understanding its potential while learning how to use it properly.

Firing a gun is not a natural thing for someone to do! It causes an explosion to go off right in front of your face, and the instinctive response is to pull the gun downwards to prevent the recoil and close both eyes. This isn't very conducive to aiming! I've seen some very big students of mine that could literally deadlift a truck who could not stop flinching against the recoil. I've also seen some very petite young women that weighed no more than 110lbs who could immediately handle it. The flinch is the first thing that needs

Controlling the gun is about proper mechanics, not size:

- *Apply leverage to your advantage in body position and weight distribution*

- *Learn to isolate just the trigger finger when shooting*

- *Crisp front sight focus!*

to be corrected in practically all students. However, fixing this problem is a question of your mental approach, and I'll cover this first.

As a first time shooter, you'll have to remember to not get ahead of yourself. Learn the basics, and don't get frustrated. I know how annoying it is to aim at something, pull the trigger, and have your shots go all over the place. Just stay calm and see if you can work out why it's happening. There's always a logical explanation for it. If you're doing well, be aware of some milestones I've listed for moving on to the next section. Don't just say "yeah I got that" and try more advanced things because if your foundation isn't strong it will come up to bite you later.

Sometimes it's difficult to follow instructions even though they're laid out for you. This is because while you can understand conceptually what to do, you don't have the muscle memory properly developed and you don't know how something is going to feel. To use yet another golf analogy, you can't just read a book on golf and expect to be good because you've memorized the fundamentals. If someone tells you that you need to change something with your swing, the correction won't be automatic. So, to help with this, I've included some exercises that explain the correct "feel." Hopefully these will be of some assistance to you.

One final point I'd like to make is the same as the one I gave for buying a gun for the first time: Don't be intimidated! It takes some nerves to try out something new. Like any other activity, there are some really nice people who are only interested in seeing you get better, and some unlikeable ones as well. Some guys think that just because they have a Y chromosome that they should know how to shoot a gun. Sorry fellas, but it's an acquired skill just like playing baseball. Everyone who started shooting began right where you are today. So if you go out there and can't hit anything the right away, just smile, suck it up, and don't be afraid to laugh a little about it. You'll get better, I promise.

MENTAL ATTITUDE

Your mental attitude will have a considerable effect on how quickly you improve as a shooter. This is true for people of any skill level, and also holds true to any sport or situation. One thing that gets in the way of development is ego. Thinking that you know everything or refusing to try out new techniques for fear of looking foolish has proven to be a hindrance to many, many athletes. Your goal is to improve, and face it, unless you've won the world championship at something, there are going to be people out there that are better than you. Putting your head in the sand is no solution.

New shooters don't want to be seen as naïve, which is understandable. They don't want to be "the new guy that doesn't know anything" so they won't ask around for advice and will shy away from shooting in front of other people. All this means is that you will not grow as quickly because you will avoid opportunities to learn. If you do seek guidance from others there's a chance that other people will know that you're not very good in the short term, but guess what? Six months down the line everyone will be applauding how far you've come in such a brief period of time.

Experienced shooters sometimes take too much comfort in their own realms, and do not seek challenges elsewhere. If you're the best shot at your own gun club, leave! Go look for someone who can beat you, or try a new discipline. There are tons of guys who can accurately shoot 3" groups at 25 yards all day long but can't shoot quickly at all. That's because they've only focused on one skill set and feel safe with it. So when they get invited to go try something else like a steel shoot, they just reply "yeah, I don't do that kind of speed stuff, it's not real shooting" or something to that effect to justify not going. I think that this is one reason why some people who are only interested in defensive shooting might decline to compete in matches. Rather than viewing it as an opportunity to learn some new skills in a different environment some people just dismiss it immediately as being not for them.

I've personally been through this twice. I was a pretty darn accurate shooter at my local static range. I knew I was better than a lot of people who came through that door every weekend I went shooting. So eventually I worked up the courage to come out to my local USPSA club and try my hand there. I thought I was hot stuff and would be able to finish really high in the standings right off the bat. I got my butt kicked! I couldn't believe how fast those guys were! After that first match I realized how long I'd been deluding myself about my true abilities. Since that time I've been trying to round out my skill set and focus on my weaknesses instead of ignoring them.

The second time I came to the realization that I was shying away from other sports due to fear of failure was when I tried skeet shooting for the first time. I went out there by myself with no idea how to shoot skeet with the wrong equipment (a tight choked tactical shotgun). I was miserable at it and embarrassed. I didn't shoot skeet again for three years. I was willing to go shoot against hundreds of people with a pistol, but wouldn't go out with friends to shoot skeet because I didn't want to look stupid. Eventually a buddy of mine asked me to come out and try it (I never mentioned my first experience until then). I said okay, and was finally willing to admit that I had no idea what I was doing and might suck. He showed me the proper lead distances, the follow through technique, and lent me an appropriate shotgun. After a short time, I was shooting great! I realized again that I was deluding myself, and should have sucked it up, admitted that I didn't know heads from tails in skeet, and asked for help. I could have been enjoying another shooting sport for years if I'd done the right thing earlier.

My overall point here is to have an open mind. You should focus on being yourself and trying to get better. Don't let your fear or your ego get in the way. And when in doubt, take a deep breath and go for it!

MUSCLE MEMORY

When you practice, make sure that you don't take any shortcuts. Load the gun in the same way as you would a real situation. Focus on your sights as if you were in a real situation. When you have a malfunction, learn to clear it quickly. These all become important because by doing them you will develop proper muscle memory.

In a stressful situation, as it's said, you don't rise to the occasion, you simply fall back on your training. You'll be so focused on the situation itself that your subconscious will revert back to what it's done countless times, while your higher brain functions focus on the threat or the task at hand. If you're running away from a bull that's charging you, you're not thinking about what your feet are doing. You're just focused on the best route to get out of there. The same goes with shooting. If you're in a dangerous situation or a competition, the stress will cause you to do what you've always done. This is why it takes lots of time to successfully adopt and implement a new technique, because you have to retrain yourself.

You will perform how you practice, so be smart and don't get lazy. If you have a holster and you draw sloppily every time on a target in practice because "it's just practice" then even though you know the correct way to do it, those hundreds of repetitions done the wrong way will surface right when you need them most.

SAFETY FIRST!

Since a gun can be dangerous if not used properly, I'd first like to cover some basic safety protocols that you should drive into your subconscious. These are the four basic rules of firearms safety which you'll see in every shooting range, gun store, and firearm manual:

- Handle all firearms as if they were loaded. When picking up a firearm you should always verify that it's loaded or unloaded, and never make assumptions. It's always loaded unless you prove otherwise. Check the magazine/cylinder, and check the chamber to ensure that they're clear of rounds before disassembly, dry fire, or maintenance. If you intend for the gun to be loaded and carried/stored, verify that there's a round in the chamber, magazine/cylinder before holstering up.

- Always keep the firearm pointed in a safe direction. Walls are penetrable by bullets, especially within a residential dwelling. Safe depends on the situation. If the gun were to fire in the direction it's pointing, who/what might be on the receiving end?

- Keep your finger outside of the firearm's trigger guard and off the trigger until you have aligned the firearm's sights on a safe target and you have made the decision to fire. Keep your finger up and away from the trigger, riding along the frame unless you're about to shoot.

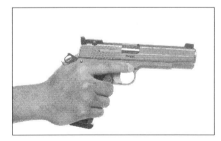

Finger rides along the frame when not prepared to shoot

- Always be certain that your target and the surrounding area are safe before firing. Bullets can travel over a mile in flight if the gun is pointed at a certain angle. Make sure that you have a good backstop and that the bullet won't go somewhere you don't intend it to.

In addition to the above, I'd like to add my own rules to the list:

- Don't be an idiot. Firearms can hurt other people if used irresponsibly. And guess, what? Sometimes the smallest little mistake can have lifelong consequences. This is a catch-all one. If you think it's stupid, it probably is.

- Don't drink or use drugs prior to shooting. Alcohol impairs inhibitions and motor control, they're just a bad combination.

- Don't shoot at water. Bullets can ricochet off water if shot at a certain angle.

- Don't shoot at hard surfaces from close range. Bullets also tend to fragment. If you're shooting steel, try to stay at least 7 yards away to prevent getting hit.

- Don't pick up and shoot random ammo. If you find a bullet on the ground in your caliber, don't shoot it. Who knows who loaded it?

- Observe the 180 rule. If you're shooting at a backstop, imagine that you're standing on an invisible line parallel to the backstop. Do not turn the gun past that imaginary 180 line. In fact, try to keep your gun pointed at the berm/backstop at all times.

- Do not handle guns when someone else is downrange.

- Always wear ear and eye protection! You can't "tough out" hearing loss or dodge debris coming at your corneas.

This may sound like a lot to remember, but it's all pretty much common sense and range safety. These rules are pretty intuitive, and all of them stem from preventing you from accidentally endangering anyone else.

LOADING/UNLOADING A HANDGUN

Follow this procedure to ensure safety. Also see Chapter 9 on Reloading.

1. ***Semi-Automatic Loading Procedure***

   a. Pick up the gun, and point it in a safe direction.

   b. Pull the slide back all the way and check to make sure that there's no round in the chamber. Lock the slide back by pushing up on the slide release lever and releasing the slide.

   c. Put the gun down and begin loading a magazine with rounds. The easiest way is to buy a magazine loader (such as an UpLula). Or just use your fingers. Hold the

Loading with UpLula

magazine in your weak hand (the one that's not holding the gun) with your weak hand thumb pressing down on top of the rounds already inserted in the magazine. Pinch the next round between your strong hand index finger and thumb and push down and in.

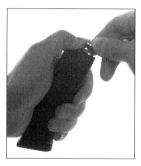

Loading by hand

d. With your finger off the trigger, pick up a magazine with your weak hand and insert it into the grip.

e. Either press down on the slide release to drop the slide, or pull it to the rear and release it under it's own pressure. This ensures that the slide will come forward with sufficient force.

f. If you want to "top the gun off" by having a full magazine and a round in the chamber, remove the magazine and insert one more round into it, then reinsert. (Do not drop a round into the chamber and drop the slide without a magazine in the gun. It causes additional wear on your extractor.)

g. Point the gun following the above safety procedures, disable the safety, and you're ready to fire.

2. *Semi-Automatic Unloading Procedure*

a. Hit the magazine release button to drop out the magazine.

b. If the slide is already locked back, then visually inspect the chamber to ensure that it's empty. If the slide is forward, then pull it back to eject the chambered round, and visually verify that there are no more rounds in the gun.

c. Drop the slide forward to close it.

d. Point the gun in a safe direction and pull the trigger to drop the hammer. (If your gun has a magazine disconnect then the hammer won't fall unless there's a mag in the gun).

3. *Revolver Loading Procedure*

a. Pick up the gun and point it in a safe direction.

b. Press the cylinder release latch to unlock the cylinder. In most cases it will swing out to the side.

c. Eject any spent cartridges.

    d. Load either a moonclip of ammo or individually load rimmed cartridges into the empty cylinder.

    e. Close the cylinder and rotate it until it clicks into place.

4. ***Revolver Unloading Procedure***

    a. Press the cylinder release catch to unlock the cylinder.

    b. Pointing the gun in a safe direction, press the ejector rod to knock out the spent shells.

    c. Close the cylinder.

AIMING THE GUN

Most handguns come with notch and post sights (sorry, no crosshairs or red dots!). In this section you're going to learn how to properly align those sights to ensure that you hit what you're aiming at. The first thing that you're going to want to do is determine which eye you want to aim out of. Then we're going to move on to discuss the two main "holds" that you'll have with the sights against the target. The work that you do with your eyes is one of the most important elements of shooting.

EYE DOMINANCE

Since people are born with two eyes, but it's important to be able to quickly switch focus between near and far objects, our brains have a natural preference for selecting vision out of a particular eye, otherwise we'd be seeing double quite a bit. This is nature's way of accounting for parallax (the effect by which when moving laterally nearer objects appear to move more that far objects). Eye dominance is just like being right or left handed. Why is it that you eat, brush your teeth, use your computer mouse, and write all with one hand? Without going into a complicated neuroscience explanation (and there's still no consensus on this) I'll say it's just the way it is!

When you're shooting a gun it's important that you get the sights aligned with your dominant eye. This allows you to aim more easily, and when you're shooting with both eyes open (covered next), you will be able to concentrate on your sights more readily and see "double" less. Sighting a gun out of your dominant eye just feels more comfortable.

Just because you're right handed doesn't mean that you're right eye dominant. This "cross dominance" exists in some people, and is often confusing because the natural tendency for a right handed person is to aim the gun out of their right eye. If a person with left eye dominance does this, then they'll either close their left eye, which is bad technique, or will keep both eyes open and have a lot of trouble aiming because their brains will want to use the visual picture that isn't aligned with the sights.

The easy way to figure out which eye is dominant is by the following:

1. Put both your hands out in front of you at arms length with your fingers together and palms facing away.

2. Make a right angle with your thumbs.

3. Put both hands together with one thumb over the other so that a small diamond of light is visible.

4. Look at an object in the distance through the hole.

5. While keeping your hands together and looking at the object, bring them closer and closer to your face.

6. When your hands are a couple of inches away from your face you will clearly see which eye you're using to look through the hole. That's your dominant eye.

7. Repeat in case you're not sure.

Eye dominance test

Occasionally there are people who do not have a dominant eye, and which eye picks up dominance changes depending on where they're looking. In this case, my advice is to do the above test regularly before you go shooting to determine which is your dominant eye for the sight picture/ distance you'll likely encounter on the range (i.e. where your front sight will be in relation to your face).

While eye dominance has been reported to change in rare cases due to injury or other factors, for pretty much everyone it won't, regardless of how much you try to "train" it. If you're right or left eye dominant don't attempt to alter it, you'll be wasting your time. Fortunately, handguns are

Right-eye versus left eye dominant right handed shooter

not like long-guns where you will need to mount the gun to your shoulder. If you're cross eye dominant just bring the gun up to the dominant eye. Don't turn your head or alter your posture. Also, don't despair, one of the best handgun shooters in the world, Dave Sevigny of Team Glock, is cross eye dominant.

BOTH EYES OPEN

While shooting a handgun, it's important to keep both eyes open. This is because of the following reasons:

- When shooting at a static target in front of you, the depth perception enables you to shoot more accurately and to quickly focus between your sights and the target, especially during rapid fire.

- When you close one eye you limit your situational awareness and eliminate a huge cone of your peripheral vision. For defensive shooting, this can be detrimental.

- As covered in the Developing Transitions section, your eyes move first to acquire new targets. Then you move your gun to where your eyes are pointed. If you're right eye dominant and you close your left eye, then it will be much slower for you to find and sight in on targets located to your left side.

- Shooting with one eye closed will really start to affect you when you have to do multiple things at once, such as move around obstacles, take cover, shoot on the move, and perform split second reloads. You will constantly be opening and closing that eye to get into "aiming mode" which will make you much less efficient.

- Closing one eye adds unnecessary facial tension due to squinting, leading to possible eye fatigue.

Some people have trouble shooting with both eyes open, claiming that they're "seeing double." This is because their eye muscles are unaccustomed to aiming a pistol correctly. To get an idea of the problem try this exercise. Pick up and hold a pencil out at arm's length. Now focus with both eyes at the tip of the pencil. Notice how everything in the background is now double? This

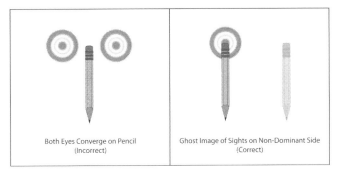

Both Eyes Converge on Pencil (Incorrect)

Ghost Image of Sights on Non-Dominant Side (Correct)

Adjusting focus with both eyes open

is because your focal point is close so the lines of sight from each of your eyes are crossing in the background. Now close your non-dominant eye and look at the pencil. Everything in the background is just a single image right? This is because there's only one line of sight.

What's happening here is that focus occurs on two different levels. When you have just one eye open, your eye muscles contract like a camera to focus on objects near and far. When you have both eyes open, however, not only does each eye change the focus distance, but the eyes turn inwards and outwards to converge on a *focal point*. Ideally in pistol shooting, you're going to want to keep the focal point off in the distance, but change the focus distance to view your sights and the target respectively. The most desirable focus for shooting will actually have two FOREGROUND objects (your sights) with a single background object. You use the sight picture from your dominant eye and ignore the non dominant picture.

This takes some getting used to. One effective method of practicing it is to first close your non-dominant eye and start shifting focus between sights and target with just one eye. Then while shifting focus, open your other eye. Unless you have a serious issue such as neither eye being dominant (which occurs in a very small percentage of the population so chances are it's not you), there's no excuse for shooting with one eye closed. Shooting this way will simply cause you to inhibit your future progress. Train to do it the right way.

SIGHT PICTURE

A standard notch and post sight picture will be one of two things:

- **A center hold.** This involves putting the top of the front sight directly on what you're aiming at and intending to hit. I find this to be by far the most useful and versatile of the two. If you're using a fiber optic or white dot front sight, then the top of the fiber or dot will point right at where you want your bullet to go. Most factory sights are configured this way as well.

Lollipop Hold (6 o'clock)   Center Hold

- **A lollipop hold.** Also known as "6 o'clock hold." This is used more for bullseye shooting where the target you're shooting at is black and you need to be extremely precise. This way instead of trying to locate your front sight and place it exactly where it needs to be in the center, you can just use the bottom of the target as a point of reference. Typically this hold requires more adjustment as distances change because there's more of an angle created between the barrel and the sights.

When you're sighting in a handgun for the first time, verify where your sights are pointed. If you're using a center hold on a gun that's setup for a lollipop hold then you'll be shooting high all the time.

Front Sight & Shifting Focus

Now that you've figured out the correct sight picture, keep in mind that the main tool you're going to be using to aim is your front sight. Rear sights are used just as a guide or reference point and are never intended to be focused on. You should be able to see peripherally that your front sight fits in the rear notch without staring at the rear notch. (Since you can only focus on one point on the gun at a time.) Obviously if you've never shot a gun before, you might want to check your rear sight alignment more often. However, as you shoot quicker and gain more experience you'll find that your brain subconsciously picks up the fact that your sights are aligned without you actually even noticing the rear notch.

You will have to shift focus between the sights and the target in order to properly aim. In order to sight in properly you're going to want to go through the following steps (assuming that you already are holding a loaded gun):

1. Look at the target that you want to shoot off in the distance.

2. Bring your gun's sights up to your dominant eye (not the other way around) while keeping both eyes open. The sights should be blurry as you're still focused on the target. Do not move your head by dipping or canting it while you do this; it's bad form.

3. Shift your focus back to the front sight of the gun. The target should become blurry. Ensure that your sights are aligned according to the proper sight picture.

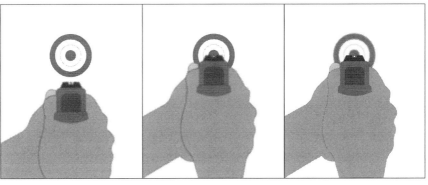

Focus on Target   Sights Brought to Target   Focus Shifts to Front Sight

4. If you're confident that the sights are aligned then pull the trigger to fire the gun (more on this later).

5. If you're not confident that the sights are pointed at what you want to hit, then shift your focus back to the target, then repeat Step 3.

This all may sound a little bit esoteric for beginners. So let me simplify what acquiring and shooting at a target should be like for you. I recommend that you try this at home, and use it to help train yourself to keep both eyes open while shooting:

When you're just walking around, riding in a car, or at your office, look at a "target" off in the distance. Make a fist with your strong hand and just point out your index finger. Then raise up your index finger to the "target" and quickly shift your focus from the "target" to the tip of your index finger. When your finger is in clear focus think to yourself "POP!" Then put your finger down and try it again with a different target. "POP!" That's how you pick up targets in the distance. You can do this anywhere, anytime, and it will really help your shooting. (Just don't try this around other people!) Do the same thing with a gun next time you're on the range.

STANCE

There are a great deal of funky stances out there that I see at the shooting range. I just don't get it. Why is it that you can hand someone a football and they'll naturally be able to get ready to throw it, or give someone a tennis racquet and they'll naturally get in a position to swing it, but when you give them a handgun they manage to contort their bodies into the most ridiculous poses? There are people who stand like they've been punched in the stomach by Ivan Drago, or who hold the gun like it's a vial of nitroglycerin. I suppose I can blame Hollywood for some of it, as new shooters tend to emulate the cops in their favorite movies like little leaguers imitate the batting stances of their favorite big league sluggers.

Let me put this one out there for you: a natural athletic stance is best. No hunching, no big leans, just standing naturally as if you were about to catch a ball thrown hard at you or hit a volleyball. If you've ever played sports, then this stance is familiar to you.

One of the central components of this technique is that you want all of the forces of recoil to come directly back at you in a straight line and be absorbed by your body and your muscles. This is because when you're firing the gun you want to ensure that you're not influencing the gun inadvertently in any direction when you pull the trigger. This causes shots to be "pulled" off target. Also, once the gun fires and recoil begins you want to reduce that recoil as much as possible so you can line up your sights as quickly as possible to shoot again. To facilitate this you want the gun to track straight back in your hands and not bounce from side to side. You're going for consistency. (More on this in the **Developing Speed** section.)

Let me explain the basics of the stance first, explain why it works, then later we'll add gripping a gun into the mix.

LOWER BODY

The basics:

1. Stand up normally facing your target. Your shoulders should be square, and your hips should be square. Your knees should be slightly bent. Your feet should be about shoulder width apart. Your toes should be in line with one another (during this step only). Your legs should feel comfortable.

Front view of proper stance

Side view of proper stance

2. Move your weak hand side (if you're right handed this means your left side) foot about two to three inches forward.

3. Put most of your weight on the balls of your feet by leaning somewhat forward. Your heels should not lift off the ground.

4. Your weak side knee should be bent slightly more than your strong side.

I can see you now, standing up and looking in the mirror trying to figure it out like a dance move. I know because I've been there before. So let me give you a couple simple exercises to try that will help you get the feel of the stance down:

Fun with weights:

1. Grab a pair for 10lb weights. (If these are too heavy for you, then go perhaps with a 5lb)

2. Stand with your feet staggered, knees slightly bent, and keep your weight on the balls of your feet.

3. Hold the weights out directly in front of you with your arms parallel to the ground. Bend your arms slightly so that they don't lock out.

4. Without moving your feet, or bending your arms, move the weights in an arc parallel to the floor so now your arms are extended at your sides.

Standing with weights in front and to the side

5. Now move one arm out front while the other is at your side, so your arms form a 90 degree angle. Reverse it, and do the other arm out front.

6. Move your arms around in front of you and to your sides.

7. At this point either one of two things can happen. You can either lean way back to balance yourself or lower your center of gravity. Do not lean back during the drill or you'll get the wrong idea. You should feel your posterior "sitting down" with the weight still forward on the balls of your feet the entire time.

8. Once you've found a place to put your feet that allow you to comfortably do this, you've found your stance. To test it, put the weights down and have a partner push you from the front. You should easily be able to not only absorb the impact of the push, but move out of the way quickly if needed as well.

The purpose of this exercise is to ensure that you're balanced properly and that your legs are ready to move quickly in whichever direction and absorb impact.

The push-over:

Another simple exercise is to have a partner hold up his/her hands, while you lean forward into them. When your partner moves his/her hands away, the shooter should not fall over forward.

This will enable the shooter to keep a solid forward balance without learning too far into the gun. Also, like the above drill, your partner should try and push you over backwards as well. If you find that you're falling easily in either direction with a little force then you need to rethink your weight distribution.

Shooter standing with a flat footed stance and weight on the heels

It's very easy to push someone over unless they have proper weight distribution

There are many reasons why this stance works:

- Once you're used to this stance, you can get in and out of it very quickly. This allows you to move from position to position (both laterally and forwards/backwards) with great dexterity and start shooting faster. It comes naturally and you won't be thinking about "setting up your stance" as you shoot.

- Your forward body weight allows you to more efficiently counteract the forces of recoil. In contrast if your weight were on your heels, it would take little effort to push you backwards and cause you to lose balance.

- Positions can include crouching or leaning around objects, in which case all you have to do is widen your base and move your torso.

- A square base towards the target gives you more freedom to rotate your torso to engage additional targets without moving your feet.

- A square base towards the target allows any recoil to come straight back at you to be evenly distributed throughout your body, and not deflected to one side.

- Slightly bent knees allow the muscles of your legs to absorb the forces of recoil.

If this stance feels awkward, then you're doing it wrong. One way to help improve it is to close your eyes and set your feet as if you were preparing for someone to push you from either the front or the sides. Once you're ready, then have a buddy start shoving you from random directions other than the rear (gently people). Your body will do the work for you.

UPPER BODY

The basics:

1. With your feet in a natural athletic position, your torso should be relatively straight with a mild, aggressive lean forwards.

2. Your shoulders should be oriented slightly in front of the hips, but not so much that you are inclined to fall forwards.

Shoulders square to the target with an aggressive posture

Weight forward, knees bent, leaning into gun

3. Your upper back should be relatively flat, and not hunched over forward or arched to the rear.

4. Your head should be up, and not "turtlenecked" into your body or craned forward or to the side. Both eyes should be open.

5. Shoulders should be more or less square to the target, and down and forwards in their sockets. Do not engage your trapezius muscles, and do not hunch your head.

Standing naturally   Hand raised   Gun raised- no additional tension or movement

6. Eyes on target.

7. Standing naturally like this, clasp your hands together and interlock your fingers. Then bring them up directly in front of you, arms slightly bent (not locked out). Do not add tension to your shoulders. They should be down and forward in your sockets. Your trapezius should not be activated, or your neck craned. You should not consciously do anything with the large muscles of your chest other than lift the arms up. (For example as if you were pointing out a low flying eagle in the sky to a friend of yours. "Hey, it's right up there!" *Points at the bird*)

One problem that many new shooters have is that they start to bend their backs either forward and down or backwards when the gun fires as a reaction to the forces of recoil. You don't want to do this. Just envision in your mind that your upper back posture should be like you were giving an old friend a handshake. Stand naturally and be comfortable.

This upper body position works because:

- Having your head up improves your peripheral vision/situational awareness and reduces tension in the shoulders. This helps you not only acquire targets more efficiently, but also reduces any negative influence that tension might have on the gun (in terms of both pulling shots off target and fatigue).

- Having your shoulders square enables the forces of recoil to come back in a straight line towards you to be absorbed by your body.

- Standing with good back posture allows you to pivot more easily and reduces tension. The moderate lean forwards will help your body control recoil by using your weight to your advantage. It also is an easier stance to get in and out of.

- It's easier for you to naturally point a gun quickly at what you're square to. Simply bring the sights up to your eyes.

- Having square shoulders enables you to get the proper hand position to form the grip.

To practice aiming with this stance, while interlocking your fingers in front of you, extend one of your thumbs up. That's your front sight. Put it on something and practice rotating and shifting your focus from your target to the tip of your thumb.

Remember: When you're aiming a gun, do not move your head down to the gun. Make sure that you move the gun to your eye level and keep your head in the same position.

GRIP

Now that you have your stance, you're going to start gripping the handgun. This part is very important, as your hands are what influence it both in firing and recoil management. What you're seeking is an even pressure all the way around the gun. This is because when it fires, the gun is going to want to move. It's your job to ensure that the gun's movements are reduced as much as possible and that the gun moves in a predictable way. Uneven pressure leads to lack of predictability and inaccuracy in follow-up shots. You also want to affirm that you're using as much mechanical advantage as possible to help counteract the forces of recoil. The correct technique puts a number of preventative measures in place that use the leverage and weight of your body as control mechanisms.

The pressure you're exerting is static pressure, and is the same before, during, and after firing the gun. It's as if you were to put a gun in a vice and pull the trigger. The vice doesn't care when the trigger is being pulled, and its clenching on the handgun will remain the same and will affect the gun the same every time. This is how you should view your grip. The trigger finger is isolated from the rest of the hand and is the only thing that's moving.

A major mistake that plenty of new and experienced shooters alike make is anticipating recoil. In this case, they utilize dynamic pressure, where they try to "pull" the gun down as its firing to act against the recoil. This doesn't work because it's not predictable, and you'll never be able to time it properly. If you try it, your shots will go all over the place.

Point of note: Once you find a grip that's fundamentally sound and works for you, find points of reference on the gun to make sure that you're putting your hands in the same place every time you form it. This helps you stay consistent.

USING LEVERAGE AS AN ASSET

Leverage is vitally important, as it acts as a strength multiplier. An example of it in action is when you are trying to change the lug nuts on your car. If the only tool available is a short wrench, then even the strongest of people might not be able to budge the nut. However, if the wrench is long enough, then your grandma could probably do it. This is a principle central to many martial arts including Jiu-Jitsu. A 150lb practitioner might be able to completely dominate a 300lb opponent not because he's stronger, but because he can use his strength more effectively. Archimedes once said "Give me a *lever long enough* and a fulcrum on which to place it, and I shall *move the world*."

Before I go into where your fingers are supposed to be on the gun, I'd like to illustrate the principle of leverage through an exercise. In order to do this, you'll need a long narrow object, such as a yardstick or golf club, and an assistant.

1. Get into your aforementioned comfortable athletic stance.

2. Grasp the club at about the middle, and point it straight up so that it's perpendicular to the ground and your hand is at about top-of-the-chest level.

If the grip is low and flat the shooter has no leverage

The club can easily be pushed back

Gripping higher gives the shooter more advantage over the club

3. Have your assistant grab the top of the club and push it back straight towards you. Try to resist. It's pretty difficult isn't it? Your assistant has all of the leverage over you and can push you around quite easily.

4. Now slide your hand up higher on the club so that there's less distance between each of your hands and have your assistant push. Try to resist. You feel much more in control now because your assistant's hands are closer to yours than before, therefore reducing his/her leverage over you.

5. Now, keeping your hand position on the club, cant your wrist at a downwards angle so that the top of the club is pointed towards your assistant instead of straight up in the air. Have him/her try to push it back at you under these conditions. You now have considerable leverage over the club and can prevent your assistant from pushing it without exerting any real force.

Canting the wrist forward with a high grip grants maximum leverage

The above illustrates how you can control force not by using tons of muscle mass, but by simple execution of hand positioning. Here you've done two things already. First, you got your hand up higher on the yardstick which reduced the length of the lever that the opposing force had against you. Second, you canted over your wrist thereby creating a mechanical advantage (a fulcrum point where your wrist breaks) over your assistant. When you apply those same principles to the handgun with both your strong and support hands, you'll find that even the smallest of people can effectively hold and control even a very powerful handgun by simply adopting the correct technique.

Remember: Your hands hold the gun. The rest of your body uses leverage to control the gun.

STRONG HAND POSITION

Proper strong hand placement will allow you to maximize your mechanical advantage over the gun. This puts you in a position to optimally resist the forces of recoil as the gun fires, and prevent the gun from moving side to side. To accomplish this, you're looking for the following points of contact between the gun and your hand:

- Gun is centered in the web of your hand between your thumb and index finger. To find out where the center is, make a "U" with those two fingers, and put a pen between them and push down. The ideal placement for the backstrap of the gun is at the deepest possible point.

- The web of your hand is up as high on the backstrap as possible. The gun should wedge in pretty firmly.

- The handle of the gun should be pointing at the small bone on the outside of the wrist.

Finding the center point of the web of the hand

Gun centered properly in the hand (SP01)

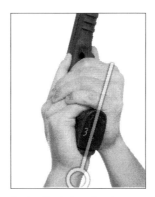

Center of backstrap aligned properly with wrist (M&P)

Strong hand thumb high up on the gun (M&P)

- Your strong hand thumb should be rotated up to be as high on the gun as possible. This opens up space for your weak hand. If you're shooting a 1911 or some other model with a thumb safety, this thumb should be on top of the safety.

- Your middle finger should be firmly in contact with the triggerguard.

- Your index finger (trigger finger) should make contact with the trigger face with roughly only the last half of the pad of the last joint. This is somewhat of a preference for many people. Some prefer a little more (usually revolver shooters due to the longer/harder pull), others a little less. Just make sure that you only use the last pad of your finger.

Firing the handgun with your strong hand in this orientation will help the gun fire and track in the most efficient way possible. One main problem that many people have is to orient the handgun over the thumb knuckle instead of in the web of their hand. This is because it feels very comfortable to do naturally. Unfortunately, it also causes erratic shooting since the forces of recoil are not being absorbed by the palm and are instead being deflected at an angle towards the outside of the hand. As a result, perceived recoil will be higher, the shooter will have a tendency to jerk the gun even during slow fire shots, and he/she will be all over the place on subsequent shots.

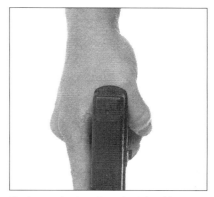

Gun incorrectly oriented over thumb knuckle (Glock 35)

Your strong arm elbow should not be locked out, ever. It should be bent ever so slightly. This is because you want your muscles to absorb the recoil of the pistol instead of your bones. If you lock your arm out, then all that happens when the gun fires is the recoil is channeled right through your elbow back into your shoulder. This will cause two things to happen. First, your strong hand wrist will then be a pivot point, causing it additional stress. Second, your upper body will be pushed back. These will both enhance perceived recoil. If you don't believe me, stand with your arms completely locked out and have someone push you at your hands. You'll fall back with minimal force.

To determine the exact amount of bend your elbow should have, completely extend and lock out your arm. Then bend your elbow so that your hand moves approximately two inches laterally from where it was. That's the correct bend.

SUPPORT (WEAK) HAND POSITION

A common misconception is that the weak hand (non dominant hand) is just there to help hold up the strong hand. That idea is a huge fallacy. The weak hand actually does more for recoil control than the strong hand does. The weak hand should be placed in a position that allows it to also be as high up on the gun as possible and deliver even consistent pressure all the way around the gun. One of the mechanisms that needs to be in place for your weak hand is called a "wrist cant." As addressed in the above section on leverage, canting your wrist forward grants you an additional mechanical advantage over a resisting force.

The first question to be answered is how do I get my wrist in the correct position?

1. Put your support hand against the top of your solar plexus. Offset it somewhat towards your dominant eye side.

2. Externally rotate your hand as much as possible and form a cup as if you were trying to hold an egg. Your elbow should be bent about 90 degrees.

3. While trying to keep the same rotation of your hand, extend it out in front of you at arms length. See if you can still hold an egg with your arm out.

4. Keep a very slight bend in your elbow (to determine the correct bend, use the same exercise as with the strong hand).

Holding egg in palm of hand   Arm extended with wrist still rotated   Normal grip
                                         & holding egg

If you look at the angle of your wrist once you perform this exercise, you'll see that it has a considerable downward bend. The bottom fingers of your hand will brace against your strong hand, preventing the gun from rotating backwards. The gun wants to rotate up and away from you. The top fingers of your hand will be high up on the gun giving it less leverage to recoil. An even pressure all the way around the gun will allow the sights to track consistently (just go up and down instead of all over the place) when you fire. Your thumbs will be forward, indicating that you have properly canted the wrist.

For the weak hand, you're looking for multiple points of contact around the firearm:

- Index finger is firmly pressed up under the triggerguard. This helps you verify that your hand is as high up on the gun as possible. Since I don't have large hands, I usually like to have my center index finger joint a little past centered with the bottom of the trigger guard. It helps me make sure that my fingers are wrapped around enough.

- Your weak hand palm should fit comfortably up against your strong hand palm. Sometimes this is not possible due to a large frame and small hands. Try to keep them in contact if possible. Avoid gaps in your grip if you can because this could result in an uneven distribution of pressure.

- Weak hand palm is as high on the gun as possible, and fits nicely in the open space on the frame under your right thumb. Think about getting the meaty part of your palm as high up as possible, this will give you a good feel for the ideal wrist cant.

Index finger under triggerguard

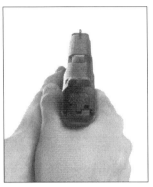

Palms wrapped around the grip contacting each other

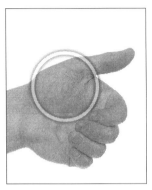

Think about getting the meat of your palm as high up as possible

- Your fingers on your weak hand are all in contact with your fingers on your strong hand. Sometimes the index finger on the weak hand rides a little far forward on the triggerguard so there's a gap between the center knuckle and the middle finger on the strong hand. This is okay, and shows you that your hand is canted properly. However, the last pads on all your weak hand fingers should be firmly in contact with your strong hand.

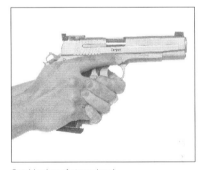

Outside view of strong hand

- Your weak hand thumb is pointing forwards, towards the target resting along the frame or possibly along the slide. (Don't try to add much pressure with this thumb. While it might be pressed into the frame as a consequence of a good weak hand squeeze, you shouldn't be thinking about intentionally applying force with it. If it's along the slide too hard then you could slow the slide down enough to jam the gun.) If you see someone giving you a thumbs-up, then they probably don't have enough wrist cant.

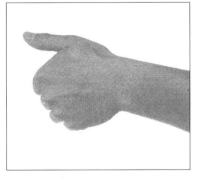

Outside view of support hand

- Think about wrapping your weak hand around your strong hand like taffy. You want lots of firm contact to be effective. Don't just pinch with the tips of your fingers, you won't get a good hold.

- Your weak arm elbow will appear to be slightly higher up and straighter than your strong hand. This is something to look for when using correct technique.

- Don't push down on your weak hand forcibly with your strong hand thumb.

Outside view of support hand with gun

Wrist cant is very important and should be stressed. It is a huge element of recoil control. Shooters trying this method for the first time might find it somewhat uncomfortable. As a result, they'll begin to reduce the angle of the wrist over time. If you're new to this, before, during, and after your shooting practice verify that your wrist is in the correct position. This is not something you'll only want to partially do, and many people "cheat" at it. Get that wrist canted.

GRIP PRESSURE

Some people talk about pushing and pulling with your hands. This is misleading and incorrect. As mentioned multiple other times throughout this section, your goal should be to produce even pressure all the way around the gun. You're holding the gun with a static force, like a vice, not doing isometrics. You should not be using your arm muscles to try and prevent recoil. Your arm muscles are there to hold the gun up, (including your biceps, triceps, and deltoids) not to add more pressure. Instead, what you need to be thinking about is SQUEEZING the gun with both of your hands. Once your hands are in the correct positions, you're going to want to squeeze in order to control the gun.

Make sure that you only squeeze with your fingers, and not your thumbs. Your thumbs are there along for the ride. To practice this, try squeezing your fingers together while giving someone a thumbs-up. Your strong hand's position will allow you to seat the gun firmly into your palm when you squeeze, and will more or less be focused on the backstrap and the front of the gun. Your weak hand's position will feel more like side to side pressure. However, since you're doubling your fingers up over the front part of the grip, you're dramatically adding resistance to recoil. The result should feel very comfortable and firm, like a completely neutral grip. Your support thumb might ride a little bit into the frame, which is okay. Just make sure that you're not pushing hard with it.

Now, how much pressure do you want to add to the gun? Go buy yourself a heavy hammer with a thick grip. Imagine that there's a stake in the ground that you want to whack with all of your might. For your strong hand, grasp the hammer using only your last three fingers (on a gun the thumb is going to be up and out of the way above your weak hand, and your index finger is going to be on the trigger). Then while gripping the hammer with only these three fingers, get the grip necessary to pound that stake as hard as possible. Do the same thing with the weak hand, except this time just grip the hammer with your four fingers and keep the thumb off.

It's impossible for me to tell you what percentage of your grip you should use, because you won't be able to duplicate it. Start with the hammer exercise, which should be about right. Keep in mind that you want to grip the gun

Strong hand grip on hammer

Support hand grip on hammer

hard, but not too hard. More strength means more recoil control, but the harder you grip the more fatigued you get, and the less manual dexterity you have. That last point is particularly important because you'll need it to precisely manipulate the trigger to be accurate. The strong hand should be firm, but not a death grip, while the weak hand should be pretty hard, but not 100%.

Once you've determined the correct grip pressure, go ahead and grasp the gun with your strong hand first, then wrap your weak hand around it. If you can easily manipulate the trigger without the gun moving around and the sights aren't shaking from the pressure then you've probably got it right.

Do not activate any of the large muscles of your chest/shoulders while you're shooting. The pressure on the gun should come from your hands/forearms alone. Doing otherwise will cause errant shots because the large muscles of your body are more difficult to control, and the application of force is too clumsy. Correct grip technique will allow you to manipulate even the highest recoiling guns without problems.

Point of note: When I talk about even pressure all the way around the gun, that doesn't mean that you necessarily have to grip with the same strength for both hands. It rather describes how you hold the gun in a firm, static position with your hands wrapped all the way around it so as not to influence the gun in a particular direction when firing it.

Instructors note: If you're showing a student how to grip a gun, it might be helpful to have them just put their strong hand on the pistol, then you can reach over their weak side shoulder and put your support hand on there. It's one thing to know theoretically how a good grip should feel; it's another to have the tactile sensation of one.

NOTES ON GRIPPING A REVOLVER

A modern revolver is typically gripped using a similar grip to the one mentioned above, but with small variations. Since there are gaps between the cylinder and the barrel/frame of the gun, when the gun fires part of the explosion is directed outwards (this is why you cannot put a sound suppressor on a revolver). Obviously you don't want to get your thumbs burned by these hot gases. Therefore when gripping a revolver, all of the same above principles apply, except the weak hand thumb will usually pin down the strong hand thumb. This thumb under thumb is done as minimally as possible, and is only used for the purpose of preventing powder burns and fitting the grip size of the revolver. Revolvers also have higher bore axes meaning that the elbows will tend to be a little more bent when shooting them. Additionally, due to the shapes of many revolvers' grips, one usually cannot achieve the degree of cant achieved with a semi-auto.

Proper Single Action revolver grip

Proper revolver grip

For single action revolvers, typically the emphasis on the support hand is to manipulate the hammer (as opposed to control recoil) while the strong hand grips the gun. As a result, the support hand thumb tends to be behind the hammer, and the index finger is in front of the trigger guard (to get higher in order to reach the hammer). To provide additional support against the resistance of pulling back the hammer, the strong hand pinky will tend to be wrapped around the handle of the gun. For rapid fire, the trigger can be held down while the hammer is manipulated to fire the gun, or for single shot fire, the thumb is rested behind the hammer while the gun fires, then the trigger is released and the gun is cocked again.

TRIGGER CONTROL
YOUR FINGER ON THE TRIGGER

The last pad of your index finger should be the only point in contact with the trigger face. I prefer to just have the last half of this pad touching, but some people like to have a bit more in there. Other than that, your finger should be bent at the center joint so that you can see light between the gun and your index finger. More trigger finger means more pull strength (such as when shooting a double action revolver) but also can result in less control. You do not want to use any more than that pad on the trigger.

Many people love to put their trigger fingers really far into the trigger guard, and pull the trigger with the joint or even the center pad. This is because it tends to feel really comfortable for people to do, and harder trigger pulls, such as those on factory double action revolvers, become a lot easier. Unfortunately, even though it might be comfortable for the novice, this type of technique will cause you to both become inaccurate and shoot slower.

Using the last pad of the trigger finger

The inaccuracy of this style is caused due to the fact that the goal of pulling the trigger is to influence the gun as little as possible while firing. Too much trigger finger will change your finger's contact point on the face of the trigger, and begin to activate more muscles in your hand than intended. To prove this, make a "C" shape with your fingers, and extend your index finger. Now curl your trigger finger down as if you were making a fist rapidly while trying to keep the others still. You will notice your other fingers start to move anyways. When pulling a trigger using a deep hold, you will inadvertently start pulling on the gun with your other fingers in a similar fashion. You have lots more manual dexterity for small movements in your fingertips than you do farther down on your fingers, and your motions will be less influential of the rest of your hand.

Too much trigger finger

You will be a slower shooter using a deep hold as well, due to the fact that it's a lot easier to make rapid movements with just the last joint of your finger than the entire finger itself. These rapid movements have a direct effect on how quickly you can pull the trigger. If you tend to shoot low left (as a right handed shooter) and you're having a lot of trouble finding your sights after you fire the gun, this could be a cause.

PRESSING TO THE REAR
There are many ways of describing the actual trigger pull, including "squeezing not pulling" the trigger. While this sounds good, new shooters tend to have a good amount of trouble understanding what it exactly means. My recommendation is that you focus on manipulating the trigger finger while keeping everything else perfectly still. At the higher levels, how this works exactly is somewhat of a preference issue, and some people have different styles of pulling the trigger. However, I'll let you know what has worked for me as well as some other really good shooters.

In order to pull the trigger, keep your last joint firm and flexed, but think about pulling from only the center joint of your index finger. This is a practical way to go because when lots of people think about activating that last joint, they have a habit of bending the rest of the fingers of their hand. To test that theory, extend your fingers forwards with a slight bend. Then try to just curl the last joint of your index finger rapidly while keeping your other fingers straight. It's difficult, isn't it? Now just bend your index finger all the way leading from the center joint. Much easier? When using the latter form to pull the trigger, especially if it's heavy or you're under stress, your other fingers will not tend to be influenced as much. This is important because the more unpredictable factors you reduce over the gun, the quicker and more accurate you can be.

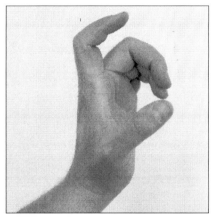

Try to move your index finger while keeping the others still.

All of your fingers other than the index of your strong hand should be exerting a static pressure over the gun. In other words, they're clenching the gun tightly, but that force isn't changing or causing the gun to move. The trigger finger is the only finger that actually causes movement of any part of the gun. If when pulling the trigger you cause your other fingers to suddenly apply more pressure, then you'll move the gun off target. This is typically a low-left pull for right handed shooters because that extra squeeze at the last moment will cause the gun to dip. You want to add even rearwards pressure on the face of the trigger.

RIDING THE RESET

If you're shooting a semi-automatic handgun, once the gun fires you have to release the trigger in order to fire another shot. There's a certain point that you'll be able to feel in the trigger when it resets and the gun is ready to fire again. When you're shooting, there's no reason to move the trigger out any more than that. This is called "riding the reset." Otherwise you're just causing the trigger to travel unnecessarily and forcing your finger to move more. Many people will tend to let the trigger all the way out which is necessary for a double action revolver but is impractical for semi-autos.

Trigger completely depressed & reset point

To find the reset of your semi-auto handgun, pull the trigger on an empty chamber (no magazine in the gun) then cycle the slide manually while keeping the trigger depressed. Slowly release the trigger and you'll feel an audible click. From this point, you can pull the trigger again to get the gun to fire. Practice doing this multiple times (I do it a lot, and recommend it for everyone) so that you can find the ideal range of motion for your trigger. In the photo, it barely looks like the trigger moves at all, which is true on a good quality handgun.

When you're actually shooting the gun, either slow fire or quickly, you're going to want to ride this reset. It allows you to shoot more accurately because less motion in the trigger finger causes less influence on the aim of the gun, and the break point is easier to indentify during the pull. If you have to pull the trigger quickly through the full travel, then you will build up momentum with your trigger pull, and you won't have a very good feel for the break point once you reach it. Riding the reset also enables you to shoot faster because you're able to manipulate the trigger with improved speed.

For the slow fire break, this is really easy to do. Just fire the gun, hold the trigger down, and slowly release it. When you feel the click, aim and start pulling back again. When you're shooting faster, your mind should know approximately where the reset is. You shouldn't be waiting for it, but you should instead subconsciously be moving your finger a short distance past the known reset point every time before pulling again.

PUTTING IT TOGETHER

By now we should already have all of the basics of how to comfortably stand and accurately put a bullet downrange on target. However, to refresh your memory, I've included a checklist that you'll want to use when shooting slow fire:

1. Put on proper ear and eye protection. Make sure that your range is safe and that you're clear to shoot.

2. Stand comfortably with your feet just about past shoulder width apart. Knees slightly bent and most of your weight forward on the balls of your feet. Your stance should be somewhat staggered with your weak side foot a few inches in front of your strong side.

3. Your shoulders should be more or less square to the target, with your head up and eyes forward on target. Your back should be mostly flat with a mildly aggressive lean forwards.

4. Pick up the handgun with your strong hand and load it with your finger off the trigger, then form your grip with the handgun close to your body (pointed downrange).

5. Your strong hand should be high and centered on the backstrap, with your strong hand thumb rotated up and out of the way. Middle finger firmly under the triggerguard.

6. Your weak hand palm should be in contact with as much of its side of the handgun grip as possible and be as high as possible. Index finger middle knuckle firmly under the triggerguard. Wrist canted over to point your thumb at the target. Strong hand thumb resting on top of the weak hand. Grip is firm but the gun is not shaking, and palms are touching if possible.

7. Extend your arms from your body to bring the gun's sights up to your eyes (don't dip your head). Arms should be out far, but elbows should not be locked. Shoulders down and forward in their sockets. Your support arm should appear straighter than your strong arm due to the wrist cant.

8. Align your sights on the target so that the front sight is centered between the rear sights and appears to be at the same height at the top.

9. Put your strong hand index finger on the trigger. Use only the last pad (preferably the last half) of your finger to contact the trigger.

10. Focus crisply on the front sight of the handgun and slowly apply pressure to the trigger.

11. Breathe slowly until you feel the break point of the trigger coming up.

12. Exhale half your lungs and slowly apply more pressure until the gun fires. Don't release the trigger immediately after it fires.

13. Once the gun fires, watch the front sight as it rises in the sight channel.

14. Allow the front sight to come back onto target. Do not muscle it down, just watch it. Keep your grip steady. This is called follow-through (See Chapter 5 for more info).

15. Slowly release the trigger until you feel the click of the reset (semi-autos only).

16. Repeat from step 10 until the magazine (slide will lock back) or cylinder is empty.

17. Remove the magazine or unload the cylinder.

18. For semi-autos pull back the slide to visually inspect a clear chamber, then point the gun downrange and pull the trigger on an empty chamber to drop the hammer.

19. Verify that the range is clear and go downrange to inspect your target.

IMPROPER TECHNIQUES

Now that I've told you what works from a shooting standpoint, I'd like to get into what doesn't work and why. Most of these problems become very apparent with multiple shots and multiple targets. Some people can shoot a handgun with a single accurate shot with just about any technique (even upside down). Keep in mind that skill level plays a role here. Just because a technique isn't the ideal way of doing something, a person that's well versed in it will beat a neophyte with proper fundamentals any day of the week. So, I'll explain the rationale behind why certain methods of shooting are not the best approach. I have refrained from talking about certain styles holistically, because I would like to break down their elements.

SUPPORT ELBOW TUCKED

One very common style of shooting involves a heavy bend in the support elbow which is tucked way into the chest. This style originated a few decades ago, and is still taught by some instructors. However, I feel it has several drawbacks. The original purpose of this was to emphasize the "push-pull" grip where the weak hand pulls the gun towards the shooter to create isometric tension.

In this case the shooter would be using his/her weak side bicep to pull, while pushing with his/her strong side tricep/deltoid. Proponents will argue that this tension is effective at reducing recoil because it locks the gun in place between the hands using the large muscles of the arm.

Hey punk, freeze!

Note the different angle at which the wrist sits in relation to the forces of recoil

As we've established earlier, leverage and mechanical advantage play a huge role in recoil reduction as force multipliers. Effectively, the correct technique allows you to distribute recoil throughout your entire body. The wrist cant forwards creates a fulcrum point in your wrist which clamps the gun in place with considerable static force. The support elbow down style eliminates this cant and changes the angle at which the recoil forces are directed at you, leaving the muscles of your arm to do the work (and get tired in the process). Furthermore, it does not allow your support hand palm to get as high on the gun as possible. While people like tucking their support arms because it "feels" like they're doing more, in practice it becomes wasted energy as you can have better recoil reduction with less expended effort. If you want to test this theory, do it with a yardstick as in the above leverage exercise. Is it easier to push something heavy with your arm tucked into your chest and bent at 90 degrees, or when the elbow is out and your arm is nearly fully extended?

Other major disadvantages arise when you are forced to deal with multiple targets. First, it's significantly easier to index on something that your shoulders are squared to. Secondly, if you have to turn to engage a target, it's much harder to shoot when rotated significantly to your weak side with a tucked elbow.

PUSH-PULL HOLD

When you create isometric tension, you're introducing opposing forces to one another. The problem is that this pressure is not consistent, and will not be consistent when other forces are applied, such as recoil. If you reduce the force applied by one while not simultaneously reducing the force applied by the other, you have motion because the forces no longer counteract one another. Try keeping everything perfectly still under lots of pressure while firing a handgun accurately as it bounces around. Chances are the hand you're pulling with (the weak hand) will at some point lose a little grip, and the hand you're pushing with will overwhelm it, causing you to push the next shot low. My question is why would you use lots of big muscles to keep something statically in place, while you can just hold it that way with your hands? Your hands can provide a steady, even pressure all the way around the gun allowing it to track in a predictable way under recoil. Also, in order to push-pull, you have to involve other muscles of your arms which leads to fatigue with no benefit.

LOCKED OUT ELBOW

A completely locked out elbow is a common technique problem that results in increased felt recoil, and additional stress on the joints of the shooter. This is because the recoil is supposed to be soaked up by the muscles of the body. When a joint is locked out, all forces delivered to that joint are transmitted directly through the bone- not the best shock absorbing material in the world. To test this theory, completely extend your arm and lock out the elbow. Then have someone grasp your hand and push you backwards. Your arm is not doing anything to control that push, it's just transferring the force back to your shoulder joint. The only part on your body that's rotating will be your strong arm wrist, which will start to take a bit of punishment if you keep doing it.

Normal elbow bend — Locked out elbow

While many good shooters appear to have fully extended arms, keep in mind that there's always a slight bend, which makes all the difference.

OVERBENT ELBOW

Be careful to not overbend your elbows either. When you do this, you reduce the mechanical advantage that your support hand has by lessening the overall amount of wrist cant available within your range of motion. In other words, the closer your hands to your body, the less you can bend that wrist over. Additionally, if you bend your arms too much, you are giving the gun more leverage to jump back at you under recoil. Extended arms brace the gun more effectively. Try doing a close-grip push up to illustrate this. It's much easier when you're at the top and your arms are extended further than when you're against the ground and your elbows are bent way in.

EXCESSIVE UPPER BODY TENSION

A lot of shooters tend to bunch their shoulders up by "turtlenecking" while shooting. Others feel lots of strain in their chest muscles as they use the pectorals to press inwards on the gun. These errors tend to be both a cause and a symptom of desire to control recoil. Typically something else is wrong in the shooter's technique which is causing either the hands to break apart under recoil, and/or increased muzzle flip. As a result, the shooter tends to compensate by "pushing down" on the gun while firing with the shoulders, or trying to crush the gun with the pecs. In either case, the shooter is usually gripping the heck out of the gun, but is doing so in an improper way, and feels like he/she has to do something else to control it. Unfortunately, this will only result in pushing shots off target, usually low.

FLAT FOOTED STANCE

This is when a shooter's entire body is square to the target, and if you were to draw an imaginary line from toe to toe, it would be parallel to the target face. This doesn't work because there's no stance offset. An average person's foot is only going to be about 10 inches long or less. This means that if pushed from the side, that person will be very stable due to having a wide base. However, if pushed from the front, there's very little resistance to them losing their balance. Try standing completely square to a target and have an assistant push you back, even a little. Have them fake pushing you a couple of times to make sure they don't anticipate it. Recoil pushes you back the same way, and you don't want to be stumbling when firing a gun.

Flat footed stance

BLADED STANCE

This case is the opposite of the above, where the body and both feet are bladed towards, or in some cases perpendicular to the target. This stance is usually presented with its hallmark tucked in support elbow to form the Weaver stance. This presents a number of problems to the shooter:

- A bladed stance is more difficult to get in and out of while moving. It takes longer to set your feet when running laterally. When running forwards, you must stop, then turn your body to adopt the stance. Additional movement required of you once you're in a shooting position will make you slower overall. Compare this to the correct technique where your shoulders will be naturally square to the target, enabling you to get a shot off faster.

Bladed stance- note the torque on the entire body to get into this position

- A bladed stance prevents you from rotating your upper body quickly and comfortably to engage targets from the sides. When your body is in the correct position, it's considerably easier to shift your weight to have a wider range of motion while keeping your feet in the same place. This is important, because every time you pick your foot up, it will disrupt your aim, reducing accuracy.

- When your stance is bladed, you're forced to essentially shoot across your body. Instead of the forces of recoil coming straight back at you in a predictable fashion, this will cause them to be deflected at an angle. This makes shooting quickly more difficult as the gun will track less consistently. (Tracking refers to how easily you can follow your sights.)

- The bladed stance becomes even less practical when forced to shoot around barricades, particularly from the weak side. Balance is difficult to maintain, and shooters used to tucking in their weak elbows won't know exactly what to do with them.

- Bladed stances have less lateral stability. Try standing in one, then having someone push you from the side. You'll quickly lose your balance.

- For defensive shooters, body armor provides much more protection from the front of the vest than it does from the sides. A bladed stance exposes your weakest side to your adversary.

- Finally, it is not a natural way to stand. You don't see people waiting for the subway train in a bladed stance. The proper stance feels more natural to people, and is more versatile. I even found it difficult to stand this way to pose for the photos!

THE LEAN

Many people while shooting want to lean either forwards or backwards at an exaggerated angle. This is usually in response to the recoil of the gun. Don't do this. Leaning too far forward will offset your balance and cause you to possibly pull the gun down below the target when firing. It also is uncomfortable and tiring. Leaning too far back will enhance the sensation of recoil and push you backwards with every shot. Your back should be at a somewhat aggressively forward, natural posture when shooting. Use your bodyweight and leverage to reduce the recoil, but don't contort yourself.

Excessive forwards lean   Excessive rearwards lean

INCORRECT GRIPS

There are a number of permutations that I've seen on the grip. Below are a few that you should avoid and why:

- **The thumbs-up**. I call this one the Fonz. "Heeeey buddy, guess who's shooting? This guy!" Someone that has their support thumb way up in the air indicates that they're not properly setting their weak hand wrist, even though they might believe that they are doing so properly. There's nothing saying that your thumb has to be pointed directly at the target, but there's no way you can have your wrist in the correct position while giving the thumbs-up.

- **The thumb under thumb.** This grip has been traditionally taught for decades with semi-auto pistols. It has its origins in revolver shooting. While easy to learn, it also suffers from certain disadvantages which are exacerbated the more the weak hand thumb overlaps. It tends to result in an uncanted wrist, which dramatically increases felt recoil. It also opens up a large gap between the palm of your support hand and the side of the gun. This uneven pressure causes the gun to track more erratically when being fired. Additionally, your support hand is prevented from getting up as high as possible on the gun, further increasing recoil. In revolvers, it is somewhat of a necessary evil, but even then, it's minimized as much as possible with the support thumb barely overtaking the strong hand thumb. In semi-autos it simply represents outdated technique.

- **The teacup.** I've heard many justifications for this one, some even as hilarious as "it helps keep the magazine in the gun." (Guns that have the magazine sporadically drop out of them are usually in terrible states of disrepair) In this case the support hand does literally nothing except help your strong hand hold the gun up, which is something that in normal circumstances you should have no trouble with anyways. Due to its low position on the grip, the teacup does not counteract any recoil in any conceivable way. It should not be used.

- **The wrist grab.** Like the teacup, this does nothing to counteract recoil and should be avoided. Do I really need to break this one down? You might as well shoot one handed the correct way.

Correct grip

The thumbs-up

Thumb over thumb

Teacup

Do I even need to explain why this one is wrong?

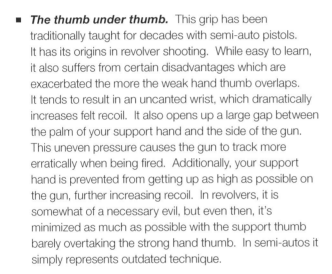
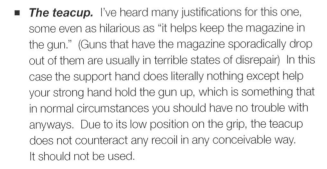

- **The backwards thumb.** In this situation, the shooter wraps his/her support hand thumb around the rear of the grip over his/her strong hand. In this case, it's impossible to develop any kind of a wrist cant, thereby decreasing the ability of the weak hand to reduce recoil. Furthermore, this technique usually causes a large gap to open up between the support side of the grip and the support hand. This causes the gun to track less consistently as there is now uneven pressure all the way around the gun. Also, if this thumb is up high enough, it will get whacked by the slide with a semi-auto. In all fairness, this technique began to be developed for the purpose of shooting single action revolvers quickly. With it, the shooter can hold the trigger down and quickly manipulate the hammer of the gun, thereby allowing the fastest possible follow-up shots. It is the preferred method in the Single Action Shooting Society (SASS) and is used to great success with those types of pistols. However, with a modern semi-auto or revolver, I would definitely not recommend it.

- **The backstrap gap**. This one is quite common as well, where the shooter doesn't have his/her hand as high as possible on the backstrap. Sometimes this is simply due to ergonomics of the gun (usually combined with smaller hands), but is often due to a technique problem. If you can see light between the backstrap and the hand the gun will likely produce lots more felt recoil, and may have a tendency to jam due to parabolic whiplash (slide moves in more of an arc than normal) under recoil.

- **The index finger wrapped around the triggerguard.** In a quest to get the support hand higher on the gun, some shooters like to wrap their index fingers around the triggerguard. In fact it's even visibly used by a very small number of shooters at the highest level (even the current IPSC World Champion in Open division). At the top, this is more of a preference issue. I don't really like this technique for the following reason: the oft quoted leverage. When holding the gun in this position, that index finger has little power over the gun because it's extended. To prove my point, when gripping the gun this way (unloaded of course), have someone try to peel your finger off. It's pretty easy because your fingers have considerably less strength in that position. Now have that person try to peel your index finger away when it's wrapped against your others under the trigger guard. It becomes a lot more difficult.

At the end of the day, I would not recommend this to new shooters. A percentage of experts have used this style to great success, but less experienced people would often find themselves making more mistakes by trying it.

CHAPTER 4

Developing as a Shooter

have structured the next sections as a general path that new shooters should take in order to start building their skills. Conceptually it works like this:

1. Learn how to shoot accurately. If you can't hit a target with regularity, then it means that you don't yet have the correct form, either in posture, grip, trigger control, or more. Accuracy fundamentals are some of the core principals to shooting.

2. Once you learn how to hit the target routinely, then we'll introduce speed to the equation. How fast can you put shots into the target?

3. Once you can shoot quickly with consistent small groups, then we'll start throwing more targets into the mix.

Take your time and master each chapter going forward!

- *Everyone loves shooting fast- that's why I do what I do. If I couldn't shoot fast, I would probably have taken up another exciting sport such as crocheting. But if you move too far ahead too quickly you won't develop the proper foundation.*

4. At this point, you'll be able to stand and hit multiple targets quickly and with confidence. Now we'll start introducing other faculties such as draws, position shooting, movement, etc.

In order to progress, there are certain drill based goals and section based tests which should give you an idea of where your skill level should be before continuing with the program. I have included these because when you're first starting out you don't want to get ahead of yourself. You'll just develop bad habits which will be more difficult to break later and your problems will be harder to diagnose. For example, if you do a little slow fire then just jump right into shooting quickly you'll be pulling shots all over the place. You might wonder why you can't hit what you're aiming at, get frustrated, and start changing things around. However, the real reason for your inaccuracy could be that the problems that you haven't fixed with trigger control were simply exacerbated when you upped the speed of engagement. Be sure to complete the challenge prior to continuing to another section.

Later on in the program, there are no more "goals" or "tests" per se, but rather some general "Milestones." The purpose of milestones is to give the non-competitive shooter some basis of comparison of his abilities to those of others. Not everyone wants to shoot standardized competition but would like to know how good they're getting at a given skill or if they should work on it more. For example, out of a holster, how long should it reasonably take you to put two rounds center mass on a target 7 yards away? 5 seconds? 3 seconds? 1.5 seconds? The answer may surprise you. Here I'll include ratings based on performance of the drill. In these segments, I assume that you already have all of the basics of that section down, and can therefore start working on what you deem to be important or can try something else. Let the milestones guide you to where you may need more practice.

DRY FIRE

Dry fire is defined as cocking the gun and pulling the trigger without any ammunition in the gun. It is a practice technique of incredible value to shooters of any level, and in many cases will give you better gunhandling skills than time actually spent shooting for real. Grip, trigger control, multiple target transitions, draws, reloads, or any other gun related ability can be improved using dry fire. Why is this? Because you're eliminating the factor of recoil, which is a major external influence, and focusing only on developing your muscle memory.

There is not a single decent shooter on the planet that doesn't dry fire, whether they're police, military, or in the competition circuits. I cannot stress its importance enough. For new shooters, before going to the range for the first time and actually shooting a handgun, I would recommend finding a pistol and dry firing it 1000 times. This will allow you to know what the gun feels like and be comfortable with its operation in a safe, controlled environment. You will be able to quickly locate the trigger break points and be able to critically evaluate your mechanics before you begin reacting to the recoil of the firearm on the range. If you can train yourself towards using good form prior to even firing a bullet, then you're well on your way.

Whether you're a beginner or an advanced shooter, before actually going out and trying any of the exercises in this book, you should practice at home dry firing them until you're completely prepared. This way you can take your time and evaluate if you're doing everything correctly, and you can gain familiarity with the procedure. Drive it into your subconscious. Whenever I try something new, such as a new style of draw from a holster (always trying to get faster), I will stay at home and do hundreds of repetitions before putting a single round downrange. Then when I go out to do some live fire, I know what it's supposed to feel like. It's great for getting used to a new piece of equipment or a new gun. You can do this without even pulling the trigger, and instead dial-in something like rapid sight pictures on different targets. Time spent on your dry fire to live fire ratio should be about 90%/10%.

There is a long circulating rumor that dry fire is bad for a handgun. This idea has its origins back with older designs and lower quality parts. When a gun is fired with ammunition, the firing pin whacks into the primer. With dry fire, the pin goes its full travel and is stopped when its shoulders hit into the end of its channel. This produces moderately more impact, and in the past you might notice more wear. Today, you can dry fire most modern handguns essentially without fear (though there are exceptions). I've dry fired my Glock 35 probably over 50,000 times (no snap caps) and never had to replace anything except springs (regular maintenance, not because they broke). I've dry fired my CZ SP01 Shadow thousands of times, and I haven't even owned it that long! Most handguns are extremely durable machines and you're not going to break them very easily. I dry fire the heck out of everything I own because I'm a shooter, not a collector. I want to be as familiar as possible with my gear, and to practice as often as I can so I can get better.

Point of note: Certain handguns are not designed for dry fire without the use of snap caps (dummy rounds). Some examples are older single action revolvers and some rimfires. In the former case, the firing pin is designed to be cushioned by the primer of the ammunition. If the gun is dry fired a lot, then the firing pin bushing can wear out and the hole towards the breechface can start to widen and burr. Modern day single actions correct this problem by using a transfer bar instead of a hammer mounted pin. In the latter case, the firing pin on the rimfire might impact the side walls of the empty chamber, which are made of hard metal, and start to wear. This is because its travel is also designed to be stopped by the ammunition. When in doubt, buy some snap caps and check your manual. It will usually tell you specifically not to dry fire the gun if there is a likelihood of damage.

Here are some tips for dry firing:

- Do it as often as possible. However, I don't necessarily mean spending a boring block of 30 minutes in your basement every day. When you get home from work, pick up the gun for 5 minutes and click around, then put it down. Maybe come back to it later when you have another minute or two. If you make it a chore, then you won't want to do it very much.

- When you're trying something new, practice it with no ammunition for awhile to get the muscle memory down before you actually head to the range.

- Buy some snap caps. If you have an external hammer semi-auto or revolver, then these will cushion the blow of the firing pin when you pull the trigger. (Striker fired handguns have to have the slide racked before every shot, so snap caps are somewhat pointless, as you'll eject one every time you reset the gun.) Snap caps are also good for practicing reloads without having to use actual ammo.

- When dry firing, try not to drop the slide (lock the slide back then hit the slide release) on an empty chamber. If you make a habit out of it, this can cause unnecessary wear to the gun because a round would normally cushion the impact. Ease the slide forward by hand.

- Always load snap caps in the gun using a magazine (for semi autos). If you just drop the dummy round, or any round for that matter, into the chamber and drop the slide on it, additional stress will be placed on the extractor. This is because the extractor usually catches the case rim as it's feeding from the magazine. This is particularly bad on 1911s that do not have spring loaded extractors.

- If you want to practice shooting reactive targets and have a more thorough training experience, airsoft is a good substitute.

TIPS ON COMMERCIAL RANGES

Most targets at commercial shooting ranges are not ideal for training. Shooting at an all black silhouette for example, is a bad idea for working on accuracy. You want to be able to see your bullet impacts when you make them without having to go check the target. This way you can get positive and negative feedback based on what you did while pulling the trigger. Completely black targets prevent you from doing this because the bulletholes blend into the background. Use a white target, such as a piece of folded computer paper taped on brown cardboard. You can buy the cardboard sheets at Home Depot. It's cheap, and if you miss, then you'll know why. Tape the cardboard frequently with brown Scotch tape, and replace the computer paper every couple magazines/cylinders.

Try to shoot in good lighting conditions. Many indoor ranges are hard to see properly in and therefore get good sight pictures. If you have to, then maybe wear a hat with a small flashlight attached to it or your shooting glasses so you can see your sights better. I've found this to be somewhat helpful when combined with a really reflective white dot up front.

There are a couple of disadvantages to outdoor ranges however. First, if you're shooting in a state that has winter, (which is something I try to avoid without skis and easy access to a hot tub) then the cold tends to be prohibitive. Also, public outdoor ranges tend to have static lines, which do not allow you to adjust target distances. The vast majority of indoor ranges have electric target hangers which can be moved to the correct distance. Many of the initial drills in this book are designed to be shot in the shooting lanes of commonly found indoor ranges for the sake of convenience to most readers.

Ideally in order to get a lot better as a shooter, you're going to want to be able to find a training facility that allows you to move around through multiple shooting bays and setup your own drills. I'm fortunate enough to have one about 30 minutes from my house. Many of the fundamentals can still be practiced from a static line, however.

CHAPTER 5

Developing Accuracy

The first thing any shooter needs to do is learn how to shoot accurately. This will help you plant the roots for your future development. Too many shooters like to skip way ahead and start blasting away. Do this to your detriment. Anyone can put a huge target at 7 yards and empty a magazine into it. It's a lot of fun, but you won't learn anything from it. If you can't hit a target consistently while just standing there, gently applying pressure to the trigger, then how do you expect to be able to shoot fast under stress? All of the shooting you're going to be doing has a basis in accuracy. Starting with slow, precise shots you will begin to get comfortable with shooting, and will soon be able to correct your own mistakes. It's a skill you will continue to rely on for years to come.

Make sure that you breathe and take frequent breaks. Hitting a small target a great distance away takes time and patience. Focus on your trigger control, as that's going to have one of the greatest effects on your success.

Accuracy is at the core of any good shooter:

- *Correcting your flinch is priority number one*

- *Master the slow fire break for the tightest groups*

- *Practice follow-through and watch your sights as they rise under recoil*

THE SLOW FIRE SURPRISE BREAK

The most accurate trigger pull technique is called the "surprise break." Its moniker comes from the fact that the shooter is more or less surprised when the gun actually fires. This surprise is a good thing because it means that the shooter has not anticipated the recoil of the gun, and therefore has kept the gun perfectly stable while firing. This is what new shooters should first attempt to achieve.

The process is simple. Just aim the gun at the target (front sight focus), and slowly, slowly apply pressure to the trigger with just your index finger. Eventually you'll feel the "break point" of the trigger, where if the trigger moves any farther to the rear the gun with fire. Continue to add more force at a very slow rate, and the gun will go off. Obviously you'll have a general idea of when the gun is going to fire, but the point is that you're increasing the force on the trigger at such a low and slow rate that you don't know exactly when.

Now why would you want to do this? Don't you just want to pick up the gun and blast away? The surprise break encourages accuracy and proper trigger control. I still use it if I'm trying to hit a tiny target at a long distance. It is a fundamental that you must learn, and from here you just pick up speed on the trigger as your skill level improves. The reason it works is because when many people know the gun is going to fire, they subconsciously start pulling the gun down or squeezing more on the grip to counteract the recoil they're expecting. This is called a flinch. This dynamic pressure on the gun will cause it to move away from what you're aiming at, and it usually comes right before the gun goes off. Then many people will exclaim "I had the target right in my sights! How come I shot way over there?!" It's very frustrating to aim at something and not hit it. The surprise break eliminates those external factors from coming into play and disrupting your aim at the last second.

Some tips on performing a slow fire surprise break:

- Breathe! Lots of people have a susceptibility to hold their breath when they're shooting a gun. This isn't a bad idea if you're shooting a rifle from a prone position and you're just about to fire. However, when you're holding up a hunk of metal at arms length for 20 seconds per shot, it doesn't work so well. Visual acuity starts to deteriorate quickly without oxygen. You might even start to shake a little. When aiming, just breathe very slowly and the gun won't really move much.

- Focus on the front sight while you slowly pull the trigger.

- Your grip will tend to be somewhat lighter when shooting for extreme accuracy. This is because holding a really firm grip is tiring, and the less you squeeze with your strong hand the more dexterity you'll have with your trigger finger. Also, you're not worried about speed of follow-up shots.

- Eventually as you get the slow fire break down, work on timing your breathing. You don't want to be holding your breath for more than 5-6 seconds. Your timing should involve breathing in and out slowly until you are right up against the break point. Then exhale slowly until your lungs are about half full. Stop exhaling and apply just a bit more pressure to fire.

- The key to slow fire breaks is to not influence the gun in any way while it fires. Keep it perfectly still. Shooting for speed requires substantially more technique. Shooting for accuracy requires substantially more patience.

- Follow through! Use good form and watch the sights back down to the target as if you were going to fire another shot. Too many people just drop the gun down to their bodies once the gun fires, then pick it up and aim again. Done due to a desire to look for hits, it usually results in bad ones. Don't do this, it becomes a bad habit to break.

- Holding the gun up looking for extreme accuracy is tiring. Take a break every couple of shots.

- Try to keep the same grip. Don't shift and reform your grip between shots every time. Many people constantly make adjustments between shots. This is a crucial component of follow through. Of course you'll have to occasionally shift it to the right place, but it should not be part of your routine.

WATCHING YOUR SIGHTS

While you're prepping the trigger to fire (starting your pull before the break point) your focus should be crisply on the front sight. Everything should already be in alignment, and you're going to want to look just at that dot on the front of your gun on the target. Try to keep it very still while you pull the trigger. Focus on your front sight while the gun fires.

Once you fire the gun, it's going to move back very sharply in your hand. Your rear sight will appear to remain relatively static, while your front sight will appear to rise. In order to help you reacquire your sight picture for a follow-up shot, or to diagnose problems in your technique, it's very important that you take note of what your front sight is doing under recoil. Ideally it should move only on a vertical plane. This allows for the fastest follow-up shots because you don't have to realign your sight picture.

Watching your sights is also a key element of follow-through. Even if you're firing slowly, you're going to want to practice preparing for another shot quickly. Do not force the front sight down! Let it settle down on its own.

CALLING YOUR SHOTS

If you maintain a crisp focus on the front sight while you're shooting, and the gun fires, you will see a quick final sight picture just as it's going off. (If you're losing the front sight just as the trigger breaks then it means you're doing something to pull the gun off target.) You should remember this flash sight picture- where the gun was pointing at that very instant of ignition. Using it, you should be able to tell with a high degree of precision where that last shot went without having to check the target. This is a valuable technique when shooting slowly as it makes up the final component of follow-through and provides feedback that you're doing things right. Once you can call your shots regularly you've made a big leap. Eventually when you begin to pick up speed, you'll just know that when you aimed and you pulled the trigger, you hit what you were aiming at.

When shooting for accuracy, do not look at the target while you're firing the gun. Your accuracy will suffer dramatically.

ACCURACY PROBLEM SOLVING

There are many types of potential problems that can result from shooting for accuracy. These can be quite annoying and will lead many new shooters to either claim a problem with the gun or to just hit a skill wall and lose motivation to improve. About 95% of the time these errors are simply caused by the shooter unknowingly doing something to move off the point of aim just before the gun is about to fire. The actual concept of shooting for accuracy is very simple. However, we're not programming androids to shoot, we're trying to convince people to be very still when they know an explosion is about to go off in front of their faces. As mentioned previously, it's an unnatural thing. Telling someone not to flinch is like an announcement telling a crowded movie theater not to panic, then following it with a 120db wailing fire alarm and flashing lights. It might take some effort to control your reaction. However, I'll give you a list of drills/hints to help overcome these problems. Many times, there is a combination of mistakes occurring at once. Focus on fixing one at a time. Also make sure you're using the correct fundamentals first.

Point of note: A "group" is a term describing the pattern of shots you've put on target.

SIGHTING IN YOUR GUN

It goes without saying that if your sights are not correctly mounted to the gun then your shots will be off center. This can happen, especially with adjustable sights that get out of alignment. Generally the way it works is that if your rear sight is too far to the left in the sight channel, you shots will go left, and vice versa. If your front sight is too tall your shots will go low and vice versa. Front sights and rear sights come in different heights as well, and it's your job to make sure that point of aim = point of impact. Typically they are fine coming out of the factory, but this isn't always the case. Examine your own shooting for problems first before looking at the sights being off, especially if you're a new shooter.

An example of a common sighting problem is that you prefer a lollipop hold (aim below the target to hit it), so you've aligned your sights to match. Then you loan the gun to your buddy that prefers a center hold (aim directly at the target to hit it). He then aims at the center of the target, but his point of impact will be considerably higher. He will shoot over the target every time until he is able to find the correct point of aim for those sights. Some people also have a natural tendency to pull shots left or right so they dial in their sights to compensate. If someone without that problem picks up the gun to shoot it then he/she will be missing the target until that person finds the correct point of aim for that sight configuration.

A similar case to the above can occur when dramatically changing ammunition, such as a huge difference in weight/design of the bullet and velocity of the round. However, in handguns, most ammunition changes at most ranges do not produce significant differences in flight characteristics or points of impact. If you're interested in absolute pinpoint accuracy for bullseye matches, and ¼" makes a big difference, then you might be more particular, but that's a tiny minority of shooters.

For either above case, the shooter that wasn't used to the sights should be able to shoot a nice tight group with the handgun. However that group will just not be in the center of the target. If you're shooting a huge group, it's highly likely that it's your fault, not the sights. In order to rule this problem out, you're going to need a bench rest of some sort. If you're not a particularly accurate shooter then you're probably not the best person to do this. Find someone more experienced.

1. Spray paint or stick a few 4" white circles on a large gray/light brown background.

2. Go back about 20-25 yards and find a seat with a table. If you can get sandbags or a bench rest device, then go for it.

3. While sitting in the seat, sprawl out across the table and support the handgun as best possible.

4. Shoot seven shots as slowly as possible into the circle.

5. Inspect. If the group is wider than six inches, you pulled some shots. Shoot this drill a few more times regardless.

6. If most groups are six inches or smaller, then you have a decent idea of where the gun is shooting.

7. Group too far left= move rear sight to right. Group too far right= move rear sight to left. (More on this in the Gun Modifications section)

8. Group too high= install taller front sight. Group too low= install lower front sight.

9. Sometimes your front sight might be way off center. This can occur if it's mounted in a side to side dovetail, such as on the Smith & Wesson M&P. Visually inspect it to ensure that it's in the right place. Otherwise, most of your adjustment will come from the rear sight.

Once your sights are in proper alignment, either take a picture of them, or find some points of reference on your gun. That way at a glance you can check to see if they're in the right position should you be unsure. Sights don't often move around, even if the gun is dropped, but it can happen over time.

CORRECTING A FLINCH

Typical low left pull

The flinch is one of the most common errors in shooting. It is characterized by someone who can practice dry firing a gun all day with pretty decent form but whose shots always end up down and to the weak side. The root of this problem is in anticipating the recoil. Just as the gun is about to fire, the shooter preempts the gun going off either by dropping his/her arms, leaning his/her body forward, or tightening up the strong hand. In either case, the muzzle of the gun drops lower or points at a downward angle. The gun then fires and the bullet misses the target. Usually this is preceded by a flawless sight picture and slow pull of the trigger. All the shooter can remember is that the gun was seemingly right on target when it fired, but low and behold the tear in the paper indicates otherwise.

The flinch is difficult to correct because its origins are psychological. It's a reflex action. How do you convince someone to not do something that they don't know they're doing? You can both encourage proper fundamentals, or if that fails, try to trick them out of it. There are a couple of methods that I recommend:

- Improve follow-through. Once the gun is slow fired on target, the shooter should watch the sights settle back down onto target and prepare for the next shot without adjusting the grip or dropping the hands. In some cases this can be encouraged by having the shooter pause the gun for a second or two after it rises up upon firing. Then the gun can be slowly, manually brought back down on target.

- Use dummy rounds (snap caps). If the shooter has otherwise good fundamentals, then dummy rounds can be used during slow fire. Have a buddy load up your magazines or cylinder for you at least half full with dummy rounds in random places. You won't know where they are, forcing you to treat every round like a dummy round. In a lot of cases, when the trigger is pulled on a dummy round, the shooter will see his/her gun immediately dip- the defining aspect of a flinch. When a dummy round is hit, rack the slide to eject the round (semi-autos), and try again. The next round might be live, or it might be another dummy round. This practice prevents people from anticipating the recoil and helps them do the same motion every time. Many people will simply align the sights correctly then mash through the trigger really quickly which causes a low pull.

- Shoot one handed. I like mixing this up a little bit because it takes shooters out of their element. Removing the supporting hand forces shooters to concentrate on their strong hand where the flinch will easily present itself. Also, while shooting one handed, the gun will always have the front sights rise (even if the shooter flinches and pulls the gun a bit low), encouraging proper follow-through technique.

- Change calibers. In many flinch situations, the downward jerk is caused in reaction to impending recoil. So to encourage fundamentals, remove the recoil. Shift to a .22LR and work on accuracy. If there's still a problem with a flinch, then the shooter should try the highest recoiling handgun that he/she can find, like a .44 Magnum. Then the shooter can blast away a few magazines or cylinders full of that without caring too much about how accurate the shots are. Then he/she should immediately switch back to the .22LR, which will feel like shooting a spitgun in comparison.

- Improve your grip. Keep in mind that a great deal of recoil is caused by shooters who aren't gripping the gun properly. Make sure that your grip is firm enough and that your hands are in the right position. Remember that you're only supposed to be pulling the trigger with your trigger finger, not anything else. The rest of both your hands should exert static pressure.

- Reduce tension in your arm/shoulder muscles. You might be trying to control the recoil too much with your upper body. Remember that you want to use leverage, not muscle. The only pressure should be coming from your hands, the rest should be only enough to keep the gun up.

- Dry fire a lot. If you don't develop the correct muscle memory off the range, you won't be able to develop the skills on the range. Pull that trigger hundreds of times at home with an unloaded gun (more on this later) to get the correct form down.

Sometimes a flinch takes awhile to get rid of. Keep at it. Persistence will pay off.

SHOOTING HIGH

Typically those who shoot groups high (and we're all familiar with the dreaded "hanger tap" at an indoor range) are having the same flinch problem, but are manifesting it in the opposite way. This can occur in two main ways:

- In a typical flinch people will push the front of the gun down to counteract the recoil. In this case, it's an issue of a shooter attempting to absorb the recoil by moving with it. Think about catching a football thrown quickly at you. The shooter will tend to bend his/her elbows dramatically and/or dip the rear of the gun with the wrist. This causes the gun to aim upwards and the shot to go over the target. A shooter doing this also tends to have a really light and/or low grip and seems to be a little more afraid of the gun firing. A backwards posture (leaning away from the gun) also occurs frequently here.

Dropping the wrists and elbows

- In the second case, the shooter is really trying hard to concentrate on follow through, and actually starts moving the gun upwards before the shot has even broken. In this case, the shooter can usually identify the problem quickly because the flash sight picture will be high.

Correcting this problem is very similar to fixing the flinch. However, if you're shooting high, then it tends to be significantly easier to remedy. The main focus here is on improving the grip and minimizing the recoil. Adopt a more aggressive posture and get a firmer grip on the gun more with your support hand. (Don't overdo it, just keep hand tension firm, but eliminate shoulder tension) Ensure that you're using correct technique with your wrist cant and strong hand position.

Also, concentrate on getting a perfect sight picture and follow-through. Make sure that your finger doesn't leave the trigger, and practice using the reset to fire the gun. One thing some people do while shooting high is immediately drop the gun from eye level once it fires and yank their trigger fingers off the gun. When you force yourself to keep the gun up there and your finger on the trigger, it becomes more difficult to start pushing shots high.

PUSHING SHOTS RIGHT AND LEFT

First off, make sure that you're using correct posture. If your stance/upper body looks good, then these types of problems tend to be more grip oriented. If you're using the proper grip, then your left and your right hands should be exerting an even, comfortable pressure all the way around the grip of the gun. This leaves two components of your grip that might be delivering lateral pressure. If the shot is at the correct vertical level but it's to the right or left of the target, then you're simply pushing too much with either your thumb or your trigger finger.

If the shots are going to your strong side, then you're probably digging into the frame too much with the thumb on your support hand. Some people like to rest their thumbs on the frame (I do). Others prefer to keep them from touching the frame. If your thumb is in contact with the frame, and you're pushing hard with it towards your strong side, don't be surprised if you push a shot over there.

If your shots are going to your weak side, then it means you could be using too little trigger finger (and also probably a pretty light grip). If the tip of your finger is just on the edge of the trigger, then you could be pushing the trigger, and therefore the gun, towards your weak side. This problem is by far the least common of all of them, especially with slow fire.

To correct this, make sure that your trigger finger is in the correct position, and if you choose to rest your weak hand thumb on the frame of the pistol, don't push too hard with it while gripping the gun.

You could also simply be steering the gun over in that direction due to somewhat of a flinch. In this case you're going steady on target, slowly applying pressure, slowly applying pressure, then just before the shot breaks you turn your body a little bit or push the gun over a little bit with your strong or weak hand. The only way to correct this is through dedication and trigger time so that you know not to move when you're firing a shot.

ACCURACY DRILLS
7-15-25 YARDS

There are no specialized drills to accuracy shooting that you can really do. Essentially at this phase of your development, you're problem solving. The purpose of your training here is to develop trigger control fundamentals. Recoil isn't a factor in your technique because you're not worried about follow-up shots. Its only impact is psychological. You just need to start slow, and once you're comfortable shooting at close range you can send the target out a little further.

If you're having problems hitting the target, make sure you consider some of the accuracy advice from the previous section. One of the most valuable diagnostic tools at your disposal is the dummy round. Have a friend load these up at random in your magazine so you can see yourself what's causing the gun to point off target.

1. Start at 7 yards. Initially put up a large target (orange torso sized is good) at close range to just get familiar with shooting the gun. Once you can put all your shots on paper move on.

2. Reduce the size of the target at 7 yards. Instead of shooting at a torso, shoot at an 8.5" x 11" piece of computer paper taped vertically to the target, slow fire. Once you can hit the box relatively consistently, move on.

3. Reduce the size of the target at 7 yards. In this case fold the computer paper twice, once lengthwise, once widthwise so that it's 4.25" x 5.5" hanging vertically. Once you can hit the box consistently, move on.

4. Reduce the size of the target at 7 yards. Now just go buy some Post-It notes and stick them on your background. Once you can hit these relatively consistently, then you're going to want to start increasing the distance.

5. Move the target back to 15 yards. Visually, doubling the distance decreases the relative size of the target by half. However, things will become more difficult because the target will require more of a focus shift. Start with two pieces of computer paper taped together lengthwise (a 17" vertical target). Once you can hit this consistently, move on.

6. Shoot at a single piece of computer paper on the target.

7. Shoot at a single piece of computer paper folded twice, as in Step 3. Try for 50% hits.

8. Finally, move the target back to 25 yards when you're confident in your ability to make hits at this distance. Start with a torso sized target to get used to the distance, then start making smaller and smaller targets until you think you're ready to take the accuracy challenge.

ACCURACY TEST

Up to this point so far you should have been practicing simple accuracy drills. Good accuracy is the core of any shooting program, and it's necessary to establish a solid base in it before seeking more advanced training. Prior to moving forward, you should be able to achieve a solid ten inch group at 25 yards while standing unsupported. By this I mean load up at least 10 rounds and put every single one of them in a row into an 8.5" x 11" vertical box. Relatively speaking, this shouldn't be a huge challenge. Your gun can probably shoot 2.5 inch groups from a bench rest. However, until you can do this, shooting rapid fire or engaging multiple targets is still beyond your grasp because you have not yet demonstrated proficiency with the absolute basics of shooting. Don't just move on because you got lucky and managed to hit your shots a couple of times. This should be something that you can do on a routine basis.

A good shooter can generally hit 4-5 inch groups at 25 yards with reasonable consistency standing freestyle. It's obviously possible to shoot to the accuracy potential of the handgun, but from what I've witnessed, this is exceedingly rare.

CHAPTER 6

Developing Speed

Congratulations! You've moved beyond the first step and are now able to shoot accurately. If you've never picked up a gun before reading this book, then if you're moving onto this section, you should be proud of yourself. From this point forward, I'm going to assume that you have a basic level of proficiency in accuracy. If you do not, then you will find yourself making basic trigger control mistakes that will be tough to diagnose within the confines of speed shooting drills.

In this section, you'll learn how to quickly deliver rounds downrange at various distances on a single target. You will learn how to properly pick up your sights and be able to unload an entire magazine into a static target with a very high percentage hit rate. Once you master this section, you'll be able to avoid the pitfalls of recoil control and engage targets with precision very quickly.

As mentioned in the previous section, trigger control is paramount to slow fire accuracy, and fundamentals of

Shooting accurately at speed comes from consistency:

- *Consistent grip and stance*

- *Consistent trigger press*

- *Consistent sight tracking*

stance and grip don't seem to matter that much. The only real goal there is to make sure you don't influence the gun while pulling the trigger. However, when you're trying to shoot fast, which is an incredibly valuable skill for both defense and competition shooting, the way you position your body and hold the gun will have a dramatic influence on you. The key is again static pressure. You want to be firmly controlling the gun with your hands and your body, but not trying to "push it" anywhere when you shoot.

It's all too common that when people start shooting multiple shots, as the gun starts moving around the shots start going everywhere. The effect is exponential. You shoot your first shot fast, and it's slightly off target, then the next one is more off target, then who knows where that third shot went. Your errors become magnified. This occurs because the recoil of the pistol is not being absorbed properly, and the sights are moving around erratically while the shooter tries to manipulate the gun into position. I liken this to a car that starts to skid on an icy road. Usually it's not the initial frozen patch that causes the accident; it's the driver that over compensates when his/her car begins to lose traction.

Ideally, when handling recoil, you're going to want your sights to track up and down in their channel. In other words when you get a sight picture as you're aiming at the target, the front sight is centered in the rear notch. When you pull the trigger, that front sight is going to lift up as the gun recoils. You want it to move only vertically and not horizontally, so that it settles down in the same place. It

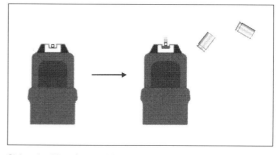

Sights should track up and down in their channel

should appear that the front sight is bouncing up and down, and not side to side. Eventually you can learn to time the front sight as it bounces up and down and hit the trigger again once your sights are aligned. As you gain more skill, this can be done very fast.

Point of note: Right handed, right eye dominant shooters will often find their sights slightly moving up and to the right (especially with high caliber handguns). Vice versa is true with lefties. This is because the support hand is coming over at more of an angle to the grip in comparison to the strong hand. Try to minimize this as much as possible with even pressure and by not "pushing" the gun in that direction.

Shooting quickly is a process of many stages. It's not simply blasting away while rapidly slapping the trigger:

1. Learn how to pull the trigger of the gun rapidly without causing the sights to move.

2. Follow through properly so that your front sight moves in the correct direction.

3. Learn how to time your front sight with your trigger pull.

4. Manage the recoil so that as you fire more rounds, the sights continue moving in a predictable way.

Focus on keeping your body in a stable, centered, aggressive posture. Do not tense up your neck or your shoulders. Keep your grip pressure constant, and focus on just utilizing your trigger finger to fire the pistol. Keep your eyes on your front sight and watch it as it moves.

In order for you to process the steps necessary to shooting faster, I've outlined a series of drills which you should use in order to improve. I would not recommend that you start shooting the drills out of order. I'll gradually give you more autonomy over your shooting as you earn it.

FAST TRIGGER PULL

As opposed to the slow fire trigger pull where pressure is slowly applied to maximize accuracy, here you're supposed to quickly press the trigger to the rear to deliver a shot as soon as your sights are on the target. The fundamentals are essentially the same in that you're going to only utilize your index finger while maintaining static pressure around the gun. You're also going to want to ride the trigger reset to ensure that you're shooting as quickly as possible. Also, ensure that you only move the trigger as much as necessary in order to deliver shots on target.

Start out with single shots to get used to pulling the trigger faster without moving the gun away from the target. At this point you're not going to worry about recoil at all. You just want to get the technique of operating the trigger down.

COMMAND FIRE DRILL

The first step to learning fast trigger control is easily demonstrated in the "Command Fire Drill." If you're shooting a revolver, I recommend that you do this only in single action for every shot.

1. Find either a timer (you can download a free shot timer app with a buzzer for your iPhone or Droid) or a buddy to help you. This is easier with a buddy so that you don't have to manually reset the timer, and can keep a focus on your front sight at all times.

2. To start, use a piece of computer paper taped vertically on a background at 7 yards. Remember my advice about using a light background so that if you miss you can see where the shot went (brown cardboard is good, along with brown scotch tape to cover bulletholes).

3. Gain a sight picture on the target with a crisp focus on the front sight.

4. Slowly pull the trigger until the gun is just about to go off at the break point. Tell your buddy that you're ready.

5. On command, either via a beep from your timer or a buddy yelling "Standby... Fire!" deliver a single shot on target. Shoot as soon as you hear the command! Do not hesitate!

6. Watch to see where your front sight moves, and slowly allow it to settle back down on the target. Follow through.

7. Once you have another sight picture on the center of the target, slowly release your finger from the rear, until you feel the trigger reset. (For revolvers, pull the hammer back to single action.) Then move your finger back to the trigger's break point, which should be not too far behind the reset on a good gun.

8. Tell your buddy that you're ready, and have him/her say again "Standby… Fire!" again.

9. Repeat until the magazine/cylinder is empty.

After doing this for awhile, you should be able to start calling your shots. When you fire the gun, a "flash sight picture" should be retained in your visual memory. This should tell you where the sights were pointed when the shot broke. Using it, you will be able to identify where that last shot went without having to look at the target. If you're finding that you're unable to pick up your sights when the shot broke, then chances are you pulled the gun off target as you pressed the trigger. Just as with accuracy, the ability to call your shots is immensely important here as it shows that your fundamentals are sound.

Take a look at your target after each practice session. If your accuracy is good, then move the target back farther a few yards at a time, from 7 to 15 to 25 yards. Keep using approximately a single sheet of computer paper as your target size.

Command Fire Drill Goals

Remember the accuracy milestone of being able to keep 10 shots within this computer paper target from 25 yards? You're going to have to do it again, but this time with command fire. However, because I know mistakes can happen and I'm such a nice guy, I'll allow you to have a 60-70% hit rate in order to continue. As long as you can put 6 or 7/10 shots in the white regularly at 25 yards, then it's time to move on.

This might take awhile, but there's no point in working on other skills until you can correctly perform a command fire drill. It's the basic motion for shooting quickly. Spend some time at the range to ensure that you're doing it right.

Problems with Command Fire

Most of the problems that you will encounter here are shots pulled low. These are caused by flinching just as the gun fires. A flinch here can be due to any of the following:

- Any trigger control issue. See the section on Accuracy.

- Stance or posture problem. See the Fundamentals of Shooting a Handgun.

- Squeezing your strong hand just as the gun is going off. Make sure that you only use your index finger to pull the trigger.

- Dipping your wrists down in anticipation of the recoil.

- Dipping your shoulders down in anticipation of the recoil. This will manifest itself in a lot of shoulder tension and a hunched over posture.

To correct these, when you have your front sight on target, you need to just move your index finger a little bit on the fire command. Keep your grip firm, so that you're not inclined to squeeze more when you're pulling the trigger. Focus on the tiny movement with your index finger while doing nothing else with the gun other than exerting static pressure. If you really want to demonstrate a flinching problem to yourself, try this drill either with dummy rounds randomly loaded into your magazine or cylinder, or try shooting one handed with your strong hand only.

RECOIL CONTROL

Once you have the basics of the fast trigger pull down pat, we're going to start including some recoil control exercises. The amount of recoil your gun has is directly proportionate to the amount of time it takes for you to deliver follow-up shots. You should not be attempting to make the gun get back to the target any faster. If you want to improve recoil control, improve your grip and stance and the static pressure they exert on the pistol.

TIMED COMMAND FIRE DRILL

Once you've mastered the execution of the command fire drill, we're going to up the speed a little bit. The objective is to get you to start prepping the trigger faster, and getting your sights on target faster. Here you will not be able to shoot at your leisure. Your buddy or shot timer will set regular intervals for you to send a round downrange. Revolver shooters should do this drill from double action.

1. Set up your target the same way as if you were doing a standard command fire drill at 7 yards.

2. Load up your gun and get your sight picture on target. Prep the trigger until the gun is just about to fire.

3. Tell your buddy that you're ready to begin.

4. At regular 5 second intervals, your buddy should call out "Fire!" If you don't have a stopwatch, just use the one-one thousand, two-one thousand method. There should be a good tempo building. Don't try to surprise yourself.

5. Watch your front sight settle back down onto the target and prep the trigger on the reset to deliver your next shot, just like in the command fire drill. (For revolvers, you're going to want to completely let the trigger out, and pull again from double action. It's easiest to pull about 90% of the way, then hold a split second and get ready to break the last 10%.)

6. Continue until the magazine/cylinder is empty.

Watch your front sight throughout this drill, as it will give you indicators about what you might be doing wrong. Your front sight should settle down in the center of the sight channel after you fire, not drift low or to the side. Calling your shots is a necessity here, as you won't have time to look at the target before your next shot. You should know where it's going already. Also, make sure that you don't try to push the front sight back on target. This should happen automatically under the correct grip pressure.

Timed Command Fire Drill Goals

Starting at five second intervals with a 7 yard target, it should be pretty easy for you to put all of your shots on paper. Improving your abilities is simply a measure of reducing the target size and the interval time. Once you can complete a string without more than a couple of misses, move onto the next one. The breakdown should be as follows with an 8.5" x 11" target:

1. 7 yards, 5 second intervals.

2. 7 yards, 4 second intervals

3. 7 yards, 3 second intervals.

4. 7 yards, 2 second intervals.

5. 15 yards, 5 second intervals

6. 15 yards, 2.5 second intervals

7. 25 yards, 5 second intervals

When you can successfully hit the target 7/10 times at 25 yards then you've completed this drill and are prepared to start taking charge of your own shooting.

Problems with Timed Command Fire

Many of the same issues that you encountered in the Accuracy and Command Fire sections might rear their ugly heads here. However you also have to contend with a new foe: speed. This drill requires you to quickly be able to get your sights back on target to prep the trigger for a new fire command. If you're too slow or cannot find your sights, then it's likely that your recoil control skills need work. The below solutions assume that you're shooting accurately, but are having trouble with speed.

- Front sight drifting under recoil. When the gun fires, the front sight should move directly up and down in the sight channel. Recoil is supposed to come straight back at you and be absorbed by your hands first, then your arms, then your body. Your front sight moving the right way is a positive indication of that. If it's not, then it means that you're influencing the gun in some fashion, typically through uneven pressure with your hands, bad posture, or an incorrect grip. Something is deflecting those forces at an angle to you instead of straight back. There are a variety of possible causes which are unique to each shooter. Start by evaluating which parts of your body the recoil hits first (hands) and continue back from there. If your accuracy is good, then you're probably forcefully pulling down on the gun once it fires or tensing up some part of your body.

- Front sight dips below sight channel when resetting. If you notice that you constantly have to lift the front sight up to aim again after shooting, it means that you're dropping some portion of your body in response to the recoil. (Usually dipping the wrist or leaning the body farther forward) This is typically associated with a reduction in accuracy and a low-left pull. Just make sure that you allow the sights to come down naturally on their own without interference.

- Sights taking too long to settle. If you find that your front sight rises in the correct direction (straight up) but goes really high while you're trying this exercise, you aren't holding the gun firmly enough. Add some more pressure on both your hands to prevent the muzzle from flipping so much. The good news is that the distribution of pressure is correct and that you have a neutral grip on the gun. Also, you can always give yourself a bit more of an aggressive forwards lean to counteract the recoil (don't overdo it).

TIMED SEMI-RAPID FIRE DRILL

In this drill, we're finally going to take away the command fire, and you'll be allowed to prep and fire the trigger on your own. The reason I've been forcing you to wait for a signal is because too many people develop bad habits when they try to shoot quickly before they're ready. Accuracy suffers tremendously. However, by now you should have been able to work all of the kinks in your trigger control out, and be able to deliver a shot on demand with a high degree of accuracy. Let's put that theory to the test.

1. Take out yet another sheet of computer paper. (Office Depot must love you by now. Just tell them you're an author or something.) Put it on a target at 7 yards lengthwise.

2. Use your shot timer or your buddy to set a par time of 1.5 times the number of rounds you have at your disposal. For example, if you have a 12 round magazine, give yourself 18 seconds.

3. Set your sights on the target and prep the trigger.

4. On the start signal (either a beep, or a "Fire!" from your buddy) engage the target with every round in the gun.

5. Make certain that you're done firing before the time limit is up, and that all shots hit the paper.

During this drill, your goal is to feel the trigger throughout the range of motion. You've already learned how to perform a fast trigger pull, to wait for your sights to settle back down on the target, and to prep the trigger for another shot. This exercise just puts everything together for you. On every shot you should be able to clearly see your sights. Do not get a good first sight picture then just blast away and hope you hit the target. Even while shooting rapid fire on a target, I see pretty much every single shot. You have plenty of time to stabilize and hit every shot.

Timed Semi-Rapid Fire Goals

Once you're able to hit the target under your own control and within the time limit, then you're going to want to move the target back further. Keep the same size target (one sheet of computer paper) and same time limit of 1.5 times the magazine/cylinder capacity. First start at 7 yards, then move to 15, then 25.

Your goal at 25 yards should be 70% hits within the time limit prior to moving on.

Problems with Timed Semi-Rapid Fire

By now, I'm assuming that you've done everything correctly up until this point, but doing this drill is beginning to cause problems for you.

- Shots being pulled low. Here the most likely situation is that you're not properly resetting the gun. Instead you're probably releasing the trigger a good distance then slapping it down while simultaneously gripping more with your hand. This causes the muzzle of the gun to dip. Alternatively, look again at tension in your arms and shoulders and for a possible forward lean in anticipation of the recoil. Use dummy rounds to check to see what's causing the issue.

- Shots coming in high. Here, you're probably not waiting for the front sight to settle down. Shoot slower and call that shot perfectly. You can't just make yourself shoot faster by getting bad sight pictures. Alternatively, you're dipping the rear of the gun as you anticipate the recoil.

- Shots going everywhere! Follow your sights and call your shots. If you can't make the time limit, then reevaluate your fundamentals to help you better control the recoil. Even though it may look like top level shooters are just spraying rounds everywhere, we know where they're exactly going almost every time. Every shot needs a sight picture.

- Grip breaking apart under recoil. Many new shooters will have their support hand start to slip off the gun as they shoot. If this happens, then your support hand is too far forward on the gun and is not in solid enough contact with the frame and your other hand. Verify that each of your support hand fingers is firmly up against the strong hand and wedged in under the triggerguard. If your hands are sweaty, which does happen, rub some dirt on them. (You could also buy a product called Pro-Grip which adds a nice tack to your palms.)

Support hand starting to slide off grip

TIMED RAPID FIRE DRILL

Now you're finally at the point where you can get acquainted with the technique behind the famous "double tap." I still like to use the term because everybody is familiar with it, even though the original technique that it described employed a fallacious style of shooting. Back when the name was developed, many people thought that the fastest way to hit a target was to aim once and shoot twice as quickly as possible. They hoped that their sights wouldn't move significantly enough to cause them to miss. Many shooters without the necessary experience still attempt to do it this way as well. Sorry, but there's a better way of going about it, and I'm going to show it to you.

All of the hullaballoo about watching your front sight as it rides up and down in the sight channel wasn't just hot air. Previously, you were supposed to allow it to settle back down nicely to give you time to prepare for your next shot. This was essentially just shooting a series of individual shots. Now things will get a little bit more complicated as we introduce trigger timing to the mix. When shooting truly fast, you're not going to have the luxury of a good second's time to carefully aim at the target. Instead of shooting a long string of single shots, you're now going to be shooting a sequence.

The goal in this exercise is to get you to follow your front sight as it bounces up and down, and to time it properly. Fire the gun and watch the front sight rise and descend. As soon as you see that front sight enter the sight channel for even a microsecond, you pull the trigger again to send another round at the target. It's called trigger timing because the recoil of your gun will cause your sight to lift the same way every time (provided that you're using even pressure all around the gun). Your grip will cause the front sight to come back to neutral, and you will fire as soon as it does. The timing of the trigger must coincide with the rate at which the front sight moves.

Point of note: I only describe looking at the front sight above, even though the rear sights will move too. Why? Because your focus should only be on the tip of that front sight, and it's the only thing you should notice.

The first iteration you should practice is called the "Bill Drill." (Maybe Bill was known to hose targets or something)

1. Set up a piece of computer paper at 7 yards.

2. Get a shot timer. Competitive Edge Dynamics and Competition Electronics both make some really killer shot timers, but they're a little expensive for basic training. (The iPhone app is good, but not as accurate) You'll need one later so that you can see the exact split times- intervals between shots. You could have a buddy with a stopwatch, but this is far less precise.

3. Take a sight picture on the target, and on the go command or beep, shoot five shots as fast as possible into the target. Record your time. You should not miss the target at all.

4. Move the target back to 10 yards, then 15. At 15 yards you will have to aim a little bit more and take your time shooting.

5. Continue to shoot as fast as possible while keeping at least 4/5 shots on paper. You should not pause your sights to aim. Try to time them so that once that front sight comes back down on paper, you pull the trigger.

6. When you can consistently hit the target at 15 yards, then we'll start adding a time element to the game.

You may be asking yourself, "Five shots? I thought I was gonna practice the double tap!" Well essentially you are. The difference here is that when new shooters tend to just put two shots on paper, they either start dropping or yanking on the gun after the second shot, failing to follow through, and/or start to lose their sight pictures. In order to formulate a proper double tap, first get an idea of what watching the front sight feels like. Find the groove. Then once you're accomplished in the Bill Drill, just reduce the number of shots down to two and fire at the same rate. Another reason they're not included specifically here is because double taps also happen to be difficult to time for beginners and are usually measured through multiple shot engagements (covered in the next chapter).

Timed Rapid Fire Goals
This drill is pretty simple, but it drives in some powerful skills. Once you're done with familiarizing yourself with shooting fast, do the following:

1. Put the target back at 7 yards. Give yourself 5 seconds to shoot 5 shots on paper.

2. Once you hit all your shots, give yourself 4 seconds.

3. Once you get all of those, give yourself 3 seconds. This is equivalent to a .6 split, which means that you're firing one bullet every six tenths of a second. Look at a stopwatch to determine what your cadence should be here.

4. Once you hit all of your shots at 7 yards (that's five shots in 3 seconds on an 8.5" x 11" piece of paper) move the target back to 10 yards. Give yourself 6 seconds to shoot all shots on paper.

5. Next, limit your time to 5 seconds.

6. When you can do this cleanly, move the target back to 15 yards. You now have 7 seconds to put all five shots on paper.

7. When you can do this, you're ready to take the Developing Speed Test.

Timed Rapid Fire Problems
This is a new skill set, which is in some ways distinct from everything you've been doing so far. Trigger timing is paramount here as you'll be shooting quite quickly. There are two main sources of errors with this drill. The first is that the trigger timing is bad and that the shooter isn't getting a clean enough sight picture. The second is again a

technique issue that causes either the gun to be pushed/pulled off target, or recoil to be absorbed incorrectly.

- Shots become less accurate as you fire. If this is the case then it's a timing issue. Those sights are moving quickly. You need to be able to get them centered and get used to the timing of your gun. Let them come to you instead of trying to force them into position. The gun naturally wants to reset back on target if you have a neutral grip.

- Sights not tracking up and down. In this situation, the forces of recoil are deflected at you at an angle. This can be caused by a wide swath of errors, many of which were covered earlier. Assuming that you've done everything correctly up until this point, what you're probably doing is applying uneven grip pressure or tilting the gun when firing. This might even be a gun related problem such as the gun may be too large for your hand.

- Sights are hard to find. To help you with this drill, I would advise you to black out the rear sights if there are dots/lines on them. (Sharpies are great!) You just want a nice front dot, either a fiber optic, paint, or tritium.

- Falling forward/back. As I've said numerous times, you're going to want to have a somewhat aggressive forward lean in your torso, with your back straight and your weight forwards. If the gun is pushing you off your feet under recoil, then it means that you need to look at your body position, because you're likely standing on your heels. If you're falling forwards, then you're overcompensating by moving too much of your weight towards the target while you're firing.

DEVELOPING SPEED TEST

By now you should have a pretty solid foundation in the quick trigger press and following your sights as they move under recoil. We're going to put those skills to the test with one more simple drill before you can move on to multiple target engagements.

This test involves 30 rounds and six strings of fire. Each string has a time limit, and shots over that par time will result in one miss per shot fired. No make-up shots are allowed. You are required to have a certain number of hits on paper in order to qualify. A real shot timer would be very helpful, but yes you can rely on the venerable iPhone. Reload between strings at your leisure.

A single piece of 8.5" x 11" paper will be your target. Tape it to a large background so that you can clearly see if you've missed. Start with your sights on target as usual and your finger on the trigger at the break point.

1. 7 Yards. Starting with your sights on target, on the start signal engage the target with 5 rounds in 3.5 seconds.

2. 7 Yards. Starting with your sights on target, on the start signal engage the target with 5 rounds in 3.5 seconds.

3. 15 Yards. Starting with your sights on target, on the start signal engage the target with 5 rounds in 7 seconds.

4. 15 Yards. Starting with your sights on target, on the start signal engage the target with 5 rounds in 7 seconds.

5. 25 Yards. Starting with your sights on target, on the start signal engage the target with 5 rounds in 9 seconds.

6. 25 Yards. Starting with your sights on target, on the start signal engage the target with 5 rounds in 9 seconds.

Required Hits = 25/30

If you cannot successfully complete this drill, then go back through the section and check your fundamentals. Don't try to get lucky and just beat it once. You should be able to nail the goal a few times first. I know that it might sound like a challenge, but your ability to control the trigger is absolutely essential. Sure you can pick up other skills in shooting, but at the end of the day you're aiming at one target at a time. You'll have to get this up to par eventually, so why not do it now? You should be able to know that you'll be able to hit whatever you put your sights on, bar none.

Point of Note: There are more advanced drills which will improve your abilities in single target speed shooting later in the book.

CHAPTER 7

Developing Transitions

The key to shooting multiple targets rests more with your eyes than your hands. If you've followed the program so far, you'd know that I've already placed a lot of emphasis on trigger control and accuracy. By now these things should be second nature to you. If you have your sights on a target you should know with a relatively good degree of certainty where that next bullet is going. Shooting quickly at multiple targets relies on this skill as a given.

Focus is a paramount resource to have here. How quickly can you shift focus between what's downrange and your sights? How crisp does that sight picture have to be in order for you to fire? You need to learn how to time your gun to your eyes so that you can not only pick up targets, but decide when it's right to move your gun away from them.

Both eyes must be left open. If you've been forgetting this simple concept up until this point it's going to really start to affect you now. Keeping both of your eyes open improves

Let your eyes lead the way!

- *Shift focus to your sights to ensure accuracy*

- *Prep the trigger so that you don't have to wait to fire the gun*

- *Make sure that you don't overrun the target*

your peripheral vision, and allows for easier shifts in focus between near and far objects. If for example, you're right eye dominant and you close your left eye to shoot, how easy do you think it will be to pick up targets on your left side?

There is some debate on if you're presented with a row of equidistant targets directly in front of you, which ones do you engage first? Left to right? Right to left? Most shooters I know shoot left to right, regardless of their handedness/eye dominance. I assume one reason for this is that in western world we read left to right, and are therefore accustomed to it. The only people I see that go right to left tend to be both left handed and left eye dominant folks, but even then it depends on the individual. Ultimately it doesn't matter which way you go as long as it works for you. Try both styles to figure out what your preference is.

At this point I'm giving you more options to go with on your training. Practice each one of the drills in this section in any order you like; they're each designed to emphasize different skills. When you're ready, move onto the test.

Point of note: In this section, many of the drills are designed to be used on a static range where the shooter only has a single lane. (More advanced versions are found later in the book.) This is because most shooters will not have access to a place where they can shoot in multiple directions. I know I didn't for years, and was forced to make do on an indoor static range. Even if you can find a place to shoot across wide angles safely, I recommend that you try these initial steps first. Many of the same principles apply and you can remove the one factor of having to turn to your body to engage targets in order to work on the basics.

WORKING ON FOCUS

One of the old adages of driving a car is that you should "look where you want to go." The same applies with driving a gun. First you look at a target, then your gun should automatically track to where your eyes are pointing. (If shooting at a large target, try to concentrate on a small point on it.) Your focus should shift immediately to the front sight as the gun is coming on target. This ability takes nothing short of hours upon hours of practice, which can only be done at home.

One easy way to practice was mentioned earlier in the book. All you have to do is use the tip of your index finger. Simply look at objects in your environment (not coworkers please!) and bring the tip of your finger up to them. As your finger is lifting, shift the focus to the tip. That's your sight picture. Look at something else, and move your finger to it, shift the focus to your finger again. Your eyes lead the way and whatever you're holding follows. It's simple hand-eye coordination.

Focus on target should look something like this:

1. Target Identifed

2. Gun Rises with focus on target

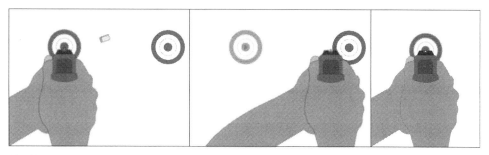

After Shooting 1st Target, Eyes Shift to 2nd Target

Gun Transitions to Follow Eyes

Focus Shifts to Front Sight

3. Focus shifts as sights come into view. You now have a crisp sight picture.

4. Bang! You fire the gun.

5. As soon as the gun fires, your eyes call the shot and quickly dart to the next target.

6. Your gun begins to move towards the next target.

7. Focus shifts from the target to the sights as they come into view.

8. Focus is crisply on the front sight.

9. Bang!

Obviously for this to work at speed, your eyes have to leave the first target the instant the shot breaks. A moment sooner will pull the shot off the first target, and a moment later will cause you to be slower on the next target. When you fire, you should know immediately where it went. If you want to be effective at shooting multiple targets, you will need to call your shots. It's that simple. You will not have time to look downrange for a hit.

For the exercises under this section, you're going to simply want to turn from the waist while keeping your arms and wrists and shoulders at a constant angle. Think of the center of your torso as a swivel. Try to keep your hips close to static for now.

PREPPING THE TRIGGER

The entire time that you're shooting multiple targets, you should be prepping the trigger in between shots. When that first shot breaks, your finger should immediately begin to let the trigger out until it's just past the reset point. This way when your sights come onto the new target, you're able to quickly set off another round. If your cadence is correct and the targets are close enough together, you should be able to shoot multiple targets just about as quickly as you would a single.

RECTANGLES DRILL

This drill will allow you to watch your sights as they bounce from one target to the next. Its purpose is to help you quickly move from one target to the next. Since the squares will be placed close together, there should be little or no delay between shots. Your front sight should rise off one target and come down on the next.

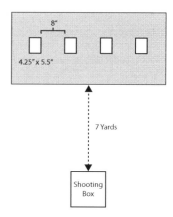

1. Your targets will be four pieces of computer paper folded over twice (4.25" x 5.5") put horizontally on a light background at 7 yards, and spread out about 8 inches from each other.

2. Start with your arms fully extended and angled at 45 degrees towards the ground below the target.

3. Focus on the first target that you'd like to shoot. Most right handed shooters like to go left to right.

4. On the start signal (whichever way you want to do it) mount the gun at the first target and shoot it.

5. Quickly engage the rest of the targets.

6. For fun, you can place these pretty much anywhere to practice sighting in on targets in different places. Stagger them for an additional challenge. Also feel free to place the targets a little more downrange to work on your accuracy.

Rectangles Drill Goals

In order to get an idea of the proper cadence, shoot four shots in a row into just one of the targets. It should take you about the same amount of time to complete this drill and hit all of the targets if they're equidistant from one another. The trigger timing is the same, and in the time you spend waiting for your sights to come back down, you should be moving over to the next target.

Try to beat the 4 second mark with all your hits on this drill.

Rectangles Drill Problems

- Trouble hitting the targets. If you've gotten through the **Developing Speed** section, then you should have no problem with trigger control at this point. This means that you have a sighting problem. You are either not getting a good enough sight picture on the target (due to focusing on it instead of your sights) or are mistiming the trigger. At 7 yards with targets relatively close together you shouldn't have to shift focus off your front sight that much in order to hone in on the next target in the array.

- Too slow on the next target. Don't hesitate after firing each shot. You should know where it went. Move onto the next target without stopping. You should only identify a miss if you call it a miss when you pull the trigger. Also, as soon as the sights come back down in the channel, pull the trigger.

- Consistently shooting to one side. Remember to not move your gun until after the shot breaks, and to not break the trigger until you have a sight picture on the next target.

MOZAMBIQUE DRILL

Here we're going to add a little rapid fire into the mix. This drill will teach you to switch up your cadence from fast to slow. Not every target is the same size. You can blast large close targets, but smaller ones farther away you'll have to aim more on.

1. Take out your dual folded computer paper from the Rectangles drill, and a sheet of computer paper. Put them vertically on a light background target at 7 yards with the smaller one centered about three inches over the larger one.

2. Start with your arms fully extended and angled at 45 degrees towards the ground below the target.

3. On the start signal, mount the gun and put two rounds into the large paper, and one round into the small paper.

4. Repeat as needed.

Mozambique Drill Goals

Shooting these targets, you should be able to audibly pick up on two very distinct strings. The shots into the center target should have very low split times (intervals between shots) with a distinct delay before the shot into the upper target. Your goal should be to produce two lower hits as fast as possible in a tight group while minimizing the time to engage the top target. Do not miss the top target.

You should be able to beat the 3 second mark at 7 yards.

Mozambique Drill Problems

- Missing the top target high. In this situation, you're lifting the gun up too much and not timing your shot properly. You should pause for a brief moment to aim at the top target before shooting it. Also, you should prep the trigger as you're lifting the gun up towards the top target. Do not tilt your wrists upwards to hit it, this is bad form and is considerably less accurate.

- Missing the top target left/right. This usually tells me that the shooter is not exercising proper recoil control on the first two shots. In this case the gun is bouncing around in his/her hands as the shooter tries to shoot really fast. When the gun is lifted up after that second shot the muzzle is pointed to one side or the other. Keep the sight picture regardless of how fast you're shooting.

- Missing the big target. In this case, the shooter has decided to shift focus to the upper target prior to finishing engaging the lower target. The first round probably was a decent sight picture, at which point the shooter thought that it was good enough and just yanked a second shot as his/her eyes shifted up. Follow through on, and call all your shots.

EL PRESIDENTE-LITE DRILL

This is a light version of my favorite hoser drill. The targets are large and you should be able to blast away. Here you will learn how to perform multiple shots on multiple targets.

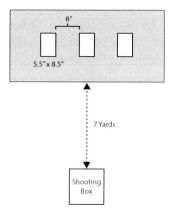

1. Grab your computer paper and fold it in half so that you have a 5.5" x 8.5" sheet. Put three sheets of it horizontally on a light colored background target. Space them about 8 inches apart at seven yards distance.

2. Start with your arms fully extended and angled at 45 degrees towards the ground below the target.

3. On the start signal, engage all three targets with two rounds each. Most right handed shooters prefer to go left to right.

4. Repeat as needed.

El Presidente-Lite Drill Goals

Like the Rectangles drill, the objective here is to perform transitions that are as quick as the shots themselves. In other words, to a bystander not looking at your target it should sound like you're firing six shots in perfect rhythm. Avoid misses. Those targets are pretty darn close. If you're feeling adventurous, go ahead and move the targets back to about 10 yards.

You should try to beat the 4.5 second mark at 7 yards with all your hits.

El Presidente-Lite Problems

Like the Mozambique drill, one of the issues that arises is the tendency to pull shots off target on the second shot. This is a timing issue, and usually involves moving your eyes before the shot breaks. Just make sure that you are able to call both shots on the target, then swing over. Don't try to move your gun or your eyes too quickly, as that will cause misses. I know, because I still do it sometimes!

CADENCE DRILL

This drill is designed to help you adjust your timing from fast to slow in your side-to-side motion. With the El Prez, you can simply hose your way through it really quickly. However, when you have to quickly alternate between large easy to hit targets and small precision shots it will mess with your mind a little bit. The cadence drill will help you learn to adjust your shot timing and movement as it pertains to the situation.

1. Get your computer paper targets. The big targets will be a piece of paper folded in half to 5.5" x 8.5". The small ones will be folded once more to 4.25" x 5.5" like the Rectangles drill.

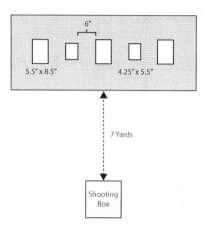

2. Place the targets horizontally in this order: big, small, big, small, big. They should each have about six inches between them. If you don't have enough space on your cardboard to put all of these up, stagger them so that the little targets are higher up than the big targets.

3. Start with your arms fully extended and angled at 45 degrees towards the ground below the target.

4. On the start signal, engage each target with two rounds each. Go from big to small to big each time.

5. Repeat as needed.

Cadence Drill Goals

You should be able to adjust your trigger timing to make all of the hits. The big targets will be easier to shoot, and you can therefore have faster split times. The smaller ones will require more accuracy, so you'll have to shoot slower. Focus on minimizing the amount of time it takes to transition between the five targets. You can move this back farther for a harder challenge, or you can reduce the size of the smaller targets to help encourage tight control.

If the targets are arranged horizontally, you should try to beat 6.5 seconds in this drill.

Cadence Drill Problems

The main problems that you will encounter here involve pulling your first shot off the small target. A lot of people tend to want to transition quickly or keep the gun moving into the shot. This isn't a bad thing per se but you're going to want to always make sure that you get your hits. Missing fast will just mean that you'll have to pick that shot up later. It is always faster to take the higher percentage route and aim.

DEVELOPING TRANSITIONS TEST

At this point, you should be very confident in your aptitude for shooting fast, accurate transitions between targets. This is the final hurdle you'll have to overcome before opening yourself up to the rest of the book. If you can complete this test, then I believe you have the necessary experience to get into higher level training and start incorporating more movement into your routine. If you're a total beginner who has followed the training schedule so far, I congratulate you for making it this far! You will have a very solid base that you can build on and should improve quickly. Good luck!

You will need two types of targets- a full sheet of computer paper, and a twice folded sheet that measures 4.25" x 5.5." In every drill these will be placed with the long side perpendicular to the ground. There will be four strings of fire, and you will have to reset your targets once. All shots over par time will count as misses. You can shoot as many shots as you want.

Array 1: Four small targets should be in a row across the top, spaced six inches apart. Centered and one foot below that array should be two pieces of computer paper spaced a foot apart. Targets placed at 7 yards downrange.

Array 2: Four small targets should be arranged in a box formation. The corners of the small targets will form the corners of the box. The box should measure 2' wide x 2' tall. In the very center of the box, there should be one sheet of computer paper.

Start with your arms fully extended and angled at 45 degrees towards the ground below the target.

Strings:

1. On start signal engage Array 1 targets with one shot per small target and two shots per large target. You have six seconds.

2. On start signal engage Array 1 targets with one shot per small target and two shots per large target. You have five seconds.

3. On start signal engage Array 2 targets with one shot per small target and two shots per large target. You have six seconds.

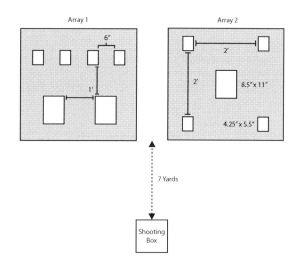

4. On start signal engage Array 2 targets with one shot per small target and two shots per large target. You have five seconds.

Your pass rate will be 25/28 hits.

If you can pass this test then give yourself a pat on the back and know that you have solid fundamentals. Congratulations! I invite you to check out some of the other more advanced training sections to build up your skills.

MOVING AHEAD

U p until this point in the book I've paid a great deal of attention to correcting certain flaws in basic technique such as trigger control. If you're reading the next sections, I assume that you've already developed a certain level of proficiency in accuracy, speed, and transitions. From here on out, I will not address fundamental problems nearly as often and will instead concentrate on building new skillsets. Additionally, I'm allowing for a great deal more latitude as far as training on your own. You should be able to understand the concepts and employ them at your own pace.

From here forward there will be no more "Tests" but rather a collection of drills with Milestone times. It's not easy to achieve the expert level goals. If you can reach some of them, then consider yourself in limited company. Even with a lot of practice, most shooters will fall into the Intermediate category. However, the point is not to just repeat one drill over and over until you get lucky and beat it. An expert should be able to perform around that level on a regular basis.

Where did the times come from? I simply went out to the range cold, and set up one of the drills, then I shot it two or three times and picked my best run as the high point. Are they possible to improve upon? Sure! However my first couple of runs indicate my true skill level. When you're at a match or in a defensive situation, you won't be able to practice what you're about to do and choose your top performance. You usually get one chance to get it right.

Point of note: Get yourself a bunch of USPSA metric targets to practice on, or something similar. All drills involve the targets at shoulder level height unless otherwise specified. This isn't a competition, and there's no reason to try and game the drills to achieve a better time.

CHAPTER 8

DRAWS/GUN PRESENTATIONS

Drawing properly is a matter of repetition. Anyone can grab a gun out of a holster, but doing it quickly while under stress is another matter altogether. While the draw can be broken down in many stages, when you actually decide to do it, it should feel like a single motion (like hitting a baseball). It will take thousands of draws to get to the point where it can be done subconsciously. Make sure that you put in the requisite practice.

Also, whether you're carrying concealed or shooting competition, remember to mount the holster in the same place every time. Use a point of reference on your body or on your equipment. This will help you better rely on your well driven in muscle memory to get the gun on target quickly.

Point of note: I discuss excessive motion as a problem quite a bit here. In some cases it can't be avoided, such as when

The best draw
is a smooth draw.

- *Get a good grip on the gun*

- *Avoid excessive and/or jerky motion*

- *Know where your support hand should be*

a shooter has a concealed carry gun that needs to really be reached for. The idea is to reduce that motion as much as possible.

BASICS OF THE TWO HANDED DRAW

MOUNTING FROM LOW READY

I think that the best way to teach the draw is to start with the gun already out of the holster. While this might sound counterintuitive, it actually will help you remember where your hands have to meet and when to extend towards the target. This is called the "low ready" position because your gun is pointing downrange, but is close to your body. Typically this involves a nearly fully formed grip (without full grip pressure) with your hands at solar plexus level, extended about 8 inches away from your chest.

The first thing that you're going to want to practice here is mounting the gun on the target. It's pretty simple, just look at a target and extend your arms into the shooting position (while forming your grip completely) and try to pick up your sights as early as possible. As soon as you start to mount the gun, your finger should be on the trigger prepping it for the first shot. (You should already have made the decision to fire prior to mounting the gun in this exercise.) Once you see your sights on target, drop that first shot downrange. The key is speed. You don't want any delay between picking up your sights and firing the gun. It's better to practice this dry at home for awhile prior to doing it on the range.

When you do get out to the range, try this for a few practice sessions. Instead of starting a shot string either with your sights already on target, or with your arms extended and pointed at 45 degrees towards the ground (from the **Transitions** drills), start from low ready. Practice mounting the gun and delivering two shots on target immediately. You should get to be pretty fast at this. Just make sure that you're extending towards the target. You want your gun to move at an upwards angle in a straight line without the muzzle changing direction.

You should be able to deliver your first shot on a computer paper sized target at 7 yards in under a second. If you want a standardized start position (because I know some people will want to cheat at this) begin with your triceps in contact with the sides of your chest and the gun pointed directly downrange (muzzle parallel to the ground). Once you can do this easily then we'll start working on actually grabbing the gun.

BASIC STEPS OF THE DRAW

There are four stages that you're going to want to go through regardless of how you're drawing the pistol from a holster.

1. ***Grab the gun.*** From here you're going to want to get a good grip on the handgun. This is vitally important because if you whip the gun out without a firm, correct hold on it, then your shots will be errant and your recoil control will be lacking. Remember to get your strong hand as high as possible and centered on the backstrap, and to wedge your

middle finger under the triggerguard. During this stage, all you should be thinking about is first feeling the middle of the web of your hand right up under the beavertail of the grip (for semi autos). This is your first point of contact and will guide the rest of your fingers. Get a solid grip right out of the holster with good pressure.

Draw Position 1

Draw Position 2

2. ***Move your weak hand into position.*** This should be done simultaneously with moving your strong hand to grab the pistol. In order to get a good draw, as soon as you move your strong hand to the gun, move your weak hand into place. Your weak hand should be placed at solar plexus height and a couple inches away from your chest (think about at the level where you might clap your hands). It should be slightly off-center towards the side of your body that has your dominant eye. Also, your hand should be externally rotated as much as possible to help you properly adopt the wrist cant. Your support arm should be in close to your body and your forearm should be angled slightly past parallel to the ground.

In order to get an idea of how much your wrist should be rotated over, go grab an egg from the fridge. Cup it in the palm of your hand in the aforementioned location on your body and practice extending while holding the egg. You want to get your wrist canted over as much as possible prior to receiving the gun from your strong hand and forming your grip. Rotating your arm over here will translate to a good wrist angle when you extend your arm. Many people who have a good initial wrist cant will train themselves out of it on the draw because it's very comfortable to grab the gun with a flat wrist.

3. ***Move the gun to your weak hand.*** This should be done while angling the gun from pointing directly downwards at the ground to aiming towards the target. It should be pointed downrange prior to reaching your weak hand. You're going to look for two main

points of contact with your weak hand on the gun. The first is your support index finger wedged up under the triggerguard. The second is the palm of your support hand pressed against the side of the grip. Start squeezing as soon as you make good contact with the support hand.

Draw Position 3

Draw Position 4

4. **_Extend towards the target._** Move the gun in a straight line towards the target (this will be at an upward slope). You can begin to extend while still forming your grip. However, wait until you get good contact between your strong and weak hands before moving the gun significantly. The wrist cant you formed while setting your support hand will translate into the correct grip while extended. Once you pick up your sights on the target, fire.

Here are some general tips for improving your draw:

- Both hands should move together as fast as possible. Don't lag behind with one of your hands. Usually I find that my weak hand will get into position first, so I like to focus on this point during my draw. If you're having trouble forming your grip, then just think "support hand position" when you're drawing the pistol. Your strong hand will do the rest.

- I generally like to keep my fingers spread apart somewhat when I'm about to draw. I don't mean wide open, but spread enough so that they're not in contact with one another. I also like to have just a slight curve in my palm, and a slight upwards bend (towards my index finger) in my wrists. Your fingers should also have a slight bend to them.

- I pretense my hands and arms a little bit prior to drawing so that I'm not going from super relaxed to lightning speed. I kind of have them "take a set" in preparation. Usually I'll bend them in, then extend them out quickly as I'm getting ready. A little tension in your hands and arms is good for getting prepared to draw. However, avoid tension in the rest of your body. You should be prepared and with full focus, but not rigid. To give you an idea of how much you'll need, try to hold both of your hands out at arms length and keep them perfectly still. That's all the tension you should have.

- Keep your eyes on the exact point on the target that you want your sights to go to.

- Breathe normally. Don't hold your breath prior to shooting or inhale too much air.

- Keep your head up and still during the draw. Bring the gun to your eyes, not the other way around. Your head should move as little as possible.

- Think about moving with your hands only. I know this sounds odd, but just think of the motions your hands need to make and where they have to be. Then do what you have to in order to get them there. You should not influence the rest of your body when drawing (such as hunching your shoulders). Don't bend or lean your torso unless you have to reach a gun way in the small of your back, such as in a concealed carry situation. The fewer muscles you use, the more consistent you will be.

- In order to get a faster shot on target, you're going to want to begin prepping the trigger as soon as the gun is pointed downrange and you've made contact with your support hand. Do this while you're extending to the target so that you time your trigger break with the point your sights line up on target.

- Try not to lift your hands up too high before extending them. It's more difficult to form the support hand cant at these starting angles.

- If you're shooting drills or in competition, it's always good to start by practicing getting a good grip by squeezing the handgun while it's in the holster prior to putting your hands at your sides. It will remind you of where your hands should be during the draw.

- If you're cross-eye dominant, then do not turn your head during the draw. Simply put the gun in front of the eye you're going to be shooting with.

FROM A HANDS AT SIDES POSITION

Here are some tips for drawing with your hands at your sides:

- Put your hands in the same position every time prior to drawing the handgun. They should be draped at your sides with your elbows slightly bent. They should also be just in front of the gun. Do not limp noodle or lock out your arms. They should have a slight bend with a little tension.

- When you're beginning the draw, think about the tip of your elbow moving in a straight line up and to the rear. Keep your shoulders down and try not to activate your trapezius muscles.

This will move your hand in the proper direction to reach the backstrap of the handgun. Your hand should go directly to the gun (do not arc the path of your hand).

- Your support hand should reach its position on your chest just as the gun leaves the holster.

Hand moves in a straight line to the gun

FROM HANDS ABOVE SHOULDERS

There are a few ways to draw with your hands above your shoulders. Ultimately it depends on the situation and on your personal preference.

- A popular method within the USPSA/IPSC circles for a "wrists above shoulders" start position is to put your hands on either your ear protection or your hat. These serve as useful points of reference. However, this might not be entirely practical for a defensive situation.

- Another starting position involves simply setting your palms towards the target in what you would expect from a "surrender position." To find this position, simply take your hand start position at your sides, and move your hands up above your shoulders by first bending your elbows to about 90 degrees and then lifting your upper arms slightly from the shoulders. Try to keep the orientation of your wrists the same and think of your hands moving in an arc upwards.

- When it's time to draw, think about leading with your strong hand elbow in a downwards and back arc. This should put your strong hand right on the gun.

- As you move your strong hand to the gun, immediately move your weak hand to the established start position.

- This draw should be just about as fast as your hands at sides drill, plus maybe a tenth of a second at the expert level.

Two competition styles of hands above shoulders

FROM ALTERNATIVE POSITIONS FACING THE TARGET

You may be required to draw from any number of alternative positions, including either with your hands on another person in a defensive situation, or on a barricade in a practical pistol sport. You might even be seated in a car or a chair.

- Practice multiple hand positions to get familiar with each of them and have the confidence to be able to draw to them if necessary. If you detect that you're having problems with one of them, practice it more so that you don't feel like you have any weak spots.

- Remember the basic principles of the draw and where your hands need to be, especially your support hand. If unsure, think about leading with your hands. Also add a little tension to your hands and arms prior to drawing.

- Try not to lean on an object using your hands prior to drawing. Moving them suddenly will put you off balance.

FROM A BACK TO THE TARGET POSITION

A time might come in which you have to engage a target behind you. Your hands might either be above your shoulders or at your sides. They could also be in any number of other places. Turning and drawing is much the same as drawing any other way, the only question is how to get spun around as quickly as possible. You'll want to rotate towards the side where the first target you're going to shoot is. Most people, including me, prefer shooting left to right so if given an option (with a target directly behind me), I'll turn towards my strong side. The below instructions assume this direction.

1. Load up your weight on the center of your pivot foot. It will usually be your weak side foot. This will allow you to turn towards the target faster.

2. When you decide to draw, immediately turn with your head first towards your strong side. This will allow you to pick-up the target and will lead your body.

3. As you're turning your head, step back and try to point your strong side foot towards the target. Transfer your weight to it as you turn your hips.

4. Put all of your weight on your strong side foot. Pick up your weak side foot, and swing it around so that it falls into your normal shooting stance.

5. Turning can be done in two steps.

6. Ensure that for safety you do not draw the handgun while facing uprange at all! Begin to draw once it clears a parallel line with the berm you're shooting at.

Foot moves back as hands go into position

PICKING THE GUN UP OFF A TABLE

To properly pick a gun up off a table and shoot, you're going to want to use two hands at once. This will allow you to quickly form the correct grip on the pistol and fire quickly. Position your gun so that the grip is pointing towards your strong side hand. However, if the gun is resting on the magazine release (especially with extended ones), be careful that you don't release the magazine by pressing down on the gun!

1. Move your fingers (down to the second joint) on your strong hand to the grip of the handgun.

2. Move your weak hand to the top of the pistol simultaneously.

3. Use your weak hand to lift the gun up and place it into your strong hand. Then slide your weak hand into your normal grip.

4. If the gun's grip is facing your weak hand, then pinch the backstrap between the middle finger and thumb of your weak hand, while rolling your strong hand under the gun. Then transfer the pistol.

5. It's always easier to pick the gun up off the table if the grip is facing your strong hand.

Gingerly picking the gun off a table

DRAWING FROM CONCEALMENT

If you're carrying defensively or shooting IDPA, then you'll have to begin your draw from behind concealment. In this case, you're going to have to move your jacket (or whatever is concealing the gun) out of the way.

- If your concealment can easily be brushed away with the strong hand, then the weak hand should just go to its normal position.

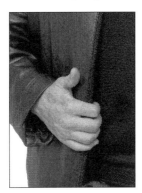  

Make precise, aggressive motions for an effective concealment draw

- Choose concealment that's easy to get out of the way to facilitate a quick draw. A gun at your hip covered by a stiff leather jacket will be much easier to get to than one in the small of your back covered by a bulky parka.

- Move your strong hand up and to your body first instead of directly to the gun. It should impact just to the side and below your navel. As you're doing this, make a hook with your fingers. Once the tips of your fingers are in contact with your body use your hand to follow along your body to catch and drag your concealment out of the way. Throw your concealment back forcefully. Then go for the gun.

- The amount you can actually throw the garment out of the way is related to how stiff the material is. Experiment and be sure to practice with different pieces of concealment so that you know what to expect if you actually have to draw.

- Depending on the position of the gun, your weak hand might be used to help pull the concealment out of the way. (Such as a gun in a cross draw shoulder holster.)

DRAWING TO RETENTION

The retention draw is an extreme close range technique which literally involves shooting "from the hip." Its purpose is to get rounds on target as quickly as possible with minimal concern for accuracy. (See the chapter title photo)

1. As soon as you make the decision to fire, the strong hand moves to the gun, getting concealment out of the way if necessary.

2. The support hand does not go to its regular position, but instead slides all the way across the body to meet the strong hand. Usually the path is will take is directly across the navel.

3. The strong hand grabs the gun, pulls it up just enough to clear the holster, and pivots the gun 90 degrees immediately.

Pushing target away while going to gun

4. During the pivot, the weak hand forms the grip on the strong hand.

5. The gun should be firing as soon as it completes the pivot.

6. The gun extends outwards to form the normal grip once the extreme close range target has been engaged.

The weak hand coming over to form the grip will not slow this draw down. Also, if you have to engage/cover multiple targets beyond the one directly in front of you, you'll want to have a two handed grip to help you shoot quickly as you extend your arms.

Sometimes things don't always go as planned. In these situations, you might need to be doing something with your weak hand such as pushing back the target to give yourself distance or controlling a weapon. So just to get used to it, you should also try shooting from retention one handed as well. In this case, you're going to want to form your grip in the normal position instead of at your strong hand hip.

Sometimes when performing a draw to retention people will have a natural inclination to put distance between themselves and the target. Make sure you practice retreating as well. (More information on how to shoot while retreating is later in the book.) There's no one right way to do this every time. You'll have to adapt to the circumstances, and should therefore vary your training. Try a bunch of different styles.

DRAWING WHILE MOVING/EVASIVE DRAWS

In competition, you'll often have to draw the handgun while moving in a course of fire. Also, there are many defensive schools which teach the evasive draw. While I don't intend to discuss the particulars of close range martial arts, I'll give you some tips to improve your movement.

- In a defensive situation, it's much harder to hit something that moves laterally than one that moves in a straight line towards or away from you.

- Practice moving/evasive draws with many different hand positions so that you're used to how to get to the gun quickly wherever your hands may be.

- If you want to move quickly to the side, load up the inside of your pivot foot (the one opposite of the direction you'll want to go) by bending your knee in laterally. This will help you immediately be able to jump off that foot and get moving without having to shift your weight very much.

Evasive draw to the left of the target

- If you have to perform a turning draw with evasion, get that pivot foot loaded up, and if possible turn to your weak side. This way, you can get the gun on target faster out of the holster. The gun can be firing on the target before you're even entirely turned around. In this case, you're likely to engage the first target one handed as you shoot around your body.

TRANSITION TO SINGLE HAND

If you need to draw to your strong hand, simply pull your support hand into your chest and extend normally to the target. To transition to your weak hand (a common feature in competition) just swing your support hand in front of your chest (solar plexus level). Do this by just bending your support arm elbow without moving your upper arm/shouder much. Pass the gun over to your weak hand, then move your strong hand in against your chest. Extend your support arm towards the target. (More information on how to shoot one handed is later in the book.)

Transition to weak hand

COMMON MISTAKES DURING THE DRAW

There are a number of possible mistakes that can be made during the draw which will either cost you time on target, or will result in you getting a bad grip on the gun:

- Many people will have excessive body motion in the draw. This is usually manifested by a sideways lean, a turtlenecked head, and/or by hunched shoulders in an effort to get the gun on target faster. These will cause a lack of uniformity between different draws, and will cost you time to get the gun on target. As we've established earlier in the book, adding tension to your body while shooting has a negative influence. So if you create it during the draw, you'll have to either shoot with improper form or will have to release it prior to shooting. It serves no actual purpose. Also, unnecessary movement isn't as fast. An old racecar adage is "Speed is economy of motion." Why add something that doesn't need to be there? Keep your head and upper body as steady as possible while drawing and bring the gun to your eyes.

Excessive lean during the draw

- The scoop is a common problem in the draw as well. This occurs when the shooter extends his/her arms at too low of an angle, causing the gun to go through its full range of motion before the sights actually come up on target. Typically here, the hands meet really low on the body and the gun is brought up at an arc. One of the appealing features of the scoop is that it feels really fast. I know, I used to do it. I would always try to rush my draws, but could never understand why my times weren't quick enough.

Ultimately the scoop will cause you to pick up your sights too late, giving you less time to acquire them on the target. This can be corrected by bringing your hands together at a position that's higher and closer to your body. Also, practice prepping the trigger on the extension.

- A bad grip on the gun will cause errant shooting and can either result from a poor index of your strong hand onto the backstrap during the first stage of the draw, or from adding your support hand too late. For the former situation, you're going to want to ensure that all of your equipment is in the same place every time you draw the gun. Additionally, don't just try to rip the gun out of the holster. Get a good hold on it before you begin to pull. If you're drawing quickly enough, you won't have time to make small corrections as you start to extend towards the target. Remember that you want to lead with your strong elbow when drawing. In the latter situation, you've bringing your support hand onto the gun too late, and are therefore having problems applying adequate pressure before you fire. To correct this, move both of your hands at the same time when you begin to draw and bring them together closer to your body.

- One final problem that I frequently encounter is the "dip." Here the gun will be raised above the target at full extension, and will then be brought down to the target (another 80's action movie staple). The gun shouldn't bounce around and you shouldn't have to make more than tiny adjustments to aim as your arms extend.

Point of note: Cross-draws are not faster by any standard but do have conceal-ability advantages. However, if you have an accidental discharge it could go uprange or into your support arm. Keep the gun on your strong side hip if permitted by the circumstances.

DRAW DRILLS

From a static position, the key to a quick, reliable draw is simply repetition. You should practice drawing from various target distances- closer ones with an emphasis on speed, distant ones with an emphasis on accuracy. If you're starting drawing the handgun for the first time, just try to get your times down with relatively easy shots. At this point, you should start transitioning to a different target than computer paper. For simplicity's sake, I'm going to use the USPSA metric target (Alpha zone measures 15 x 28 cm) as a point of reference, but you can use whatever you have access to. Also, mix it up a little bit, but for now don't start throwing in multiple targets just yet. Ultimately you're going to want to practice just your draw and not complicate your life by working other skills in. If you do so, then you'll simply make it more difficult to indentify errors.

If you're an advanced shooter trying to improve draw times, set up a hard to hit target far away and draw to it. I'll sometimes shoot a 10" steel plate at 40 yards from the holster. Why do I do this? Because when I start hitting the plate at that distance (and I can work my times down in the 1.4 second range) then when I move closer that target seems HUGE. Suddenly you'll have a lot more confidence at short distances.

Point of note: These drill milestones assume a kydex friction retention side mount holster and a striker fired semi-automatic pistol. If you're shooting with a behind the back or inside the waistband holster, it might take a little bit longer to get the gun out. When I say "loaded and holstered" it means that it's in ready to fire condition. If it's a DA/SA, the hammer is down with the safety disengaged. If it's a single action only, then the hammer is back with the thumb safety engaged.

Another point of note: If you want to practice these from a wrists above shoulders position, add about .3 seconds for beginner, .2 for intermediate, and .1 for expert to the draw times.

SINGLE METRIC TARGET @ 7 YARDS SINGLES

For this drill, you're going to want to initially start by putting just single shots on paper. Once you're comfortable, you can add any number of shots to it. I prefer practicing with two. The reason I say start with one shot is because it's easier to just wing a quick and get your hit, but adding in recoil control to your draw requires more sophisticated coordination. Start position is hands relaxed at sides (let your arms and hands hang).

All alphas milestones for this drill:

Beginner- 2.2 seconds

Intermediate- 1.5 seconds

Expert- 0.9 ~ 1.0 seconds

SINGLE METRIC TARGET @ 7 YARDS DOUBLES

Here you're going to have to focus on getting two hits on paper. This requires some recoil control, but at 7 yards, you don't have to be perfect to be fast. Start position is hands relaxed at sides (let your arms and hands hang) or wrists above shoulders.

All alphas milestones for this drill:

Beginner- 2.6 seconds

Intermediate- 1.75 seconds

Expert- 1.10 ~ 1.2 seconds

SINGLE 8" STEEL PLATE @ 10 YARDS

In this situation, you just need to get one shot on the plate, but it's pretty small, so don't miss! It's always faster to get your first hit than to try to get a makeup shot. Start position is hands relaxed at sides (let your arms and hands hang) or wrists above shoulders.

All alphas milestones for this drill:

Beginner- 2.4 seconds

Intermediate- 1.5 seconds

Expert- 1.15 seconds

SINGLE METRIC TARGET @ 25 YARDS DOUBLES

For this last basic drill, you're going to really press on that front sight and have a good grip to pull a clean run. First shot accuracy is paramount to the draw, because you can't miss fast enough! This drill forces you to get your hits. Start position is hands relaxed at sides (let your arms and hands hang) or wrists above shoulders. Fire two shots on the target.

All alphas milestones for this drill:

Beginner- 3 seconds

Intermediate- 2.2 seconds

Expert- 1.55 seconds

TURNING DRAW DRILL @ 10 YARDS

To mix things up, let's practice starting with your back to the target, facing directly uprange, with your wrists above your shoulders. On the start signal, turn and fire two rounds into the target.

All alphas milestones for this drill:

Beginner- 2.75 seconds

Intermediate- 1.8 seconds

Expert- 1.45 seconds

RETENTION DRAW DRILL

This one involves three USPSA targets. Place one at arm's length in front of you, with the other two about five yards downrange, spaced about two yards apart and centered with the first target.

Start standing with your gun loaded and holstered and your hands relaxed at your sides. On the start signal, draw and engage the first target with two rounds from retention. Then extend your arms and engage the other two targets with two rounds each.

All alphas milestones for this drill:

Beginner- 3.5 seconds

Intermediate- 2.75 seconds

Expert- 2.10 seconds

Keep in mind that a good retention draw can be executed in ¾ of a second with a kydex holster mounted on the hip without concealment.

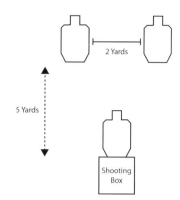

LATERAL MOVEMENT DRAW DRILL

The drill encourages lateral movement with the draw. To do it, you'll need two USPSA targets, one with the no-shoot side facing it. Place one no-shoot USPSA target at arm's length in front of you. Then directly behind that target, about three yards downrange, place a shoot target.

Start standing with your gun loaded and holstered and your hands relaxed at your sides. On the start signal, simultaneously sidestep around the no shoot target and engage the shoot target with two rounds.

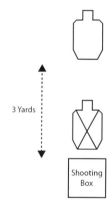

All alphas milestones for this drill:

Beginner- 1.9 seconds

Intermediate- 1.4 seconds

Expert- 1.05 seconds

Remember to load up the inside of your pivot foot, then do all of your motion at once- including the draw.

HOLSTER SELECTION TIPS

Whether you're a competition shooter or a defensive shooter, you're going to need to find some way of carrying a gun on you.

- A good competition holster is usually made out of plastic and the gun is held in place by friction. Many of these are dual purpose and can be carried on the streets as well. However, an outside the belt plastic holster isn't the most concealable available. Unless you're wearing a long coat, people will see you're armed. It will give you a quick draw if needed though.

- There are specialty race holsters available for competition use only which barely hold the gun in place for as fast of a draw as possible. These simply have slight pressure on the triggerguard, and have a knub on which the end of the barrel rests.

- Other more defensively based outside the belt plastic holsters include an active retention system. Here, you're going to need to perform some action to release the gun, such as by pressing a button that holds the gun in place. While your draw is slower on these, you can perform all sorts of motions and the gun won't dislodge. These are good for plainclothes officers. Some people have reservations about using holsters that require you to use your trigger finger to release the gun. There is a higher possible accident rate with these, so train accordingly.

- You will find a vast assortment of inside the waistband holsters, ankle holsters, etc. which can all be had. These are typically made of leather/plastic/nylon and hold the gun via friction. Ultimately you need to weigh the pros and cons of each in terms of comfort, concealability, and draw speed. Comfort will ensure that you're going to want to wear the gun out, and that it's not going to be a pain to put on/remove. If it's a huge hassle, guess what? You won't carry very often. Concealability is also very important. This isn't the wild west. If you're carrying you should at least put a modicum of thought into hiding it from sight. Do you really need to brandish that 5" Government model 1911 to help you deter possible threats during your dinner at Applebees? Finally, the gun needs to be accessible to improve your time on target. An ankle holster won't work if your armed adversary is right in front of you. It's going to be a balance for you to determine the best combination. I personally like an inside the waistband a few inches behind the hip because I don't have to bend too much, and a good shirt will cover it completely. Pocket holsters work well too.

CHAPTER 9

RELOADING THE GUN

Much like anything else that involves high speed manipulation of the handgun, when you're reloading, you're going to want to minimize auxiliary movement. Many people have a tendency to do a little "reload dance" whenever they need to do a mag change. This all takes time, and is easier to screw up. Work of being efficient and develop proper muscle memory. As a matter of fact, when I use a magazine loader prior to shooting, I will actually use proper form to "reload" it every time. The reason I started doing this is because I found that I would drop my hands too much when I was actually shooting, so I decided to correct it by always doing it the right way, even when I wasn't even holding a gun. As a result, everything improved tremendously because the motion was driven into my subconscious. You'll know that you have the muscle memory dialed in when you can reload a gun blindfolded. Give it a try!

Reloads should be
a quick, compact motion:

- *Try not to shift your grip too much*

- *Keep the gun up and in*

- *Look where you want the magazine to go*

One major factor that will come into play during your reloads is hand size and working with the gun's ergonomics. If you have to significantly shift your grip to hit the magazine release button (semi-autos) then it will not only cost you time on the reload, but you'll also be less consistent in rotating the gun back on target.

If you're just getting started learning the reload, just do drills with it as a primary focus. Later on we'll add some movement into the situation, which will affect you considerably (because you're bouncing up and down). Don't try to do too much else as you'll want to ensure you get the form down in a controlled environment. Work on both situations in which you drop your magazines to the ground and you retain them. The situation will dictate the proper procedure.

Mimicking the reload with my mag loader

Point of note: Label your magazines. I like to use a silver Sharpie on the baseplate. Magazines can cause jams. When you're dropping them a lot (like I do) then they're bound to incur some wear and tear and get dirty. If you find that a certain magazine isn't falling free from the gun, or you tend to have malfunctions associated with the magazine, you're going to want to know which one it is.

Another point of note: Leave your magazines on your belt so that the bullets face forwards. This will make reloading a lot easier as you won't have to turn the magazine to insert it in the gun.

PROPER SEMI-AUTO RELOAD TECHNIQUES

When performing a reload, you're going to want to follow the below guidelines. I'll start out by doing the simplest style, which is changing a magazine with a round left in the chamber, then we'll add in some particulars. The finger always comes off the trigger immediately preceding a reload:

1. When you decide to begin your reload, move both your hands simultaneously out of full extension.

Steps of a proper reload

2. Your strong hand will bring the gun in towards you. It should move in at around eye level and stop at around a foot from your face. While you're moving the gun inwards, you're going to want to hit the magazine release with your thumb. (Left handed shooters without ambidextrous magazine catches will use their index fingers.) How this is done is both a matter of preference and hand size. Some shooters like to "flip" the gun to the outside to hit the release button. This motion is fine, but I don't recommend overemphasizing it. Larger handed shooters will not have to shift their grips much to drop a magazine. Ideally you want to move your hand as little as possible.

3. At the same time, your support hand should be reaching for a new magazine on your belt. It should move in a straight line towards the magazines. Your hand should open up and you should focus on making contact with the magazine with the base of your palm and the tip of the index finger. When grabbing the magazine, your support hand index finger should ride along the front of the magazine pouch.

4. Once you've dropped your old magazine, you should tilt the gun so that the magwell is at about a 45 degree angle directed towards approximately your support side hip bone. This will place it in perfect position to accept the new magazine. Your eyes should be focusing on the inner lip of the magwell.

5. Move your support hand in a straight line towards the gun, and "point" your magazine into the magwell using your index finger. You are using it as a guide, because it's natural for people to point towards things they're looking at.

6. Seat the magazine firmly with the base of the support hand palm. To do this, extend your fingers out of the way and slam that magazine in there.

7. Rotate your hands back to form your grip and extend your arms towards the target as you prep the trigger.

Correct points of contact on the magazine

Except in certain situations, you should always load with the easiest to access magazine first. In many cases this will be the frontmost one. You'll want to reduce the amount of time to get back on target as much as possible.

SLIDE LOCK RELOAD

The slide lock reload is very similar to the one with a magazine left in the chamber. In many guns, if you seat the new magazine hard enough, the slide will come forward on its own and you won't have to hit the release manually. However, this doesn't happen all the time, so you'll have to familiarize yourself with the other three methods of getting the slide back into battery.

1. Press on the release with your support hand thumb. Don't try to use your strong hand to do this, as you won't be able to get a good reach, and the lever can be under some tension. Once you hit it, get your support hand back into position. This is the fastest way.

2. Once you seat the new magazine, you can reach back and pull on the slide with your support hand. Left handed shooters that don't have access to ambidextrous slide releases will have to get used to doing this. The fastest way is to keep the gun at eye level and pinch the slide between your index finger and thumb and pull back.

3. The third way is to move the gun towards you and downwards somewhat, grab the slide with your entire hand and pull back from the serrations. This works well with heavy recoil springs, and in slippery conditions. Also, it can be argued that it's easier to train new shooters on for stressful situations and unfamiliar guns.

Pulling back on slide

MAGAZINE RETENTION RELOAD

In some situations, you're going to want to retain the magazine on your person instead of letting it drop to the ground. This can be either for defensive reasons, or you could be shooting a competition (such as IDPA) where you're required to stow your magazine. Either way, the mechanics are the same.

- The easiest way to keep a magazine on you is to put it in one of your pockets assuming that the pocket is large enough for you to toss it in with minimal effort. In this case, as you're hitting the magazine release, your support hand comes under the gun and grabs the magazine between your thumb, and index/middle fingers. Put it in your pocket (not recommended with super tight jeans) and go for the next magazine.

- You can also stow the partially full magazine in one of your magazine carriers. This is easy when you have a spot open, but what if you have two mag pouches on your person and they're both occupied? In order to do this reload, first grab a magazine with your support hand. Then bring your hand up to the gun, and drop the partially full magazine in between your index and middle fingers. Next, insert the full magazine and seat it with the base of your palm. Finally, put the partially full magazine into the now empty space on your magazine carrier. This type of reload is typically done in a secure location as it takes the most amount of time and dexterity. If you're doing it, think about loading from the rearmost (or most difficult to access) magazine carrier. This way if you need a full magazine immediately it will be the easiest one to get to.

Removing old magazine & inserting new one

LOADING OFF A TABLE

If you have to pick up a magazine off a table to perform a reload, then place the magazine so that the bullets are pointing up towards the sky. This way when you grab the magazine, you can easily lay your index finger across the front of it so that you can point it into the gun more easily.

RELOADING FROM CONCEALMENT

Similar to the concealment draw, you're going to want your support hand to first make a hook up against your body to clasp and throw the concealment (such as your jacket) out of the way. This time, since the hand will be coming directly off the gun, it should appear to be a single continuous sweep. Make solid contact between your fingertips and body so that you'll be sure to catch the concealment for a quick reload. Follow your hand along your body until you make contact with the magazine. If you attempt to "throw" the garment out of the way, it might come back before you can reach a magazine. If you grab a piece of the jacket along with the magazine, you might accidentally drop it.

Magazine position is important in reloading from concealment. Since the magazine is thinner than the gun, and since there are likely going to be two magazines on your belt, the concealment garment has an increased likelihood of getting snagged when it's brushed back. Magazines that are placed farther forward are easier to access, but might result in less wearing comfort.

Like with the draw, each piece of concealment will handle differently. Make sure that you're familiar with what you're using and have practiced on it extensively.

PROPER REVOLVER RELOAD TECHNIQUES

The revolver is a considerably more difficult firearm to reload than a semi-automatic. Many things are happening at one time. Instead of simply hitting a button and plunging another magazine into the gun, you have to perform several different precise actions at once. There are two common methods to reload the revolver, one involving loading with the support hand, and the other with the strong hand. The support hand load is significantly easier to learn because during the entire process you're still hanging onto the gun with your strong hand.

Point of note: There are many different revolver designs, including breakaways. These techniques apply to the standard swing out cylinder, which is typically loaded with moon clips (but also work for rimmed ammunition as well).

SUPPORT HAND RELOAD

1. As soon as you're ready to perform the reload, remove the support hand from the grip, and begin to tilt the rear of the gun downwards with the strong hand. The gun should be moved closer to the body, no more than a foot away.

2. Swing the support hand up so that your thumb is on the cylinder release lever and your fingers are cupped along the top of the gun to reach the front of the cylinder.

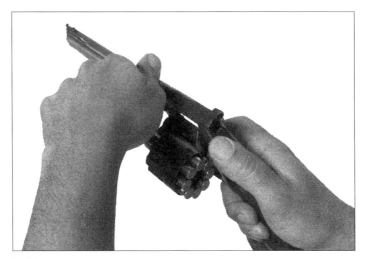

Emptying the gun

3. As you press the cylinder release with your support hand thumb, push the cylinder to the left with the index finger on the strong hand.

4. With the rear of the gun now at a significant downward angle and the cylinder fully swung out to the left, hit the ejection rod with the index and middle fingers on your support hand. This should eject all of the spent cases onto the ground.

5. Immediately swing the gun so that the muzzle points down towards the ground with your strong hand. Your support hand should leave the gun and pick up another moonclip of ammunition.

Inserting a new moonclip

6. The support hand should then place the new ammunition into the cylinder.

7. Simultaneously close the cylinder with the support hand thumb and bring the gun back up on target.

8. Reform your grip and fire.

STRONG HAND RELOAD

1. Once you're ready to reload the gun, immediately drop your hands down to about center chest level and bend the arms inwards. The gun should be no more than a foot away from you.

2. The strong hand hits the cylinder release as the support hand does a major pivot so that the middle and ring fingers can push out the cylinder from the right side of the gun. The index finger on the support hand is resting more or less around the top right of the barrel, the middle and ring fingers are resting on the cylinder, the pinky is resting on the frame, and the thumb is extended ready to hit the ejection rod.

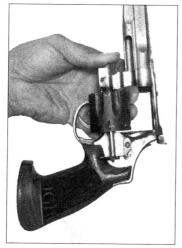 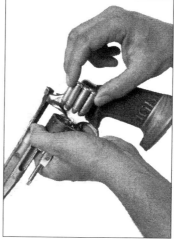

Hand positions on gun during strong hand reload

3. The strong hand leaves the gun and goes for more ammunition on the belt.

4. Simultaneously, the middle and ring fingers continue to push out the cylinder to the left while the rear of the gun is rotated downwards.

5. Once the cylinder is open, the support hand thumb hits the ejector rod, and the middle and ring fingers (now in the gap where the cylinder has swung out from) brace the gun against the opposing force.

6. The gun's muzzle is now tilted somewhat downwards to allow you to drop in some fresh ammo.

7. The strong hand comes back with the ammunition and loads the cylinder.

8. The support hand thumb/palm closes the cylinder as the strong hand comes back up on the gun.

9. The grip is reformed as the gun is brought back on target.

COMMON MISTAKES ON THE RELOAD
THE STIFF ARM RELOAD

One of the most prevalent alternative methods I've witnessed is called the "stiff arm reload." This technique asserts that it allows you to have improved situational awareness while reloading and keeps your gun on target. It advocates keeping your strong arm in the shooting position (nearly fully extended), and your eyes downrange the entire time. To reload, the magazine is brought out to the gun which remains up with the sights relatively vertical. I personally do not advocate this style because I feel it has a number of disadvantages.

Proponents will argue that by using a stiff arm reload the gun will still be pointed towards where you were shooting, which is theoretically supposed to be a threat deterrent. However, in the best case scenario you now just have a single bullet left in the chamber. If you have to fire, you will be shooting one handed while manipulating the pistol with imperfectly aligned sights, which isn't the best combination for accuracy. If you're shooting a revolver, you went to slide lock, or you have a magazine disconnect on your pistol, you now have no bullets remaining in the gun while you're performing your reload.

Proponents will also argue that the stiff arm reload prevents you from having to move your gun much from the point of aim. They claim that this will save you time and will increase your accuracy when you start shooting again. However, it's much more difficult to reload a handgun when it's that far away from you and as a result you'll actually be significantly slower overall. There are many reasons for this. First, you cannot see the magwell because it will be below your line of sight, and you will therefore have to rely on muscle memory alone to guide the magazine to its destination. Second, you will be mostly using your front deltoid muscle, which is not noted for its fine motor control, to raise a heavier arm (due to the extension of your elbow) towards the gun. Your movements will not be as precise. Third, since the stiff arm reload requires you to cup your reloading hand to hold the magazine, you will not be able to lead it into the magwell using an easy, natural motion (such as pointing the magazine into the gun). These effects, combined with pressure and stress can result in a higher potential to fumble one's magazine, which is a big distraction and time waster. The problems become even more magnified if you're trying to do a stiff arm reload while you're on the move.

Finally, proponents might state that you are able to keep your "eyes on target" with the stiff arm method, in spite of the price of a substantially slower and less precise reload. The method taught by this book recommends that you shift your focus to the magwell for a split second during the reload. However, that's simply a recommendation. You can reload by bringing the gun in close to you while still looking at the target if you believe it to be necessary. It's even possible to reload in total darkness. However, if you shift focus, another factor to consider is that human peripheral vision works based on motion. If you happen to be looking the magazine into the gun and during that split second a target moves in the background, you will be able to instantly snap your eyes onto it.

In general, those who support the stiff arm reload will laud its "situational awareness" and "defensive" benefits. But there really aren't any. A reload performed close to your body will be far more quick and consistent- even if you're looking downrange while doing it.

OTHER ISSUES

- Dropping the hands. I'm guilty of this one sometimes too. It's very comfortable to drop your hands down to your chest when reloading. However, doing it will cause you to be slower, and to move your eyes considerably lower to complete the load. This will increase the time to get the gun back on target. It happens sometimes, but you should make sure that you try to keep the gun just below eye level.

- Not moving the gun in far enough. As established earlier, keeping the gun out too far in front of you will make getting the magazine in the gun more difficult and time consuming. Don't bring it in too far so that you're all scrunched up, but don't be fully extended either.

- The reload dance. I referred to this one earlier as well. Lots of people like to lean to their strong side when dropping a magazine, then lean all the way back to grab another one. I've also seen people swing their strong arms way out and to the side when performing a reload. It should be a compact, quick movement along the center of your body. Doing otherwise is just slower and serves no purpose. Don't bend your body at the waist unless you're reloading a revolver.

- Improperly seating the magazine. This occurs either because you're not pushing hard enough with the heel of your hand as you insert the magazine. It should be a firm shove, not a little tap. This problem can be exacerbated with reduced capacity (due to state law) magazines which are loaded all the way up. Follow through with the base of your palm to really get that magazine in there.

RELOAD DRILLS

Since this section covers basic reloads, there hasn't been any movement or multiple targets included. For now, just worry about getting your reloads down to acceptable times. Then you can create more complex drills that rely on a wider variety of techniques. I recommend that you try working with steel targets so you know you're getting your hits.

Point of note: These drill milestones assume a kydex friction retention side mount holster, and a side double friction retention mag pouch.

THE DOUBLE SHOT EMPTY BELT DRILL

In this drill you're going to want to practice your basic reload fundamentals. You can experiment with various distances and types of reloads (for semi autos). Doing it is pretty simple. Just start with your gun at low ready, then engage the target with two rounds then perform a reload. Repeat this until you've expended all of the magazines on your belt. I've included some sample times based on each one of the different types of reloads that are discussed above. All milestones have been tested with a 10" steel plate at eye level. (Do not shoot at steel closer than 7 yards away. You will get fragments flying back at you.)

7.5 Yard, 10" Plate Dropped Magazine Reload Times

Best Interval time (exact duration of the reload between shots) milestones for this drill:

Beginner- 2.6 seconds *Revolver +1.25 seconds*

Intermediate- 2 seconds *Revolver +0.8 seconds*

Expert- 1.5 seconds *Revolver +0.5 seconds*

Point of note: It's possible to perform an under one second reload at this distance with an unmodified semi-auto. A revolver can also be reloaded in the low one second range by some of the top shooters in the world.

20 Yard, 10" Plate Dropped Magazine Reload Times

Interval time (exact duration of the reload between shots) milestones for this drill:

Beginner- 2.9 seconds *Revolver +1.25 seconds*

Intermediate- 2.2 seconds *Revolver +0.8 seconds*

Expert- 1.75 seconds (Some people can get much faster than this.) *Revolver +0.5 seconds*

The Staggered Distance Reload Drill

In this drill, you're going to take three 10" steel plates (or equivalent) and stagger them at various distances. This drill emphasizes the necessity of getting certain sight pictures on targets prior to breaking a shot after reloading. It's pretty easy to just get a flash on target at 7.5 yards (minimum safe distance away), but you're going to have to have incrementally better grips and sight pictures to hit the target twice quickly at 14 and 21 yards. Place one steel plate at eye level at each of these distances in front of you, slightly offset from one another so you don't have to move to see all of them. (Center the 12 yard one in front of you, with the others 3 yards off the center line.) Start at low ready, with your triceps touching your chest down to the elbows, and the muzzle pointed directly downrange. On the start signal, engage the first target with two rounds. Then perform a non-slide lock reload and engage the first target again. Then perform a reload and engage the second, then a reload, then engage the third. If you don't have access to a range in which you can perform this drill, substitute targets of decreasing size in exchange for increased distance (2nd target is half as big as the first one, etc).

Two hits on each piece of steel (six total) milestones for this drill:

Beginner- 11

Intermediate- 8.75

Expert- 7.40

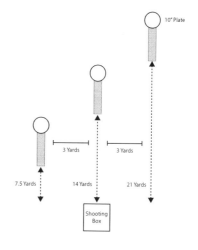

BLINDFOLDED RELOADS

In order to emphasize the muscle memory behind your reloading technique, try doing it blindfolded on command. This will help in a defensive situation where your attention might need to be focused downrange, as well as in a competition setting if you have to be moving dexterously through a field course. Also, if you ever have to shoot at night, you won't really be able to see your magwell anyways, so it's always nice to have this skill developed.

Your eyes serve as a guide in the reload and improve the speed and consistency. However, you should be able to easily do reloads without looking.

These help develop good muscle memory

POSITION SHOOTING

Y ou won't always be able to engage a target while just standing there. As your abilities progress (and as the situation requires) you will have to shoot around objects and from uncomfortable stances. This section will cover some of the basics of barricade shooting, as well as how to quickly get in and out of positions. I will also go into shooting strong and weak hand only. Remember to keep your finger outside of the trigger guard while performing any movement. You don't want an accidental discharge.

One of the main things you're going to want to remember in this section is to allow the position to affect your shooting as little as possible. Some things are harder to do than others. Shooting weak hand will be slower and less accurate than shooting strong hand. The gun will move around more when you're shooting from a contorted position than from a more natural one. However, the same fundamentals of shooting apply. If you have to shoot from a position, you're going to want

Sacrifice as little technique as possible when shooting from a position:

- *Keep your weight forward at all times*

- *Set a wide base and a low center of gravity*

- *Try to keep your head up while shooting around objects*

to prevent it from changing your basic mechanics of sight picture/grip/body dynamics as much as you can. Each of the exercises below will force you to mix it up a little bit. Just keep in mind what you should be doing ideally, then make the needed changes to shoot from that position.

Sometimes you'll have to make sacrifices in your stance to hit multiple targets. For example, let's say that you have a target on your left and a target on your right which requires a mild swing transition between the two. The best place for your feet to be would be squared up mostly directly between them. This way you merely have to turn your torso to engage both. If you were to square up entirely to the target on the left first, then in order to shoot the target on the right, you'd have to tweak your body, thereby costing speed and accuracy.

Standing is always the easiest position to shoot a handgun from. If you have the option, stand up. Also, stretch! If you're going to start moving around quickly, you don't want to pull anything during practice!

It's better to keep your feet in the same place during transitions

Point of note: In competition, always shoot from the easiest positions first. You'd rather end a stage or an array in the place it's hardest to get in and out of. This way you'll just be worried about getting up and moving to the next position instead of trying to shoot while you do it.

Another point of note: You should know whether you prefer to shoot left to right or vice-versa. Take advantage of this if you have the easy option to. However, remember this is not a high priority and there are far bigger concerns to account for (such as difficulty and location of the shot) which relate to the order of target engagement than this preference.

STANCE CHANGES
CROUCHING

The crouch is the second most stable position for shooting quickly and accurately next to standing. It applies when you're forced to shoot under something low, or if just want to keep your head down. If you must choose between kneeling and crouching (all other things being equal), definitely crouch. Your weight will be supported by the muscles of your legs instead of the bones, which will allow you to enter and leave the position faster, and will allow you more freedom to shift your weight and swivel your body. Furthermore, the forces of recoil will still be coming back at you in a direct line, instead of at the angle of the bladed stance that kneeling mandates. (Of course if you plan on being there for awhile, kneeling is the best option so you don't get tired.)

Here are some tips:

- If you have to crouch, use a wide stance. This will allow you to get lower and will reduce the pressure on your knees. Having your knees shake or hurt while shooting won't help you. It will also provide a much more stable base than a narrow stance. Your feet should be ideally about three quarters of a foot wider than your normal stance (or a few inches on each side wider than shoulder width apart).

Correct crouch

- When crouching keep the weight on the center of your feet as much as possible. Putting it on the toes is not only bad on knees (especially important for older shooters), but is also less sturdy.

- Sit your butt down directly, and keep your torso and head as upright as possible, but leaned forward from the waist in an aggressive posture. You don't want to hunch over with your upper back. Many people like to do this, then are forced to crane their necks upwards to see the targets. If you're going to stress muscles, don't do it to those which will affect your shooting. All of the supporting tension should be in your thighs, not your spinal erectors or shoulders. Lower yourself with your legs.

Incorrect crouch

KNEELING

One stance that you'll find in a wide variety of situations including tactical training and many pistol competitions is the kneeling position.

1. To enter the kneeling position, swing your strong leg back a good bit before starting your descent. Kneel down on your strong knee if you have a choice. It enables you to have an easier time swiveling around to engage targets around you. This is especially true when it comes to shooting to your strong side. If you kneel with your weak side knee down, then you tend to get bunched up when turning to your strong side.

2. Your weak knee should be bent at a little wider than a right angle.

3. When kneeling, you're going to want to focus on keeping a wide base with your weight forward. Leaning back here will augment the sense of recoil, and you'll get pushed around more easily.

SITTING

The seated position involves a weight shift back from the kneeling position to engage targets through a lower port. This is the hardest position to get in and out of in comparison to the others in this section because your legs are under/in front of you.

Kneeling

1. In order to enter the seated position, you're just going to roll back your lower body over your strong side foot from the kneeling position.

2. People who are more flexible can sit on the side of their strong side foot. Others will have to make full contact with the ground and fold their strong side leg in front of them (I'm one of those people).

3. Make sure that from this position, you still try to keep your weight aggressively forward to prevent recoil from taking too much hold of the gun. Super low ports might require you to bend even further at the waist. You might have to bunch up your shoulders a little bit in order to make that tight shot, but try to keep your head up and back as flat as possible. Bend from the waist.

Sitting

4. Try not to bend your weak side leg too much, as it'll just take you longer to stand up from this position.

5. Standing up easily is a three step process. First put your weak hand down to the ground on your side while keeping the pistol pointed downrange. Second, swing your strong foot out in front of you and put it on the ground. Third, while putting your weight on your weak hand and strong side foot, swing your weak side foot out behind you. Then move!

SITTING IN A CHAIR

At some point you might have to use a gun while seated in a chair. This is a common occurrence in USPSA/IDPA matches, or if you frequently play high stakes poker with unsavory characters. While engaging targets while seated, spread out your legs to form a good base and bend them under you then lean your upper body forward. It's always better to stand up and shoot though. You'll be faster and more accurate.

PRONE

Unlike when shooting a rifle, going prone with a handgun probably produces the least amount of rapid fire accuracy in comparison to any other position. There is an assortment of possible ways to shoot while prone, but I tend to prefer two above all others. The key here is to not create pivot points on your body, like your elbows. Doing this will just cause the gun to bounce off of those angles and will make the recoil harder to control.

1. In order to properly get into the prone position, you're going to want to perform three steps. While keeping the pistol pointed downrange simultaneously bend down and put your weak side palm onto the ground and swing your weak side leg way back (place the ball of your foot on the ground). Now bracing yourself with your weak side arm and leg, settle down your strong side forearm onto the ground. Finally, lower the rest of your body onto the ground and extend the handgun forwards.

2. The first way to shoot prone at low targets is to place the heel of the gun directly into the ground. Make a lot of contact with your forearms and the ground so that the gun won't move all over the place when you fire. Your arms should be extended well in front of you if possible. The farther they're extended and the more contact between your forearms and the ground, the easier it will be to shoot from this position. However, if you have to shoot targets significantly above ground level, you'll have to lift your forearms and rest on your elbows if you stay flat. In that case, I recommend the next method.

Low prone

3. The second way to shoot prone is by rolling somewhat over onto your strong side and resting your entire strong side tricep on the ground. From here, you can bend your elbow without problems to lift the gun and your forearms up to engage substantially higher targets. From this position, your support arm will be entirely off the ground, and your legs will be swung out towards your weak side for balance. The advantages here are more mobility for shooting at targets that are far apart, and decent recoil control. Also, if you're wearing prescription glasses, you'll be able to look more straight ahead and will not have to worry about any distortion from the top of the lens.

High prone

4. Create a wide base with your legs and keep your feet on the ground. Lifting them up will cause strain in your lower back, and will want to pull the gun up under recoil.

5. To stand up from the prone position, simply put both your hands in the push-up position then swing your legs under you to jump up. Keep control of the gun and your finger off the trigger. If you're not that flexible, then go to your knees first.

SHOOTING STRONG HAND

Shooting strong hand only should be relatively straightforward to you at this point. I haven't included it up until now because by far the most stable and accurate way to shoot a handgun is with two hands. There are only two instances in which you should be shooting a pistol one handed. The first is in a competition, the second is in a serious defensive situation in which you've either been injured or it's a tactically sound idea. (Sorry John Woo fans, there will not be a "guns akimbo" section in this book.)

There are a couple of things that you'll want to keep in mind while shooting strong hand only:

1. Blade your stance towards the target. If you're right handed, then your right foot should be moved forward. I like to have my feet at a little less than a 45 degree angle to the target, with about 60-70% of my weight on my front foot, which should be pointing more or less towards the target. My shoulders are a little more square than my hips. This helps recoil absorption and prevents the gun from moving you or your firing arm off kilter. If you were to stand in your normal stance, the gun would have more of a tendency to move up and to your weak side because you'd be shooting across your body with no support from that side.

2. Rotate your firing hand in a little bit towards your weak side (counter clockwise for righties). This will turn the gun slightly sideways. This will help align the bones in your arm and hand more naturally, and will turn the sights into your field of vision. When you point at something in the distance naturally, your wrist is not perpendicular to the ground, it's always at an angle. (Try it as if you were pointing at a mouse on the ground "Hey lookout for that mouse!") The same is true with holding a pistol. Don't overdo it, but adopt a natural posture.

Strong hand

3. Your grip should be the same as if you were holding a handgun two handed. If you're using a particularly heavy trigger or one that's hard to reach, then it's acceptable to move your thumb a little bit lower on the handle for better leverage, but this isn't the best method normally.

4. Your face should be square to the target, and your head should be up and level.

5. Your weak hand should be up and in against your chest. This will help with balance.

SHOOTING WEAK HAND

Shooting weak hand looks a great deal like a mirror of shooting strong hand. You're going to want to blade your weak side towards the target in a similar manner, and keep your face pointed straight at the target. The one thing that you might want to do a little differently is to rotate your weak hand over a little bit more so that it's in line with your dominant eye. By this, I don't mean shift your arm position. Actually rotate the wrist in (clockwise for righties) so you can see your sights without moving your head. This way you can avoid shooting across your body, where the forces of recoil will cause the gun to jump around unpredictably.

Weak hand

BARRICADES
PORTS

You'll find that ports are quite ubiquitous whether you're shooting in a defensive situation from behind cover, or you're in a competition and are forced to shoot through a barrel or a window. Here are some key points to remember if you have to contend with one:

- Don't stick your gun deep into or all the way through a port. In a defensive situation, this will expose your hands to possible return fire. For competition, it will cause you to have a slower time. Every second you spend pushing your gun way in there will be time you're not spending engaging the target. This is in addition to the time it takes to extricate yourself from that position.

- Be careful of parallax of ports against your sights. For example, if you have to shoot through something that's a few feet away from you, you might call a hit because your sights are on target. However, your barrel could actually be aligned with the side of the object you're shooting through. Even a small amount of contact with a pistol round will cause the bullet to deflect errantly, and often the ricochets are significant. Know how much clearance you have.

- Practice shifting your weight between your legs. It will dramatically improve your transition times when shooting through a single port. To quickly shift between a target on your far right, then to your far left, come into the port already loaded up on your left leg, with your knee bent and your body twisted at the waist. Then when you're ready to shoot the target on your far left, immediately transfer most of your weight onto a bent right leg and twist your waist over to engage it. These wide swings can all be done without moving your feet much, thus granting you as much stability as possible.

- Have a wide base in your legs. This allows you to be more maneuverable. If you're shooting through a window for example, spreading your legs wider allows you to be able to shift your weight and pivot your upper body without moving your feet. Every time you take a step, your sights will bounce. A wide base enables to you move in and out of cover, rotate to engage targets at different angles, or possibly to shoot through multiple ports without having to move your lower body that much. This part is essential to speed and accuracy. Also, if you have to get lower, you can more easily control your descent as your body weight is braced on your thighs instead of your knees. Your stance will naturally be about a foot wider than normal if you expect to move a lot within your position.

Transitioning between two ports

- Do not rest your wrists on the barricade while using a two handed grip. It will create a pivot point that the gun will bounce off.

SHOOTING AROUND A BARRICADE

Shooting around barricades is another vital skill that you'll need both in defense and competition. Obviously the emphasis on the former is to remain as much behind cover as possible, while the goal in competition is speed. Try practicing both to get a feel for how quickly you can pick up and engage targets around doors and walls.

- The foot that's on the same side as the side of the barricade you're shooting from should be ahead. This helps you keep your body weight forward, and also allows you to lean farther around the barricade to engage deeper targets. This knee should be bent to absorb the additional weight and help you move out of position quickly. Try to keep the rest of your body as square as possible.

- When shooting around an object, make sure that you keep your head and your gun as vertical as possible. Many people will start by leaning their heads over (clockwise if shooting from the right side of a barricade) and will tilt their guns to match. This will cause inconsistent

Shooting around a barricade

recoil tracking, and will hinder your speed and multiple-shot accuracy. Gravity will act as a force that pulls your gun laterally instead of up and down, and you won't be used to it. Lean from your lower torso instead.

- Stand back from the barricade you're shooting around if you can. Pushing yourself directly up against an obstacle will limit your mobility and gun extension. Also, you won't have to move as much to engage multiple targets the farther back you're standing. If you get too close while coming around a wall in a defensive situation this becomes an issue as your adversary will be able to see your gun before you can see them. In a competition, it's simply slower, and will cause you to be more contorted when shooting. I like to have at least an arm's length if the situation allows it.

- If you have to shoot around both sides of a barricade or go back behind cover for some reason, bring your gun in with your elbows and keep it pointed downrange. Some people like to raise their muzzles up to the sky or point them at the ground. For both defense and competition, this will cause you to be slower in getting rounds back on target. If you bring your elbows in, then you can still pivot and shoot at close range. You can also extend your arms to bring the gun up to eye level fast. If your muzzle is aimed up in the air, then if a threat comes around the wall, you're pretty much screwed. In competition, it will take you more time to aim again because you'd be bringing your hands down, and will have to settle them prior to touching off that next round.

- Bend your outside knee in (that's on the side of the barricade you're going to shoot from), and put your weight on the inside of that foot. It will help you lean around more efficiently and keep your balance. This knee should be bent significantly to support your weight.

- If you're shooting around the barricade on your weak side in competition (with a fault line), and have to bend in deep to shoot a target that's way around it, get your entire strong arm around the barricade so you can turn your arms from the shoulder.

- If you're shooting around the barricade on your strong side in competition (with a fault line), and have to hit a deep target, it's better to bend the weak arm in and bring the gun closer to you than to force it around the barricade.

Weight on the inside of the foot, knee bent in

- In competition, if you come up to a position where you have to shoot around a barricade with a tight fault line, it's always better to engage the targets that require the hardest lean last. This is because a big lean will put you off balance. When you're done with that target you want to be able to book it out of there instead of having to regain your balance to shoot again.

- In a defensive situation, try and expose as little of your body as possible. This includes your foot and lower leg. Ideally the only visible parts of your body should be your head, hands, and gun.

COMMON MISTAKES WITH POSITION SHOOTING

Most problems that arise while position shooting come from bad setup. If you get into a position improperly then it will make shooting from it more difficult.

- **Feet too close together.** You want to be able to shift your weight, change your stance orientation (go kneeling or prone), and lean with ease. If your feet are too close together, then in order to move your upper body, you'll have to start using your feet. This is undesirable because this "sideways shuffling" movement will cause you to be slower on target. Also, when you're crouching down, it starts to be really hard on the knees and is quite unstable.

- **Too bladed of a stance.** This can occur when shooting one handed or around a barricade. If you start putting one foot directly in front of the other then you'll begin to not only lose your balance, but will be obligated to shoot across your body. The gun will be harder to control. Plus this position takes way too long to get into.

- **Too slow into position.** Regardless of it being a defense or a competition situation, you want to get in position fast. This will help you get rounds on target as soon as possible. Be aggressive with your leans and your body movement. Get your feet wide and pivot quickly. Keep your gun as close to the shooting position as the situation will allow while you're transitioning. Try to minimize whatever movements you have to make.

- **Head and shoulders canted.** It's comfortable for many people to hunch and roll over their upper bodies in order to shoot. Keep them as vertical as possible to ensure that you're as consistent as possible.

- **Improperly squared to the target array.** When you're shooting multiple targets from a position, you need to place your body in such a way that you'll be able to engage them without having to lift your feet. Get into a wider stance that allows you to pivot your torso across a big variety of angles.

POSITION DRILLS

Point of note: These drill milestones assume a kydex friction retention side mount holster, a side double friction retention mag pouch, and a striker fired semi-automatic pistol.

Another point of note: When I say that you need a piece of steel for a drill, you should set it so that it doesn't fall over when you shoot it. You can always use a paper substitute but I like steel because it gives instant feedback on your hits.

MULTIPLE POSITION DRILL

In this drill you're going to go through three different positions- standing, kneeling, and prone. Simply set two paper USPSA metric targets at 15 yards, with their shoulders about level with yours. They should each be spaced about 7 yards laterally apart. You'll need at least three magazines/speed loaders with this drill (the reloads are so you don't cheat and start moving from one position to another while you're shooting). Start standing, facing the targets, hands relaxed at sides with your gun loaded in your holster.

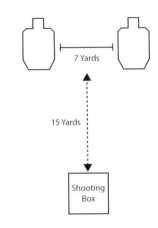

On the start signal, engage each target with two rounds. Perform a reload, and engage the targets again with two rounds from the kneeling position. Perform a reload and engage the targets again from the prone position.

All alphas with one or two charlies milestones for this drill:

Beginner- 16 seconds

Intermediate- 13.5 seconds

Expert- 11 seconds

NARROW PORT DRILL

This drill requires the use of a front fault line (spraypaint or a piece of wood will work) and two barricades. Place the two barricades a foot apart from one another. Place three USPSA targets 15 yards downrange from the barricades, each spread out five yards from one another. The center target should be aligned with the port created by the barricades and be visible with the other two obscured. Start standing about arm's length from the port, facing the targets, hands relaxed at sides with your gun loaded in your holster.

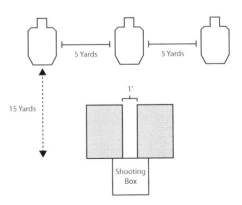

On the start signal, draw and engage the center target first, then both of the other targets with two rounds each from behind the fault line. Focus on shifting your weight and moving your body gingerly into position to shoot all of the targets. For added variety, you can put more targets up on the sides at deeper angles.

All alphas milestones for this drill:

Beginner- 8 seconds

Intermediate- 5.5 seconds

Expert- 3.75 seconds

To improve at this drill, don't move your feet. Just shift your body using your waist and your knees.

AROUND THE BARRICADE DRILL

For this drill, you're going to need another barricade with a fault line drawn at the edge of the barricade on your strong hand side. The fault line should be perpendicular to the backstop you're shooting at and should not allow your foot to get around the edge of the barricade. Place four USPSA metric targets 15 yards downrange from the barricade, each spaced three yards apart from one another. The fault line should be pointed directly at the second target from your strong side, with one visible target and two obscured by the barricade that you'll have to lean around to shoot.

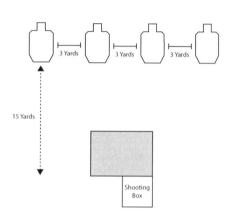

Start with your strong side foot on the fault line at arm's length from the barricade. Position yourself so that you can only see the first target. Hands begin relaxed at sides, and your gun is loaded and holstered. On the start signal, draw and engage all targets with two rounds each. Do not step over the fault line during this drill. The purpose of the fault line is to limit your movement. You will be forced to lean around the barricade to hit the deeper targets without moving your feet.

To shoot this drill on your weak side, simply reverse everything. You should be able to run it in about the same times.

All alphas milestones for this drill:

Beginner- 8.5 seconds

Intermediate- 6 seconds

Expert- 4.75 seconds

WIDE BARRICADE DRILL

For this drill, you're going to need four USPSA targets, and a 4' wide barricade. (If you don't have access to the barricade, simply put the no shoot sides of three USPSA targets next to one another.) Place the box about one yard behind and centered with the barricade. There will be two arrays of targets. On each side and aligned with outward edge of the barricade put a target 15 yards downrange. Put another target 5 yards to the outside of these two targets. There should be two targets engaged from the left side of the barricade and two to the right.

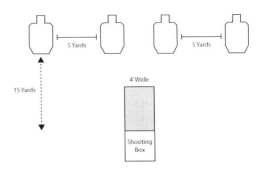

Start standing centered behind the barricade about arm's length away with your gun loaded and holstered, and your hands relaxed at your sides. On the start signal, draw and engage the four targets- two from each side of the barricade.

All alphas milestones for this drill:

Beginner- 9 seconds

Intermediate- 7 seconds

Expert- 5.5 seconds

This drill will encourage you to learn how to cover a short distance with the fewest possible steps. Try to literally jump over from one position over to the next. If you try to shuffle your feet, you'll get caught in between steps and will be slower. Try not to overrun the barricade on either side; just go as far as necessary. Also, shoot the target on the outside first.

THE DIP DRILL

Sometimes you'll not only have to shift back and forth, but also up and down. It's kind of like a boxer bobbing and weaving. This drill will help you get used to bending down to shoot. You'll need one barricade that's a foot and a half wide (or one tall USPSA metric target with the no shoot side facing you that you can't see over), and one USPSA target. Place the USPSA target 10 yards downrange of the barricade. Staple or tape a piece of wood, cardboard, (or anything that's about two inches wide) at about chest level to the barricade so that it extends well past the sides. This will create four quadrants, one above and one below the barrier on each side of the barricade.

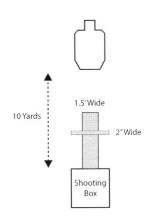

Start standing with your gun loaded and holstered at arms length away from the barricade. On the start signal, draw and engage the target with two shots from each quadrant without moving your feet.

All alphas milestones for this drill:

Beginner- 9.5 seconds

Intermediate- 6.75 seconds

Expert- 5 seconds

To improve at this drill, practice shifting your weight around. A lot of the bending can come from your knees to keep your torso as upright as possible.

MOVING AND SHOOTING

Finally we get to move around! In both the real world and the practical pistol competition circuit, chances are if you're shooting a handgun, you're not going to want to stay in one place the entire time. The ability to not only get from point A to point B efficiently but to be able to hit targets while you're doing it will prove to be incredibly valuable. Shooting on the move is difficult and it's always preferred to plant your feet if you can. In this section, I'll concentrate a great deal on footwork. Initially you'll want to practice setting yourself up while you're moving to a position so you can start shooting as soon as you get there. When you're familiar with that, you'll want to start adding more shooting as you're moving in and out of those positions. Later on you'll be shooting between those positions.

When you're adept at shooting on the move, you'll be able to make everything into one fluid motion. The key is to be smooth and not jerky. The difficulty of the shot will be your gas pedal. The harder the shot, the slower you'll have to go

Maintain stability during movement:

- *Be fluid while entering and exiting positions*

- *Roll heel to toe with your knees bent to prevent bouncing while firing*

- *Make smart decisions about when to move and when not to*

in order to hit it. If it's a close range target in a competition, I can blast it while running sideways at almost a full sprint and still get two center mass hits. If it's a long range shot, then I'll go from a run to a stop and will get two crisp shots on it, then accelerate again.

Point of note: A skill you're going to want to learn is an awareness of your own limitations. You need to know when it's prudent to stop and fire, and when to continue dropping rounds. You'll also want to gauge speed. Walking and shooting is a ton more accurate than running and shooting.

Another point of note: When you're moving, keep your finger off the trigger. You don't want to trip or stumble and get an accidental discharge.

ENTERING AND EXITING POSITIONS

By now you should be familiar with shooting around and between objects. However, you need to get to those positions fast. Furthermore when your feet stop moving your gun should be up and you should be shooting immediately. Here are some tips for improving your speed:

- While moving over a long distance, I like to keep my gun up around eye level with my arm extended towards the targets I'm about to shoot next. I can run just as quickly, and it makes it easier for me to mount the gun on those targets when I arrive to my next shooting position. I just have to bring my support arm up to form the grip at the right time. I usually rotate my arm so that the gun is pointed sideways downrange because I feel I can run faster that way and not cause the gun to bounce around that much. While moving a medium distance, I'll usually keep my two handed grip and bring the gun in closer to my chest. Then I'll re-extend it to the target just before I arrive. While moving a short distance, I might just keep the gun extended with both hands.

- Mount your gun before you stop moving from position to position. If your gun is up and you have your sights ready as you come around a barricade then as soon as you clear the obstacle, you can put rounds on the target. Do not wait until you're in your next position before you get your gun up.

- The correct way to slow down from a run is to break down your steps. If you've played baseball, basketball, or football, you're undoubtedly familiar with this concept. You can't just go from a full sprint to a stop. Attempting to do so will cost your balance, and might lead to injury. To correctly slow down from a run do the following:

Gun stays up while sprinting

- Shift your weight to the rear. This starts by moving your shoulders then your hips backwards.

- Bend your knees so that they absorb the shock better and lower your center of gravity.

- Start taking smaller, quicker steps. You'll feel the balls of your feet hitting the ground first, then your heels coming down.

- Once you start to slow down enough keep your hips back, but bend your torso forwards and mount the gun on the target. The forward lean of the torso will reduce the recoil of the gun and set you up to start shooting.

- At this point, you can either continue moving at a slow pace while shooting, or you can plant your feet into your regular stance.

- Get a good stance if you stop from a move. Lots of people let their momentum carry them forwards and they end up shooting off their toes. Practice breaking down your steps into a sound shooting base.

■ Know where you're going to put your feet in advance. In competition this is especially vital because you will not waste time shuffling your feet around when you get into a position. They will set themselves up naturally. Placing your feet in the right position the first time will allow you to simply pivot your upper body to shoot multiple targets without having to change up your stance. An ideal foot position will allow you to engage as many targets as possible from a reasonably neutral stance. For defense, you don't want to have your lower leg exposed or force yourself to shoot from an uncomfortable/difficult body orientation.

■ Running will get you there faster, but it will take you time to get ready to shoot. In a competition, you're going to have to be running constantly because it's a game of speed. You'll have to know when to start breaking down your steps so that you're not looking at the target and waiting to mount your gun. In a defensive scenario, if you run out from behind cover then it's going to take you awhile to be able to slow down enough to accurately put shots on target.

■ In competition, in order to exit a position quickly, you're going to want to start shifting your weight out of the position as you're finishing shooting the array. This will ensure that I don't waste any time moving after I'm done shooting.

Shooting while entering and leaving a position at 10 yards

- Whether you're coming from a sprint or just a quick position change, practice keeping your knees bent. This will prevent bounce and will allow you to stay low for future movement. A stiff frame will easily sway.

As you improve, you should be able to start shooting when you start setting your feet and also as you're leaving a position. For example, let's say I'm coming up to a closely spaced eight shot (four target) array at about 10 yards from a full out sprint in a competition. I'll break down my steps so that I've already shot the first target while I'm slowing to a stop. I'll shoot the next two targets while I'm stopped. Then I'll begin to lean out of the position while I shoot the last target. This is the most efficient way to be in and out, without sacrificing accuracy.

SHOOTING WHILE MOVING

The most crucial element to shooting while moving is stability. If your gun is not stable then you won't be able to fire accurately. Each step you take can produce a bounce that will send your sights off target and bullets in an unpredictable direction. However, someone that's experienced in these techniques can keep the gun perfectly level while travelling at a respectable rate of speed.

One of my favorite ways to demonstrate this is using a full beer bottle. (Probably the only time you should have beer out there on the range!) Open up your hand, palm towards the sky, and extend your arm to about the length you'd use while shooting. Take a full 12 oz beer bottle, open it, and put the base in the palm of your strong hand. Then while holding the beer bottle there, try to move around the room without spilling the beer. You'll quickly notice that it's not as easy as it looks! This is the type of stable platform that you're going to be looking for while shooting. Your legs act as shock absorbers while your torso and arms remain flat and relatively still. The only movement you're doing is with your legs.

Balance drill

- Keep your knees heavily bent. This lowers your center of gravity which gives you a nice shooting platform.

- While bending your knees, to get an idea of the correct position, sit your hips backwards as if you were trying to sit down in a chair.

- Keep your torso and arms stable, and maintain an aggressive forward lean to control recoil.

- Keep a crisp focus on your sights to see how much they're moving in relation to the target.

Sit backwards into the moving posture

- While moving forwards, you're going to want to roll your feet heel to toe. Land on your heels and keep your weight centered over your feet.

- While moving backwards, do exactly the opposite. Roll toe to heel.

- While moving side to side, you're going to want to move your feet in the direction of travel with the same mechanics as if you were moving forwards. However, you should turn at the waist to square your shoulders as much as possible to the target.

Rolling heel to toe

- If you're running really quickly and have to shoot a target at speed, it's best to mount the gun at the last possible second. Your body will instinctively know to mount it correctly on target based on what your body is doing at that moment in time. However, if you try to aim for longer than a split second, all the bouncing from the run will throw you way off. Look at the target, mount as fast as you can to get a quick sight picture, fire, and keep moving.

- Sometimes if you're moving really quickly, it's easier to stop your legs for a brief pause and let your body keep moving (so you're falling for a moment). The gun will arc in a very predictable way until that foot comes down and you regain your balance. If you can time the shot, then you're good to go.

SHOULD I SHOOT ON THE MOVE?

There are many considerations which affect whether or not you're going to want to move and shoot at the same time. These include the difficulty of the shot and the quality of the terrain. Trying to hit a huge target at 7 yards while walking on a paved road will produce dramatically different results than trying to hit a plate at 20 yards during a jog down a muddy hill. The question is how much confidence you have.

Keep in mind that movement isn't an on/off switch. In order to win a competition or survive in a defensive scenario, you're going to want to be able to incorporate varying degrees of movement based on the situation. If you have to lean out from around a barricade to shoot, can you hit the target while the gun is still moving, or do you need to pause? Be sure to know your limitations. Based on your speed of travel, how long is it going to take before you can deliver shots with a high probability of hitting the target?

DRAWING ON THE MOVE

If for some reason you have to cover a lot of distance and draw your handgun, you're going to want to begin the draw as soon as possible then run with the gun in your hand. If you're drawing from a full sprint, I would recommend slowing your run a little bit before taking the gun from the holster. You don't want to fumble around with it as the gun bounces, or get a bad grip, step on a bump, then drop the handgun. Make a clean draw.

RELOADING ON THE MOVE

One thing you're going to want to practice is reloading on the move. While this type of reload is frequently found in USPSA competitions, it also has defensive applications (such as when moving behind a large piece of cover). Generally if you have to perform a reload as you're leaving a position, try to complete the load as soon as you're finished firing at the previous array. If you fail to initiate the load as soon as possible, then as you begin to move your hands will start to bounce. It's not the easiest thing in the world to run at full speed and reload a handgun. Try to maintain focus on the inner lip of the magazine well as you seat the new magazine.

Reloading on the move

PROBLEMS WITH MOVING AND SHOOTING

Problems that people frequently encounter while attempting to shoot on the move typically arise due to a lack of stability of the shooting platform. The sights appear to be bouncing around all over the place, especially during recoil.

- **High center of gravity.** When I was working on my shooting on the move awhile back, a buddy of mine commented that I "look like someone going for a stroll through the supermarket." In other words, I was standing fully erect and was simply walking through the course of fire. It was little surprise to me that I would miss high when engaging a target while moving towards it. My first shot would always be center mass, then I would take a step and my sights would bounce up. Wham! Another miss. A high center of gravity will cause every little bump to go straight through your legs and manifest itself in a parabolic movement of the gun. Make sure that you sit yourself down towards the ground.

- **Timing problems**. Sometimes in order to hit a target, you'll have to lean way out or take a big step. As soon as that next foot comes down, the gun will move around a lot. If you're making big motions with your legs, then learn to time the gun with those motions so that you can maintain a good sight picture on target without it suddenly jerking away.

- **Not aggressive enough.** If you're speeding from position to position, it's vital that you be aggressive when mounting the gun and shooting. If you spent too much time watching your sights, they'll begin to bounce around more. When you're moving, get to the speed that you want to be at, then mount the gun, pick up the front sight, and deliver your shots all in one continuous motion. Don't wait on the gun. Mount it to your eyes.

- **Not setting the proper stance.** While breaking down the steps after a run, many people do not focus on getting their feet set. I see a lot of feet placed way too close together, and people almost falling forward when they stop. How you set your feet will play a large part in how quickly you can shoot targets from that position. Pay attention to it when you're slowing down.

MOVEMENT DRILLS

When performing these drills, take careful note of safety. Move with your finger out of the triggerguard. Also, keep the gun pointed directly downrange the entire time. Do not break the 180 with your muzzle (an invisible line parallel to the backstop) at any time.

Point of note: These drill milestones assume a kydex friction retention side mount holster, a side double friction retention mag pouch, and a striker fired semi-automatic pistol.

Another point of note: When I say "inside the box" I mean that neither one of your feet is touching the ground outside the box.

LINE BOX DRILL

For this drill, you'll need two USPSA metric targets, and three boxes. Put the three boxes in a line parallel to the berm you're shooting at. Space them four yards apart. Put the two metric targets 10 yards downrange of the center box one foot apart. Start in the box on your weak side, gun loaded and holstered, hands relaxed at sides.

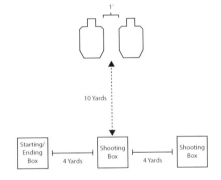

On the start signal, engage the targets with two rounds each from the box. Move to the center box and engage the targets with two rounds. Reload while moving to the strong side box then and engage the targets with two rounds from the box. Move back to the middle box and shoot two rounds at each target. Reload while moving to the first box and engage each target with two rounds from it. There should be a total of 20 shots.

All alphas with one or two charlies milestones for this drill:

Beginner- 26 seconds

Intermediate- 20 seconds

Expert- 16.50 seconds

You can improve your times by feeling the balance of your body as you lean in and out of position. Add more movement within the boxes. When I hit that third box, I'm leaning in on the first target and leaning out on the second. I don't stop moving during this drill.

You can also practice your barricade shooting by shooting around a bunch of them instead of from boxes.

SQUARE BOX DRILL

The box drill is one of my favorites for practicing movement. To do it, you'll just need three USPSA metric targets and three magazines. Arrange four boxes in a square, with each of the boxes four yards from one another. The front and rear lines of the square should be parallel with the backstop you're shooting at. Place the three USPSA targets 10 yards downrange of the two boxes closest to the berm, with each of them one yard from each other. The middle target should be directly centered between the two frontmost boxes.

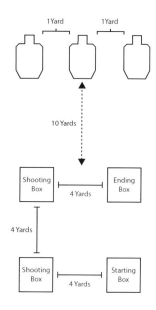

Start in the rearmost strong side box with your gun loaded and holstered with your hands relaxed at your sides. You should be facing downrange with your shoulders and toes square to the berm. On the start signal, draw the handgun while moving to the box on your weak side. Engage each target with two rounds each from within the box. Perform a dropped magazine reload while moving to the box in front of you. When you're inside the box, engage the targets with two rounds each. Perform a dropped magazine reload as you're moving laterally to the last box on your strong side. When you're inside the box, engage the targets with two rounds each.

All alphas milestones for this drill:

Beginner- 18 seconds

Intermediate- 15 seconds

Expert- 12.25 seconds

You can improve your times by getting your feet properly set and mounting your gun as you're entering the box. Also, practice leaning out of the position while you're engaging the last target in the array.

Try different variations of this drill by starting in different boxes.

LATERAL STABILITY DRILL

For this drill, you'll need four USPSA metric targets, along with two boxes. Place the two boxes four yards from one another on a line parallel to the berm you'll be shooting at. Place an array of four USPSA targets 10 yards downrange spaced one foot apart with the last target centered with the box opposite your start position.

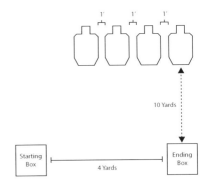

Start standing in either box, gun loaded and holstered, hands relaxed at sides. On the start signal, engage the three targets from between the two boxes. Engage the final target from within the opposite box.

All alphas milestones for this drill:

Beginner- 9 seconds

Intermediate- 6 seconds

Expert- 4.15 seconds

Try to keep your gun at eye level and your motion steady as you shoot the three target array on the move. It's the fastest way to complete this drill.

ACCELERATED MOTION DRILL

This drill will demonstrate how quickly you'll have to move in order to be able to be fast while getting your hits. To perform it, you'll need four USPSA metric targets, one box, and markers, barricades, or spraypaint to create fault lines. You're going to want to create a path at a 45 degree angle to the berm you're shooting at. Place the box at the beginning of the path as your start position. Place one fault line two yards away from the box along with three more fault lines down at two yard intervals going at a 45 degree angle towards the berm. These fault lines will create shooting positions that you'll move through while engaging a single target. Put the USPSA targets directly downrange from each of the shooting positions.

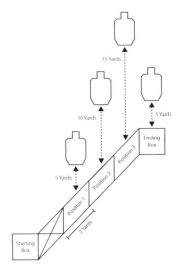

Shooting Position 1: 5 yards

Shooting Position 2: 10 yards

Shooting Position 3: 15 yards

Shooting Position 4: 5 yards

Start standing in the box gun loaded and holstered, hands relaxed at sides. On the start signal draw and move to Shooting Position 1. Engage the target with two rounds. Move to Shooting Position 2, engage the target with two rounds. Move to Shooting Position 3, engage the target with two rounds. Move to Shooting Position 4, engage the target with two rounds. You'll be moving at a 45 degree angle to the berm.

All alphas milestones for this drill:

Beginner- 11 seconds

Intermediate- 7.75 seconds

Expert- 5.15 seconds

You should be able to drill the first target really fast, then will be forced to progressively slow down as you move between positions. At the end you'll have to move quickly from your position to get the last target. This drill can be run with targets to either your weak or your strong side. The times should be pretty close to one another.

To improve your times here, know at what pace you'll want to shoot each one of the targets, then adjust to that speed immediately before you engage the target. If you're doing the drill right, you'll find yourself running to a position, slowing down to shoot, then running to the next position.

SPRINT TO A STOP

This drill will emphasize how much you actually have to stop moving when trying to engage targets. To perform it, you'll need four boxes and a 12" steel plate. Setup the boxes in a straight line perpendicular to the berm you're shooting at. Place the boxes at the following distances from the steel plate:

Starting Box: 35 Yards

Shooting Position 2: 25 Yards

Shooting Position 3: 15 Yards

Shooting Position 4: 7.5 Yards

Start in the farthest box from the steel plate with your hands relaxed at your sides and your gun loaded and holstered. On the start signal, draw the gun and run to the second box. Engage the steel with two shots. Once you hit it twice, run to the

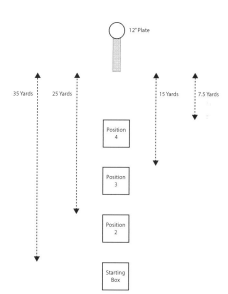

third box and shoot the steel twice. Then run to the fourth box and hit the steel twice.

All hits milestones for this drill:

Beginner- 16 seconds

Intermediate- 13.5 seconds

Expert- 10.75 seconds

To improve your times, determine exactly how much you have to stop in each box and break down your steps. I find that I can hit the target out of the 7 yard box with enough forward momentum to carry me out of the box. In other words, I'm still running pretty fast as I deliver those shots.

POSITION TO POSITION DRILL

For this drill, you're doing to need three 4' wide barricades, or barrels, cones, or some form of position marker. I like barricades because they help me get used to mounting my gun as I'm coming up on a target, but whatever you have at your disposal will be fine. You'll also need a box and two 12" steel plates. Setup the steel plates downrange about 12 yards apart. Place the box directly between the steel plates about 30 yards away. Imagine a center line going from the box downrange directly between the steel plates. Place a barricade along this center line at:

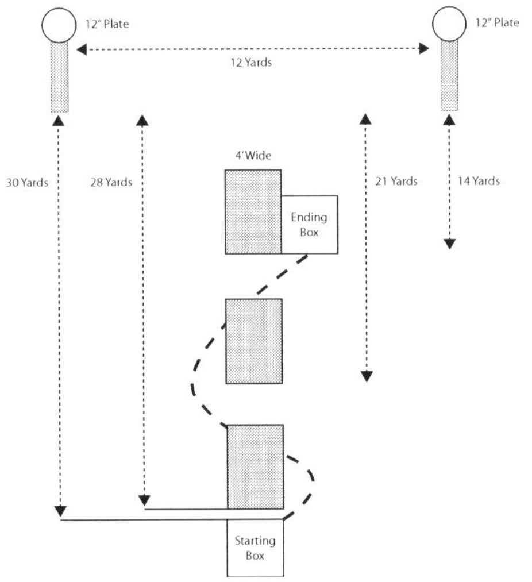

Barricade 1- 28 Yards

Barricade 2- 21 Yards

Barricade 3- 14 Yards. Put a box on the right side of this barricade. It will be your finish position.

Start standing in the first box, with your gun loaded and holstered with your hands relaxed at sides. On the start signal, move to the right of the first barricade and engage the plate on the right with two shots, then the plate on the left. Then move around the left side of the second barricade and engage the target on the right with two shots, then the target on the left. Finally, perform a reload, then move past the last barricade to the ending box and engage the right target with two rounds, then the left with two rounds. The idea is to weave your way between the barricades and gauge your speed as you shoot the targets.

All hits milestones for this drill:

Beginner- 20 seconds

Intermediate- 16 seconds

Expert- 13 seconds

In order to get better at this drill you should focus on only moving when you have to. I like engaging the second array of targets while aggressively on the move. Then I drop a quick reload before I come around the last barricade, get my gun up, and quickly shoot the last array from the box. Movement and speed will help you here, but you have to be accurate and not sacrifice your hits, otherwise you'll be standing out there trying to get them before you can move on.

ADVANCED SHOOTING MECHANICS

By now you should be pretty well versed in the fundamentals of modern shooting. As an advanced shooter, you're going to be looking for something that will give you a little bit of an extra edge to hone your skills. This section builds on the basics established in the intro chapters on accuracy, speed, and transitions. It contains tips and tricks that will help you continue to improve, as well as drills that you can try out to drive everything home. This section assumes that you already have read and learned everything up until this point.

There are a few main points that you need to remember in this section as an advanced shooter:

- Accuracy comes from precise trigger manipulation.

- Speed comes from the application of pressure through grip strength and leverage over the gun.

Tension is the illusion of speed:

- *Fluidity and economy of motion will give you the best results*

- *Develop your natural shooting index*

- *Learn exactly what you need to see in order to make a shot.*

- *Master changing focus levels rapidly while shooting.*

- Transitions come from how quickly you can focus your eyes on a target as well as how quickly you can pivot your body.

If you've opened this book for the first time and have decided to skip "all of that beginner stuff" I recommend that you go back and peruse it. While the drills might seem a little simplistic to you, the techniques described are not. Perfecting your fundamentals is something people should strive for at every level. Just because you consider yourself an advanced shooter doesn't mean that you have all of them correct. Some people are quite proficient at shooting the wrong way. Also, the "wrong way" doesn't even have to be that far opposed to the right way. You might just have developed some bad habit that needs a minor tweak to set you right again. A main problem with doing something incorrectly is that you will have longer plateaus in performance that will be more difficult to overcome. Have an open mind and always try to understand the why behind what you're doing. Constantly look to improve yourself even if it means going back to check your basics.

With the above being said, try out some of the stuff I've listed below. Remember that there are plenty of other drills to experiment with out there, and these are just a fraction.

Point of note: You might even learn something from people who you might not consider as good as you. Perhaps even if 90% of what you're doing is better in comparison to someone else, they might have some unique knowledge about the 10% that you're deficient in. It's still possible to beat someone with better mechanics than you by a huge margin in a competition now, but it's possible that they might have more long term potential.

Another point of note: These drill milestones assume a kydex friction retention side mount holster, a side double friction retention mag pouch, and a striker fired semi-automatic pistol. Keep in mind that I've simply put an "all alphas" milestone for the sake of comparison so I can avoid starting a long discussion about scoring targets. If you occasionally throw some Charlies (hits just outside the Alpha zone on a USPSA target) doing these drills then it's usually fine. I do it all the time. It just depends on what your training goals are.

ADVANCED ACCURACY

There are three things that I like to practice when it comes to accuracy. The first is the zen game of perfect trigger control. The second is to work on my split times and following my sights on difficult shots. The third is to run my standard drills using reduced size targets incorporating either no-shoots or hard cover (hits there don't count). All three require a highly developed sense of shot calling. You should be able to know exactly where every shot that you're firing lands. At this level if you miss, or even just don't hit the center of the target, you should know nine times out of ten without having to go look for bullet holes. If you can't do this, it means that you're not an accurate enough shot to move on.

One of the benefits about practicing accuracy is that when you add other elements into your shooting such as movement, then your accuracy cone widens. If you're naturally more accurate, then there's a lot more you can do from a speed perspective with the knowledge that you can still hit your targets. For example, if I'm moving through a course of fire and my sights are bouncing around, then I get a quick sight picture on something, I know that when I pull the trigger I'll hit what I'm aiming at. If I wasn't an accurate shooter, not only would I have to worry about the movement affecting the position of my sights on target, but also where my shot will impact if I fire. There are more variables for those that don't practice accuracy.

60 YARD PLATES

Usually when I'm done practicing for the day, I'll watch the sunset over the horizon, take a nice deep breath and relax with this drill. There are a bunch of plate racks setup on my home range. (In case you don't know what a plate rack is, it's six 8" plates arranged usually with about six inches between them.) I'll set one up, then go back about 60 yards and start shooting the plates. Speed isn't a factor here. Your goal is to not miss the plates. While it's possible to go 6/6, I would say that you can consider yourself an expert if you only miss twice while shooting the array.

DISTANT STEEL BILL DRILLS

I like to setup a 10" steel plate and put it a long ways away, then practice bill drills. 30 yards is usually a good place to really focus on your accuracy and control. Simply start loaded and holstered, with hands relaxed at sides. Then draw and engage the target. When you get five hits, look at your time.

Five hits milestone for this drill:

Expert- 3.60 seconds

It's a good idea to work on your draw times by trying to see how fast you can get on a little target at distance. This drill also encourages positive recoil control. Watch your sights to ensure that they're coming back down on target as much as possible in a straight line.

REDUCED SIZE TARGETS

These combine both speed and accuracy, and are a fantastic tool. You should add them sporadically to your regular drills to ensure that you actually can make tight shots. I have some drills which use them listed in the transitions section coming up in a few pages. Here are some examples of reduced size targets which you can use to force yourself to improve:

- Hard Cover Target

- No Shoot Overlap

In competition and defensive scenarios, you'll need to learn to quickly shoot at irregular targets which are obscured in some way. Mixing your usual targets up with these encourages precision and prevents misses. I would encourage you to include these in all of your drills, especially those where you don't currently have a high degree of accuracy- such as movement. It's always easy to throw rounds downrange.

Targets with hard cover and a no-shoot

However, when there are no-shoots in the way, you don't want to miss what you're aiming at. Once you know your overall accuracy cone, you can determine how far from a no-shoot target or piece of hard cover you'll have to aim in order to give yourself a good chance of preventing an accidental hit. If you run drills with nothing but reduced size targets and can hit them with regularity, imagine how much faster you'll be able to shoot when you're trying to perform the same drill with regular sized targets?

ADVANCED SPEED

Speed drills will become more important to you as you improve. How fast can you get rounds on target? I've seen plenty of people that are incredibly accurate who will put a one inch group on target at 10 yards, but will take forever to do it. Your speed will come from how quickly you can follow your sights as they bounce up and down on target. It will also come from how controllable that bounce is. One crucial element here is your split times. You should be able to drill a close range target as fast as you can pull the trigger. There are two major complaints that I hear at the higher levels from some very proficient handgun shooters:

- **My sights are not tracking properly.** Your sights will be a good diagnostic tool for what it is you're doing wrong. For some people, their sights simply don't get back on target fast enough. People find themselves waiting on the gun, and consequently their split times are slower. "How can I fire the gun when I know the sights aren't back on target yet?" For others, they are forced to "steer" the gun back on target after firing.

- **My hands are breaking apart under recoil.** This becomes evident in multiple shot arrays, and especially reveals itself during bill drills. In this case, the support hand starts to move off the strong hand and creates a gap between the fingers.

Assuming that the gun is not way too big for your hand (which could be the source of the problem) then both of the above issues tend to be derived an uneven amount of pressure. This can come from a bad grip, or the desire to push the gun with the larger muscles of the body. Hands breaking apart under recoil can be corrected by adjusting the position of the support hand to give it more leverage or by closing a gap on the gun between the palms.

If all of your fundamentals are 100% correct, then look at how tight you're holding the gun with each hand. For a little while my sights were going excessively up and to the right with a particular new gun. I could still shoot really fast with it, but wanted to get the maximum consistency possible. Due to the unfamiliar ergonomics, the grip that had worked for me previously was to blame. When I asked a good buddy of mine who is a champion revolver shooter, he pointed out that when I shot strong hand only, the gun tracked just fine. Therefore, he suggested, I should try applying more pressure with my strong hand. (The logic was that I was applying an imbalance with a really hard support hand grip. pushing at an angle) I did, and my problem immediately disappeared.

Try and understand how a recoiling gun might act on a weak point in your grip (such as a gap between your hands), or how some inconsistency in pressure might cause the sights to move in an undesirable direction. Also, keep in mind that when you're manipulating the handgun with draws, reloads, or movement, you might be positioning your hands poorly as you rush to re-engage targets.

DRIVING THE GUN AT CLOSE RANGE

In USPSA, we call this "hosing the targets." For targets at around 7 yards or less, you should be able to break .20 splits easily. Many shooters can get into the .12-15 range. In order to accomplish this, you're going to really want to squeeze that grip tight and time the trigger as it resets and the sights descend back into their channel. A good point of reference for the grip is to hold just hard enough with your strong hand so that the sights don't shake. Don't try to apply downwards pressure with your shoulders or wrists, and don't overly accentuate your forwards lean. Also, don't squeeze with your chest muscles or arms. Think about using only your hands while relaxing everything else. Your grip pressure will change somewhat based on the difficulty of the shot. If you have to hit a hard long shot at distance, you might ease up a bit. If you have to drill close targets, you might tighten it up a bit. Here your emphasis is on speed so you want those sights getting back on track as soon as possible.

There are many guys and gals out there that exhibit what's called a post-firing "flinch." A normal flinch that pulls the bullet off target occurs when the gun drops PRIOR to the gun going off. This second type only occurs once the trigger has been pulled, the primer has ignited and the bullet has left the barrel. It doesn't affect accuracy, but instead results as a reaction to the CONSTANT force of recoil that comes from multiple shot rapid fire. In other words, people are simply leaning more into the force pushing against them. You can see this when someone is shooting really fast, then they get a light primer strike and their gun dips forwards. While this happens to many people at one point or another, nobody at the top level consciously thinks about trying to do it. It's not a technique or necessarily an error, but rather something that can occur naturally while trying to time the gun. If your accuracy is good under recoil and this happens, don't worry too much about it. If your accuracy is poor under recoil, do not attempt to incorporate it into your technique. It should not be done intentionally, nor should it happen when you're shooting any slower than your fastest splits.

The difference between a normal flinch and one that comes subconsciously (and that's the important part) as an element of recoil control is that the former anticipates recoil, the other reacts to it. To get an idea of how this works, stand in your normal stance with your arms outstretched and your hands clasped together. Then have someone start pushing back on your hands with a decent amount of constant force. In order to maintain your stance, you will start to lean into that person. Your hands and shoulders will maintain the same height, and your head will be in the same place as before, but since you're focusing on keeping stable you end up pushing back. If that person were suddenly to release all pressure, then you would dip forward. Now have someone try to fake you out by leaning on your outstretched grip a bunch of times, but deliberately missing your hands occasionally. If you fall forward in anticipation when they miss, that's a pre-firing flinch.

Leaning into partner's hands

At the end of the day, recoil control will come from your grip and the position of your arms, legs, and torso. Do not try to compensate for poor recoil control by manually pushing and pulling with any part of your body, especially your shoulders. Your technique should only consist of you worrying about exerting a static pressure over the gun. If you can't control the recoil properly, build up your grip, don't try to shove the gun down.

EL PRESIDENTE DRILL

This is one of my favorite recoil control drills. I like the fact that you're going to have to go at a really high rate of speed, and guarantee that you're forming your grip properly during the draw and reload. You're going to need simply three USPSA targets and a box. The targets should be 10 yards downrange of the box, and spaced one yard apart, with the center target aligned with the box.

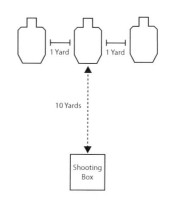

Start standing in the box with your gun loaded and holstered, wrists above respective shoulders, facing uprange (back square to targets). On the start signal, turn, draw, and fire two shots on each of the targets, perform a reload (dropped magazine) and reengage each target with two rounds.

All alphas milestone for this drill:

Expert- I've shot this one in 5.5 on a particularly good run at a match with all alphas. It can be done in the 3-4 second range with some Charlies. Be careful not to break the 180 with your gun on the draw

THE "FLYING-V" DRILL

The difficulty of the shot is your effective "gas pedal" when it comes to shooting fast. How quickly can and should you engage targets? Your splits should increase at a constant rate as distance or no-shoots get added. Here's one drill I like to use to practice this:

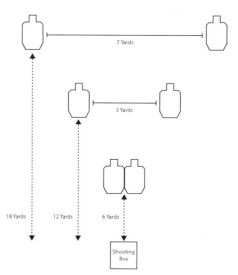

You'll need six USPSA targets and one box. Place the box on the center line between the targets. Stagger the targets with two at 6, 12, and 18 yards. The targets at 6 yards should be right next to one another. The targets at 12 yards should be 3 yards apart. The targets at 18 yards should be 7 yards apart.

Start standing in the box with your gun loaded and holstered, hands relaxed at sides. On the start signal, draw and engage one target at 18, then one target at 12, then one target at 6 yards with two rounds each (farthest target first). Perform a dropped magazine reload, and engage the other three targets from the inside out (closest first) with two rounds each. You must work out-in-out.

All alphas milestone for this drill:

Expert- 6.10

This drill will encourage you to track your sights, and to adapt your speed to the position of the targets.

HOT AMMO DRILLS

We all know that there are ways to reduce the recoil on your gun. This can be accomplished through either light training/competition loads, reduced power recoil springs, lightened slides, etc. If you want to improve your recoil control, shoot with some more powder in your ammo with a heavier than factory spring. Watch how the gun moves and how your times differ from the drills you've been running so far. You'll be surprised at the results. Hotter ammo might make people want to physically try to reduce the recoil on the gun with your larger muscles. You can't. You can only exert a higher amount of static grip pressure and maybe lean a little more forward. Too many people become complacent using their target ammunition, and start easing up on the grip pressure. This exercise will get you back to the proper form. When you switch back to your normal loads things will go more smoothly.

ADVANCED TRANSITIONS

Transitions are some of the most important things that you can practice. In competition lots of time is saved being able to hit multiple targets with speed and precision. In a defensive situation, there will be a lot of movement. You need to be able to steer your gun towards what you need to hit. Your eyes are going to lead the way.

WIDE ANGLE TRANSITIONS

As covered extensively in this book, you're going to want to encourage consistency in your shooting, both in terms of how you control the gun and how you absorb recoil. Your body should be as square as possible to what you're shooting at to ensure that recoil is evenly distributed. But how do you reconcile that concept with engaging targets to your left and right, as well as those which are below or above you?

The correct technique involves keeping your wrists and arms bent at as much of the same angle as possible, and as straight out in front of you as possible. A small range of motion can be driven from the shoulders, followed by rotation of the waist, and if necessary moving your feet. Lifting up your feet is the least desirable out of all of these as your sights will bounce when you do. Most swivels should be done from the waist alone.

Here are some pointers for a wide angle transition:

1. When entering a position to shoot the array which contains a wide transition, arrange your stance as if you were shooting somewhere between the targets. This is very important. Lots of people will square up too much on the first target. This causes a slow transition because aiming at the other target(s) will require more of a turning range of motion at the waist then their body allows. They will then have to shuffle their feet and reset their stance.

2. The same principle as the above applies when drawing to two targets at a wide angle. Square up your lower body to somewhere between the targets. Keep your head and upper body directed at what you want to shoot first.

Wide angle transition without moving feet

3. Make sure you call your shot on the target that you fired on before beginning the transition. A lot of people will pull off prematurely and throw a miss.

4. Lead with your eyes.

5. Rotate from the waist and keep your shoulders and arms square.

6. If it's a really big angle, you might want to bring your hands in a little bit to turn faster.

7. Prep the trigger while your body is turning. As soon as your sights get on target, you should be shooting.

8. Decelerate your motion at the end of the swing so that your gun doesn't go past the targets and have to come back.

9. Do not move your wrists to turn the pistol. While this might be the best technique while playing Time Crisis in the arcades, it won't help with a real gun.

Wide Angle Transitions Drill

You'll need two USPSA metric targets and a box. Arrange the two targets and the box in an equilateral triangle with 20 yards between everything. Start standing in the box with the gun loaded and holstered with your hands relaxed at sides. On the start signal, draw and engage one target with two rounds, then shoot the other with two rounds, then back to the first with two rounds, then back to the second with two rounds.

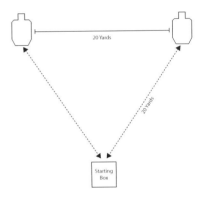

All alphas with one or two close charlies milestone for this drill:

Expert- 5.75 seconds

Watch out for throwing shots off target because you're leaving the target you're shooting at too quickly.

POINT SHOOTING

Point shooting is one of those skills that you will hear about in every gun store, in every magazine, and on every firing range. Some people call it "natural point shooting" or a "natural index." I like these terms because they allude to the things that your innate hand-eye coordination is capable of doing. If you have to throw a football or baseball to someone, you just look where you want it to go, and perform the motion. Your brain makes the minute adjustments of your arm and release point in three dimensional space in order to get the ball to its destination. Further practice means further refinement. So what really is it anyway when it comes to shooting?

I would describe point shooting as looking completely at the target while pulling the trigger. If you think of the amount of focus on your sights as a scale, this would be a zero. This is just your head telling your hands where they need to be pointed to put a round where you're looking. The amount of focus on your sights is inversely proportionate to what I call your "cone of accuracy." This is a hypothetical cone of where your bullets will impact if you pull the trigger at that moment in time. With all other things being equal, if you just look at a target in the distance, your cone is going to be its widest (least accurate). With a 25% focus on your sights, that cone is going to tighten up, all the way to maximum accuracy at 100% focus. Every time you perform a transition, you're point shooting somewhat. When you're looking out in the distance to find a target, then swiveling around to get your sights on it, you're using this index to get your body aligned. It's quite valuable in this regard. At very close range, there's not any real reason to see any more than a glimmer of your sights on the target in order to hit it, so there's no reason to take the time to focus more. Point shooting can be very fast.

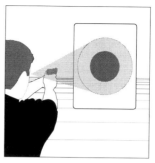

100% focus on target is fine at close range

One problem that many people have when attempting to point shoot is to drop their hands lower and peer out over the top of the gun towards the target. This is a bad idea because you're disrupting your normal point of aim, and you'll have trouble getting your hits. Your hands, arms, and body should be in exactly the same position as if you were taking a sighted shot. The only difference is that your focus will be on the environment instead of your sights.

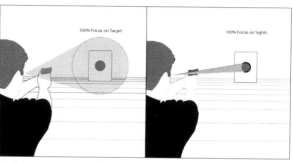

At distance you will need to see your sights more clearly

This way you will be shooting the same way you always do, except relying entirely on muscle memory and hand-eye coordination to aim. Also, if you need to shift some focus to your sights to make a tougher shot, then they're right in front of you.

Obviously there are environmental and tactical limitations which may inhibit your usual mounted gun position such as going around a tight corner. In these cases, you'll have to shoot from either a low ready, or possibly even from retention. As mentioned above, "shooting from the hip" will be considerably less accurate than normal point shooting. In this case, the best advice that I can give is to practice doing it so that your body accommodates. For you baseball players out there, it's kind of equivalent of trying to make a throw from second base to first underhanded. It can be done, but good luck trying it without practice. Get the gun mounted properly when you can.

Smoke & Hope

My favorite point shooting drill which involves some sight focus at the very end is called Smoke & Hope. It's one of the stages shot every year in many Steel Challenge Shooting Association (SCSA) matches. Some of the top shooters on this stage will produce simply inhuman times. To try it, you'll need the following:

- Four 18" x 24" rectangular pieces of steel mounted at 5.5' from the top of the target to the ground.

- One 12"round steel plate mounted at 5' from the top of the target to the ground

- One 3' x 3' box

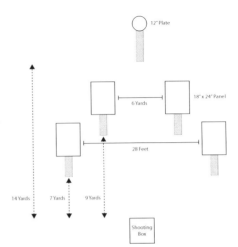

Don't worry about being too exact to run this drill. You can do it just fine with four paper targets instead of the rectangular steel, you just won't have the auditory feedback.

- Place the round steel plate 14 yards downrange from and centered with the box.

- Place the leftmost steel rectangle 7 yards downrange and 14 feet to the left.

- Place the second leftmost steel rectangle 9 yards downrange and 9 feet to the left.

- Mirror the rectangles on the right with the rectangles on the left.

Start standing in the box with your wrists above respective shoulders, gun loaded and holstered. On the start signal, engage the four rectangles, THEN the round plate last. Don't shoot the round plate until you've hit all of the other targets.

All hits milestone for this drill:

Expert- 2.5 seconds (Shooters have broken the 2 second mark on this stage in competition before using factory guns and basic holsters. In the race gun division with tricked out equipment and red dot optics, the world record is 1.84 seconds.) You should be able to run this milestone time CONSISTENTLY. Doing it one time on a really lucky run doesn't mean anything.

In order to improve on this drill, you're essentially supposed to point shoot the first four rectangular targets, then get a quick sight picture on the last plate to get your hit and stop the time.

FLASH SIGHT PICTURE

There's a saying in shooting that "your sight picture is only as good as you need it to be." When you're shooting fast, it's not necessary to get a crisp clean focus on your front sight, especially when the targets are at close range. One of the main reasons that I like using a red fiber optic in my front sight is because it glows really brightly and I can pick it up easily even when shifting focus. If I can find that dot, even if it's still somewhat fuzzy, I can deliver a round on target.

It takes time for your eye muscles to contract and your lens to focus on the foreground. However, you don't have to wait on it all the time. You sight picture serves as your gas pedal. If

I'm shooting a small target at distance then I go for a very crisp view of my front sight because a small aiming error might cause me to miss completely. However, if I have to hit something large that's right in front of me, I usually get what I call a "flash sight picture." The amount of time I take to focus on my sights will improve my accuracy cone.

1. I start by looking in the distance to acquire my target.

2. My gun follows my eyes.

3. My eyes lock onto where I need the bullets to go.

4. My gun now arrives near the target and I start prepping the trigger.

5. I start shifting my focus back to my sights.

6. While I'm shifting my focus, my gun locks onto where I need to shoot.

7. I can see a slightly fuzzy picture of my sights and a slightly fuzzy picture of the target as my focus is coming back into the foreground. But I see enough of my sights to know that they're on target. Focus levels are constantly changing between targets/shots.

8. I begin to shoot.

Keep in mind that this whole process takes well under a fraction of a second. I'm relying on multiple abilities to accomplish this. First, I'm proficient at point shooting, or a natural index of my gun to wherever I look. Second, the timing of my arm movement is precise enough so that I'm quick on, but don't overshoot the target. Third, I know what a "good enough" sight picture is in order to hit the target. Fourth, my trigger control is so dialed that I can prep the trigger in anticipation of the shot so it goes off right as my sights come on target. Fifth, my accuracy is such that I know I won't pull the shot off target when I do fire. This is one of the hardest things to do in all of shooting. How much the gun has to stop and how much of a sight focus you need is always determined by the situation.

Flash Sight Picture Drill

For this drill, you'll need a box, a full size pepper popper and two USPSA targets. Place the USPSA targets 7 yards downrange of the box, spaced four yards apart. Place the pepper popper 10 yards downrange of the box centered between the USPSA targets. It's a good idea to prop up the popper so that it doesn't fall when hit.

This will be a four string drill. Write down the times of each string, then add them up. Start standing in the box with your gun loaded and holstered, hands relaxed at sides.

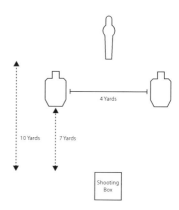

String 1: On the start signal, draw and engage the two USPSA targets with two rounds each and the steel with a single round going left to right.

String 2: On the start signal, draw and engage the two USPSA targets with two rounds each and the steel with a single round going right to left.

String 3: On the start signal, draw and engage the two USPSA targets with two rounds each and the steel with a single round going left to right.

String 4: On the start signal, draw and engage the two USPSA targets with two rounds each and the steel with a single round going right to left.

All alphas milestone for this drill:

Expert- 8.6 seconds

In order to improve on this drill, you're going to want to drill the outside targets really quickly, then get a soft focus on your sights for the center steel and hit it as you sweep through it. Try not to stop on the center steel, as it'll cost you time. However, don't just stare at it and pull the trigger hoping you'll hit it either- because you usually won't. Determine what your ideal sight picture for that shot is. If your draw isn't very good, then you can always just start this drill from low ready. Obviously the milestone won't apply, but you'll be able to work on just your transitions.

You can also try a version of this drill where you set the transitions even wider, such as 90 degrees. Try to pick up on the target even when it's completely outside of your initial field of view.

Hard and Soft Transitions Drill

I might take a soft sight picture on a close range target that I have a high degree of certainty that I'll hit, but will get a nice crisp focus on the tighter shots. You need to train this adjustment to be automatic. Your body and eyes should know exactly the amount of focus required to hit a hard shot. I like this drill because it forces me to adjust throughout the entire array. The only way you'll be successful is if you know what it takes to not miss shots.

For this drill, you'll need one box, three USPSA targets, and two 8" plates. Put the USPSA targets at 5 yards downrange, with their shoulders about at your shoulder level. They should be spaced one yard apart from one another, with the middle target centered with the box. Put the two plates at 15 yards downrange spaced four yards apart (centered between the middle target) so that each one appears centered between the paper targets. Start standing in the box with your gun loaded and holstered, hands relaxed at sides. On the start signal, draw and engage each of the paper targets with two rounds each, and each of the plates with one round.

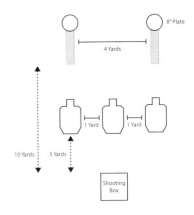

Make sure that you go paper, steel, paper, steel, paper.

All alphas milestone for this drill:

Expert- 3.75 seconds

As opposed to the flash sight picture drill, in this one, you're going to have to stop the gun on the distant plates to get a hit. Ultimately, the speed of your transition has to come from the difficulty of the shot.

Other versions of this drill:

- A good alternative involves removing the center target, and placing the steel plates back at 20 yards. With this presentation, you'll be forced to do some very precise transitions, then some very fast transitions.

- Another version involves two paper targets at 25 yards placed 15 yards apart. There are also two paper targets at 7 yards placed one yard apart directly in front of the shooter. You engage the outside 25 yard target, then the two close ones, then the other 25 yard target. It trains precision, speed, then precision.

PICKING UP TARGETS

Target identification is an important part of any training regimen. How quickly can you decide between shoot and no-shoot targets? How quickly can you react to a target? This skill is something that should be practiced for both competition and defensive situations. The technique that's driven in here is based on not only indexing in on an unknown target, but also being able to successfully avoid hitting no shoots.

An excellent approach to this type of training would be an entirely blind course of fire through a multi-room environment where the shooter has no clue where anything is and what he/she is expected to fire upon. However, even many police departments don't have facilities that inclusive. One fantastic training tool is called the PRISm® device. It utilizes lasers (similar to the technology in a golf simulator) to track your bullets as they're fired at a screen. The screen depicts some sort of prefilmed dangerous event (or even a practice range) to which the shooter must react. Such movies can unfold in any possible manner of directions, limited only to the imagination of the course designer. These are available at some commercial shooting ranges, and are extremely useful.

While realistic 3d targets and extended courses are wonderful, many people don't have the resources to setup scenarios that detailed. Fortunately there are many permutations of target ID drills which can be conducted with a small range and a small group of people. These usually involve the shooter standing either with his/her eyes closed, or back to the targets. The gun would either be at low ready, or a table, or in a holster. One version of this drill is the following.

Pick a Feature

For this drill, I recommend that you paint portions of targets multiple different colors in different configurations, and stagger them around a shooting bay. It's possible to use the "dude with a gun" paper target, but I find that it never looks realistic enough. Plus with my version of the drill you don't have to change around the targets after every string- you just have to call out different combinations.

To perform this drill, you're going to want to get a bunch of USPSA targets and some different color spraypaint. Paint the targets each in a certain color or pattern. For example you could have:

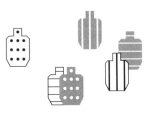

- Target with yellow vertical stripes.

- Target with yellow horizontal stripes.

- Target with red circles.

- Target with red vertical stripes.

- Target with green circles.

Shooting Box

- Target with green horizontal stripes.

Preferably don't allow the shooter to see the configurations of the targets in advance of running the drill. Once he/she steps up to the line, the instructor/range officer running the clock will call out a certain feature or combination of features such as: "Circles!" or "Green!" or "Yellow Horizontal!" Upon hearing this, the shooter will draw and engage all targets meeting the description. Any target that didn't have the feature(s) called out would be considered a no-shoot.

This drill allows multiple strings of fire with the same targets. Also, if you're an instructor grading your students, you can mix up the order of the calls a little bit so that people don't get used to shooting the same test every time. I find that as people shoot this drill, they get faster on indexing in on the threat target every time and avoid the other targets better.

TRANSITIONS INTO NO-SHOOTS OR HARD COVER

The concept of the accuracy cone has been addressed a couple of times already. When shooting around no-shoots or hard cover you're going to want to give yourself a little bit of room on where you're aiming to prevent yourself from clipping them. However, when shooting quickly many people tend to pull shots because they either shoot before their sights are entirely on target, or start to move the gun before they're finished engaging a target. You should often practice making tight shots by putting no-shoots next to and around your targets. This will teach you to call your hits and not rush past a target.

For example, if you have an array of two targets with a few yards between them, and also each with a no-shoot on the outside edge, you will have to slow your gun down during your transition so that you don't pull past the target and can get a precise shot. You'll also have to "stick" your sights on each target a little bit longer to ensure more accurate shooting. If you're used to just blasting away then these will force you to improve your timing of the transition based on the difficulty of the shot.

MOVING TARGETS

In competition, you're going to see lots of moving targets. These can include swingers, drop turners, and targets on rails. In a defensive situation, your target is never going to stand still. You have to be able to quickly locate a moving target, determine its direction of motion, and get some rounds downrange on it. At close range this is pretty straightforward and usually involves a decent amount of point shooting. At distance, you're going to have to be more precise.

With a distant rifle shot or skeet, you're going to have to really lead targets. With a pistol, a lead may also come into play, but not as significantly. This is because of the relatively close range of engagements, and the speed of the targets.

Imagine a target at 25 yards (75 feet) moving at 15 mph (a good running speed for a person). That translates to 22 feet per second (fps). Now let's take a pistol round moving at 1000 fps. Simple arithmetic will show that bullet will reach its target in 7.5 hundredths of a second. Within the amount of time that the bullet takes to reach the target, the target will have moved only 1.65 feet. In other words, if you were shooting at a target moving 15 mph perpendicular to you at 25 yards, you would only have to lead maybe one target width in front of it.

How you shoot a moving target with a pistol largely depends on its speed and distance. There are two ways to do this:

- Let the target come to you. In this case, you just look downrange and aim where you think the target is going to be, and wait for it to come into your sight picture. When doing this, you point your gun downrange while maintaining focus on the target. Just as the target is coming into your lead (if you're giving one) then your focus shifts back to the sights and you deliver the shot. This is more for a flash exposure target where you're only seeing it for a brief moment. Also, it works if you the target changes direction frequently and you just want to unload a bunch of shots at it with the hope of getting as many hits as possible.

- Follow the target. In this style, you rotate your body at the waist as if you were doing a normal swing transition, and keep your sights moving at the same speed as the target. When you're at the correct lead distance (if any), you start shooting. I tend to prefer this method if you have longer exposure to the target as you can call your shots more easily. The downside is that this becomes very difficult if the target is moving erratically in and out of cover.

I would recommend practicing both styles of engagement. If your target is popping up randomly and moving around in an erratic pattern, then it's going to be hard to match its speed with your sights as method 2 advocates. You might constantly be behind it. However with method 1, if you screw up the timing, then you might also miss altogether. It all depends on the situation, each type has advantages and drawbacks. You might find that you're using a blend of both.

Per moving target drills, there are a whole bunch of props that involve motion that are discussed below in the Competition section. I'll give you strategies on how to conquer them there. However, I've shot all of those props so many times that I know pretty much what's going to happen. It's very hard to simulate fast, unpredictable motion unless you have a specially built range, are using the PRISm® system, or are performing force on force drills using Simunitions® (a proprietary system that shoots paintballs out of modified duty firearms) or airsoft pistols.

WHILE HOLDING A FLASHLIGHT

Sometimes you'll have to use a hand-held flashlight along with your handgun. There are a variety of different holds that you can use depending on the size of the flashlight and the situation.

- **The neck index.** This is my personal favorite when shooting in the dark. I simply hold the flashlight up around jaw level about couple of inches away my your face. I prefer it because the light will follow where my shoulders are pointing, and I can make small adjustments with my wrist. Also, very importantly, some light from my beam is reflected across my sights. This allows me to get a positive sight picture when engaging a target. It works with any flashlight, and the strong hand is free to shoot the gun normally with an aggressive posture. Also, the weak hand is free to turn the beam on and off if necessary.

Neck index

- **The cigar hold.** Ideal for small flashlights, this hold allows you to get some support hand contact to stabilize the gun. The sight picture looks somewhat equivalent to as if you were using an accessory rail mounted light. To do this one, just hold the flashlight between your middle and index fingers on your support hand. Try and maintain as much contact with your support hand and the gun as possible. Also, watch that you don't accidentally turn the flashlight off when you're firing if it has a rear mounted on/off switch. I like this one too, but it's a little cumbersome for my taste, especially when it comes to getting the light pointed exactly where I want it.

Cigar hold

- **The cup hold.** The cup is a substitute for the cigar hold where the flashlight is held between the index finger and thumb on the weak hand and the remaining three fingers grasp the strong hand. Recoil control is pretty good with this one and it's easier to form your grip. However, reloading with your hands like that might be tough.

- **The backhand hold.** This is the traditional flashlight hold that you'll see widely circulating. To do it, hold the flashlight in your weak hand and bend your wrist so that your hand is perpendicular to the ground. Then set your strong hand in the curve created so that the backs of your hands and wrists are firmly in contact. The origin of this technique was with the Weaver stance. I don't generally like this hold because I find that when I rest bone against bone, the gun will jump around in an unpredictable way. This is made worse because in order to get in this stance, I have to put my support shoulder way too far forward which causes me to shoot across my body. This hold seems to be the most awkward for me, and actually reduces my ability to control recoil.

Cup hold

Backhand hold

Other tips:

- When shooting one handed, make sure to get your strong side foot forward if possible.

- How you reload a handgun while holding a flashlight will depend on your technique for shooting with the flashlight and the size of the flashlight.

- For the neck index and backhand holds, I generally like to get my thumb, index finger and middle finger in contact with the new magazine while holding the flashlight in my last three fingers doing a reload.

- While using the cup hold or cigar hold, you might have to shift the flashlight around in your hand (perhaps wedge it between your index finger and middle finger) so you can grab the new magazine.

- Make sure to seat the new magazine firmly with the base of your hand once it's inserted.

- Beware of lanyards getting in the way of gun manipulation in the dark. They could get stuck in the magazine well. If you're going to use them ensure that they're secured.

DEFENSIVE SHOOTING

T he subject of "how to shoot defensively" is one of the most oft-discussed topics in all of shooting- from weapon and ammo selection to room clearing. There are countless opinions on this from countless authors. Some are of course vastly more plausible than others. A thorough comparison of all of the alternatives is beyond the scope of this book. However, there are some central principles which you should keep in mind when you're thinking about protecting yourself which I'll detail below. These should get you on the right track and give you some food for thought.

MINDSET

The first thing that I wanted to bring up is the mindset of shooting defensively. If you draw your firearm you are doing so with the intent to kill another human being. It's not something to be brushed off lightly or trivialized. It is a

Defensive shooting is a very serious topic that should not be taken lightly:

- *Check your ego and your "toughness" at the door*

- *Have a plan and train for different contingencies*

- *Extreme stress will cause your abilities to deteriorate*

decision that you'll have to live with for the rest of your life, both from a moral and very possibly a legal standpoint. Also, keep in mind that if you're drawing your firearm, it's very likely that there will be fire returned towards you as well.

Many firefights are going to be fast, brutal, and at close range. Most people simply train by shooting slowly for accuracy at a single target on a static range, usually at a long distance. Statistically speaking, this type of training will not adequately prepare you to deal with real world threats. According to the 2009 FBI Law Enforcement Officers Killed and Assaulted Report, from 2000-2009, approximately half of the police officers killed in the line of duty were killed at a distance of less than five feet. Over 80% were killed at a distance of under seven yards. Of these reported deaths, over 70% of the officers were killed with handguns.

The events of a firefight will also be massively unpredictable. At a short engagement distance, people are going to be running around all over the place point shooting at one another. Luck plays a large element in the outcome at close range. You might be the best trained person in the world, and nine times out of ten you would win that conflict, but today your adversary gets a lucky shot and hits you in the head or the femoral artery. Even a high school basketball player will beat Kobe Bryant in a free-throw contest every now and then. During a one-on-one high speed engagement your training will dramatically improve your odds but it won't guarantee victory.

If you're a member of the law enforcement community or military, then part of your job description requires you to be in dangerous situations and carry a weapon. However, if you're a civilian then you have many choices that you can make. These include where you go, how you behave, and even whether or not to actually draw your gun if confronted. If someone pulls a knife on you and demands your wallet, do you shoot him? You could be legally justified in doing so (which will have to be established after a very long interview with the police). Or you could decide to just give that person the $50 you have on you and go on about your life. Some might say that defending one's property is an essential right. Others may only choose to use a firearm if they believe that they or someone they love will be injured or killed.

If you're thinking about preparing for defensive shooting, my advice to you is to have a plan and train for a wide variety of situations. Decide beforehand what you would do should something go a certain way. Also, be realistic. Know the law and know your limits. Avoid being "macho" and allowing your pride to get in the way of your decision-making. Many people have lost 20 years in jail, but have successfully "defended their honor." Have a results based approach. What are the possible outcomes to your actions? Which ones are the most desirable? Carrying a firearm simply gives you another option that you can choose.

SHOOTING UNDER DURESS

One of the main misconceptions that I think many people have is that they expect to be able to perform as well in a life threatening encounter as they do on the practice range. Multiple things happen to the human body under extreme stress. Heartrate rises tremendously, adrenaline starts blasting, and you begin to experience what many refer to as "tunnel vision." (If you'd like more information on this, I suggest you read an excellent article out of the Police Policy Studies Council entitled "Vision and Shooting" by Edward C. Godnig) Focus will usually go directly on the threat, which is counter-intuitive to sighted shooting. Also, fine motor control will deteriorate, preventing you from dexterously manipulating that trigger or the controls on your gun.

Those targets that were static on the range are now moving everywhere and taking cover. You know that if you don't perform, you very well may die. What might have been a really small group in practice will now become a very large one. Under these circumstances this old soldier's adage applies: "You never rise to the occasion. You merely fall back on your training."

There's an old story circulated amongst firearms instructors, which everyone has heard but nobody can quite point to the exact incident. It involves a number of police officers found dead at the scene of a shooting with empty revolvers and a pocketful of brass. How did they get this way? The saying goes that because those cops were trained to store their brass in their pockets when reloading so as to not have to pick it up after practice. On the scene, they did exactly that under pressure, and the additional time required to stow the brass prevented them from getting the bullets in their guns fast enough.

The story has its origins in the annals of law enforcement training, most notably the California Highway Patrol's tragic Newhall Incident where four police officers lost their lives in a gunbattle. In the aftermath of the massacre, it has been widely concluded that poor training procedures may have significantly contributed to the deaths of the four officers. These procedures included practice on lower recoil rounds than those issued in the field, poor shotgun training, and a lack of issuance of speed loaders. Had these officers received better instruction and equipment, they might be alive today.

This is why if you're going to train to defend yourself, regardless of your profession, it's important to develop proper muscle memory and tested equipment. Go outside of your comfort zone and practice a variety of situations. Let's say you're sitting in your car and someone threatening comes up to your window. You might be the master of the quickdraw standing up, but now you're sitting on the gun or you can't find it in your glovebox because there are too many keys rattling around in there. Even if you only try something once, it's better having done it before should you need to call on that skill or repetition to save your life.

Another thing that you should keep in mind is not to run standards all the time in your drills. In USPSA/IDPA for example, we almost always shoot two shots on every paper target. While two shots is usually a good idea, let's say that your adversary is wearing body armor or is high on drugs and he doesn't go down. If you're so used to just putting two rounds on paper, then perhaps this is what you'll do in real life as well. The same goes with scanning for threats after shooting your targets. Even though it may seem silly to those doing a course of fire to scan for threats when they know there aren't any, it's still good practice to get into if training for a defensive environment.

You should know exactly what you're capable of doing. If you're wearing a jacket that you've worn and shot with many times before, then you'll know about how long it takes you to draw a gun and hit a target at a certain range. If there are two threats standing seven yards from you, how long is it going to take you to engage both of them? What order are you going to engage both of those targets? Two shots on the left, then two shots on the right? One shot, then two shots, then one shot? Head shots or body shots? All of these should already be drilled into your memory so that not only can you plan realistically, but you can carry out your plan as efficiently as possible.

POINTERS FOR DEFENSE

I'm assuming with these pointers that you're the only person "on your side" with a gun. (The theory/application of team based tactics could be the subject of another entire book!) If you're a civilian, don't go looking for a fight if you don't have to. Most home defense situations can be defused by simply getting behind a large piece of cover, leveling your gun at the door, and calling the police. When you're in that position, you have a huge advantage against anyone who enters that room. However, there's no panacea for defensive shooting. Sometimes you end up in harm's way and it's up to you to survive.

SLICING THE PIE

Cover is a very important element. The less you expose yourself to your adversary the better. The idea of slicing the pie comes from your field of view as you're moving around an object. You're going to want to lean your torso out (as covered in the **Barricade Shooting** section) so that only your gun and your head are visible from around the object you're shooting behind. Don't just run into a room. Take your time and evaluate your surroundings.

1. Give yourself some space from the wall or door if possible. This will allow you full extension of your arms, and the ability to rapidly move back behind cover if necessary. You don't want to get bunched up. This will also prevent your gun from coming around a corner laterally before you do. Take a wide arc approach.

When behind proper cover, you're minimally exposed

Giving yourself room behind a barricade improves mobility

2. Load up your outside foot (the one closest to the opening) and side step around the barricade. Pick up your inside foot, put it next to your outside foot, then take another small step with your outside foot- leaning with your torso the whole time. If you try to pick up your weighted foot, then your muzzle will drop and you might stumble.

3. If you're coming around a tight corner and you can't get any space from the barricade, then bring your gun into a low ready position. Keeping the gun close to you will allow you to contend with any adversaries who could come right up in front of you.

4. If it's really quiet wherever you are, people will be able to hear you coming- even while slicing the pie slowly. Determine your rate of speed based on the situation.

CONCEALMENT IS NOT COVER

Unlike movies or video games where a potted plant or a signpost provides all the cover in the world, bullets often will penetrate materials. Just because they can't see you doesn't mean they can't hit you. Depending on the strength of the object (a sturdy wooden dresser vs. a plastic chair) the bullet will stop, fragment, deflect, or penetrate. Usually it's going to be some combination of them. Although the walls in your house may be a few inches thick, you have to keep in mind that most of that thickness comes from drywall, plywood, and insulation. None of those materials is particularly good at stopping bullets. Just because you're hiding behind something doesn't mean that you're going to be safe there. If I'm a person about to go to jail for his third strike and I hear a police officer approaching from a certain direction, I might just dump a magazine into the wall he's hiding behind and hope to get lucky. Pick your cover wisely.

BLIND STAGE PRACTICE

One of the main problems with any type of shooting training is the fact that you know where all the targets are. Even if you're doing target ID drills, chances are you've done a version of it before. To mix up your training, I recommend that you try blind stage drills. Setup a few barricades, or some sort of a vision barrier based structure, then send a member of your group downrange to find and engage targets with no clue as to the layout of the course of fire. Obviously you can't do this one on your own, but it's definitely a good thing to try out.

AIRSOFT

The best form of practice for shooting defensively is to actually shoot defensively against an opponent. Airsoft gives you a great tool to do just that. The guns are realistic in weight and size, and can duplicate any sights that you currently have on your pistol while fitting in your holster. Although they're not as accurate and are much easier to shoot than their real world counterparts given that they have zero recoil, at least with airsoft you'll get used to shooting a moving target. For close range engagements, airsoft will allow you and your training partners to get acclimated to the skills of movement, suppression, and quick reflexes that are needed in the real world. I know quite a few law enforcement instructors who swear by them.

If you want to practice some force on force training, ensure that you do so with a smaller private group of people that are organized and familiar with tactics. If you end up at a public airsoft field, you'll find that a lot of people don't follow any sort of organization and it's everyone for him/herself. In this case don't expect to learn that much from getting shot- although you will quickly figure out how to keep your head down!

Point of note: Use black BBs with an airsoft gun that has a realistic magazine capacity so that you don't point shoot and hose.

Another point of note: Airsoft pellets will bounce off everything and therefore cannot distinguish cover from concealment.

COMPETITION SHOOTING

There are a variety of disciplines which fall under the umbrella of "competition shooting" including high precision accuracy, standards courses of fire which involve lots of speed, and practical pistol matches. Like auto racing, the equipment ranges from out-of-the-box to tuned to the razors edge. Some of these are represented by worldwide sanctioning bodies while others are simply the fun local matches that involve seeing who can chop a 2x4 in half the fastest with a 1911. Regardless of the type of competition, each one involves a combination of pressure, fun, and community. To excel in these you'll need to spend lots of time developing the skills and the mentality required of you. Ultimately what you get out of the sport will be proportionate to what you put in.

Shooting matches can be of tremendous value to any firearms owner:

- *Expose yourself to match pressure*

- *Vary your training*

- *Learn valuable marksmanship skills*

COMPETITION SKILLS TO REAL-WORLD ENVIRONMENTS

When people think of competitive shooting versus the real world, they are likely to compare something like 10 meter Olympic Air Rifle to being a Marine in combat, where there are few overlapping parallels with the exception of trigger control. Much of the skepticism from the defensive world about competition handgunning assumes both the techniques learned and the equipment used in competition is too specialized and far removed from what you would see on the streets. This is a misrepresentation. Practical pistol courses of fire are designed to test diverse skills sets including rapid fire, shooting on the move, and engaging multiple targets very quickly. Every course is different, and there are thousands of variations. To succeed, you have to be good at everything with your gun from extreme speed to extreme accuracy under pressure.

In many divisions of USPSA/IDPA (I compete in Production and Stock Service Pistol respectively) you will find the same guns with that are used by tactical units with few modifications save an individual shooter customizing it to his/her preferences. While practical pistol is entirely a sport, a great deal of the abilities learned from this type of environment can easily translate to a defensive scenario. Some courses of fire are even identical to those found in defensive/offensive training schools. This concept is evident in the numerous USPSA champions, including those from the venerable Army Marksmanship Unit, who regularly instruct for both police and military organizations.

Competition shooting builds on your ability to hit targets on demand- which is a skill that I don't think anyone can argue is a bad thing. Techniques such as the "thumbs forward grip" and other techniques that were developed exclusively by competition shooters have since found their way into the instructional programs of a substantial percentage of elite tactical teams. Competition is a marksmanship proving ground. It has very few variables, unlike combat. If you don't have the right fundamentals, you won't be able to shoot as fast, and therefore you'll lose more often than not. You can't win consistently by getting lucky all the time. In this environment it's very apparent what works and what doesn't.

Of course you'll find many more rules in competition than in the real world. These are necessary to ensure a safe and level playing field. In auto racing it's about who the fastest is but you don't want people pushing other drivers into the wall. In MMA, it's about who can get a knockout or submission the quickest, but certain strikes that could kill or maim an opponent are not allowed. However while the rules of shooting don't allow a perfect simulation of a defensive scenario, to survive a gunfight you need both marksmanship and tactics. Competition is clearly the best environment to train the former. If you're a great tactical guy but a really lousy shot, then you won't get very far. If you're a great marksman that just runs into the open while everyone else takes cover then your marksmanship probably won't save you.

I encourage anyone interested in shooting defensively to try out USPSA or another shooting sport. Lots of people will say "I'm interested in winning a fight not a trophy." I think the argument that shooting the occasional match will somehow override your tactical knowledge is without merit. Competition shooting will expose you to stress and pressure, and will help you vary your training. One major goal you should have is to be adaptable. There are a nearly infinite number of possibilities for what might happen in a gunfight. You should be comfortable with shooting in all sorts of ways. Seek out challenges and overcome them; it will make you a better and more confident shooter.

Point of note: I encourage all competition shooters to take defensive tactics classes as well. As discussed in the Defense section, competition shooters should not become so ingrained in the sport so as to ignore real world factors (such as that two shots aren't always enough). But a person from either the defensive or competition side saying "I just don't like what those guys are doing, so I won't ever try it" simply inhibits their development potential.

GAMERS

Some people may question the internal logic behind the shooting sports when it comes to all of the specific rules of the game. IDPA (more info on this later) for example, is incredibly detailed in each scenario about precisely how each target can be engaged, with little room for interpretation. I've heard a couple of my buddies with some bona-fide tactical backgrounds that have asked me "Why do I have to do such and such? I would never do that in the real world!" The answer is simple: gamers.

The shooting sports, regardless of the intentions that they were developed for, are still competitions. And in competitions, people want to win. How do you determine who the "best" shooter with a handgun is? Some people might declare that it's the person who is the most accurate. Those guys will take up a bullseye sport where he/she with the smallest group is victorious. However, then people will start modifying their gear to squeeze the highest degree of accuracy out as possible. Rules will then have to be created to constrain what can/can't be done. Other groups might say that if you actually get into a gunfight, you'll have to shoot quickly with a limited sight picture on a humanoid target. So then a sport like IPSC/IDPA is built. Yet one guy might use cover as if he/she is really shooting at a target while another will just jump out from behind it in order to get a faster time.

There will always be gamers. I know because I'm one of them. If you leave me any ambiguity in your course or sport design, I'll seek it out for an additional advantage. The rules exist to minimize those opportunities and keep the focus on shooting ability. The unfortunate side effect of this is that even the basic concepts behind the origin of the sport will have to be defined and categorized in a rulebook. This could lead to some sacrifices in the game's original purpose.

SHOOTING UNDER PRESSURE

In many self defense and law enforcement training programs there is an emphasis on lots of physical exertion prior to shooting. Cadets will be forced to run through an obstacle course or something of that effect to tire them out prior to picking up a gun for a test. This is supposed to duplicate the feeling of "shooting under pressure." I find that all of those efforts are completely misguided. While being able to function at a high level while fatigued is certainly something to strive for, physical stress through exertion is nothing in comparison to what the intense influence of the sympathetic nervous system can do when you're in a stressful situation.

One cliché line about public speaking is that some people would rather be in the casket than giving the eulogy at a funeral. Plenty are terrified at the prospect of having to deliver an address in front of their peers. Why is this? Fear of failure? Fear of being judged? There are a multitude of reasons. The same thing goes with shooting. I've seen some very big and tough guys have their hands start to shake a bit when I put the clock on them in front of a large group.

Being able to perform when you're on center stage where your actions count and all attention is on you takes mental focus and fortitude. Confidence plays a significant role. A major component of shooting competitively which applies to all facets of life is the ability to manage your stress level and perform at 100% efficiency on command. I've been in major matches where I knew that in order to do well I would have to shoot my very best on every single stage. For example, a stage would have to be run in 19 seconds flat- 20 or more would be utter failure. How can you deal with pressure and still be successful?

Lots of stress management comes from experience. Before I ever started shooting competitively I had to do a lot of public speaking at my job. One particular memory I have was when I first got involved with a new company and didn't know the space (corporate social media applications) or the technology. We were scheduled to be as part of a trade show panel in London, and due to a large client issue, two of the guys that were supposed to be there couldn't make it. So I had to go with no agenda, no preparation, virtually no familiarity with the business, and a week's notice. Also, there weren't going to be any written speeches; it was all impromptu and I was supposed to be the "expert" from my company. I ordered some books on the subject and crammed as much as possible on the 14 hour plane ride over. After about 6 hours of terrible jetlagged sleep, I got over to the conference hall and discovered that the panel was only four people deep and was in front of a crowd of 300 executives. To boot I was one of the only Americans there.

I'll admit that I was nervous! However, I just settled down and said to myself "It's go time." I cheered myself on, and even chuckled a little at the sheer ridiculousness of the situation. Because I remained positive, I was able to go onstage and use some hastily written notecards to deliver a 15 minute monologue as well as deal with the Q&A session. I accepted the situation for what it was, and did so with the confidence that I knew I could do it. Your mental mindset goes a long way, and the more stress that you're exposed to through your sympathetic nervous system, the easier it is to manage.

How do you improve at shooting under pressure?

- Remember that in the competitive world, everyone else has been where you are today. Also as with many other pressure situations, you just have to say "the heck with it" and go for it. Everybody fails at one point or another- it's nothing to be ashamed of. It's how you get back up that counts. Tell yourself that you can do this!

- You might want to try a pre-game/pre-stage process. Don't make it too elaborate or be too compulsive about it. (If you do that and something gets out of order then you'll be too focused on missing it and might screw up.) I like to practice visualization of the stage in advance so that I know where everything is and I can just hammer it out. I always try to grip my gun to get a good feel for it just prior to shooting a stage and then put my hands in the same position. When the range officer is reading the commands prior to the buzzer going off, I remember to breathe.

- Be sure to get a good night's sleep in advance of the match and show up on time the next morning. If I'm travelling, I like to arrive at the hotel early so I can get into my normal routine. (I hate rushing to get to bed for an early match because then I can never sleep!)

- Pack your equipment the night before and do a gear check. Make sure you have enough ammunition and you know where everything is. Your focus should be on the competition the next day.

- Take time to calm yourself down and maintain a positive outlook. Be deliberate and mentally prepared.

- Shoot a lot of matches!

COMPETITIVENESS AND BEING HARD ON YOURSELF

I train very hard when I'm prepping for a match. I'll go to the range and shoot hundreds of rounds as often as my schedule will allow. I'll train in the middle of the night with just my car's headlights while shooting at white steel. I'll train in the rain standing under my hatchback. I put a lot of myself on the line to go shoot a big match. If I fail, it will be because of me and I know it.

Sometimes things go badly in matches. Nobody is harder on myself than me when they do. However, it's not the losing which gets me. There are people who have put in longer and harder hours on the range, and who deserve to win because of it. I have lots of respect for them because I know what it takes to get as far as I have. What I find that digs into me is the idea that I didn't perform up to the level that I thought I should. (Occasionally my equipment will have issues which will induce a similar angry response.) I've been known to wear my frustration on my sleeve so to speak. It almost feels like sometimes my performance in the match is beyond my control.

One thing that I've learned is that this is all natural. Each person has a theoretical performance spectrum. They have their averages, their highs, and their lows. However, depending on how often people practice, the standard deviations off their mean will tighten. Let me give you an example with the most frustrating sport ever: golf. I'm a decent golfer because I've known the game since I was young, but I rarely play and never practice. Now if I just sucked at the game, then I could probably live with that. However, I've shot some pretty good scores out there, sometimes in the low/mid-80s. Unfortunately, those good scores are also intermittently peppered with 95s and even 100s! Needless to say if I've just shot a few strokes over par on the front nine, then throw it all away on the back nine with a handful of quadruple bogeys, a club or two might be in need of repair by the end of the round!

So how can I explain my aggravation? Have my skills just disappeared, never to return? Instead what I've come to realize is that I always will remember that really good performance, and will be disappointed whenever I don't reach my theoretical potential. But I forget about all those times I wasn't even close. Let's create an imaginary bell curve of my last 30 golf scores. We'll say that I shoot a 90 on average. Because I don't practice, I'm inconsistent. The more I practice, the more consistent I'll get and the standard deviations will narrow while my average scores will improve. When you look at your performance and you're getting down on yourself for screwing up, just ask yourself "how realistic were my expectations?" Keep in mind that you might not be able to do as well in a match as you did in practice because there is actually something at stake now.

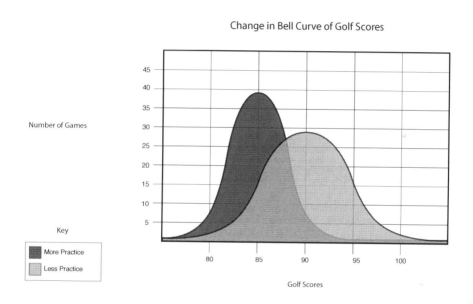

Change in Bell Curve of Golf Scores

There's nothing wrong with being driven. Getting angry at yourself for failing is a good thing. It will force you to go back to the drawing board and practice even more so that you will succeed the next time. I know that every time I lose, I critically analyze why it happened and try to figure out a plan to give me a better chance the next time.

One thing that I did want to point out though is that most games, but especially shooting, are social. Even at the highest levels of competition, your reputation needs the same attention as your performance. Nobody is going to remember that time you completely missed an array of targets or when your pistol had a light primer strike, but they'll certainly remember you blowing up and going ballistic about it.

I come from a baseball background where if you struck out during an important at-bat then it was more or less acceptable to start cursing or maybe throw something in the dugout. It showed your team that you cared and were going to work on improving. If you just shrugged and sat down then people would think that the fact that you cost the team didn't matter to you. However, when I recently had something bad happen to me on a stage due to a prop issue, I got really mad. It could very well have cost me the match. After spouting off for a minute, I noticed that everyone was either staring or deliberately trying to avoid eye contact with me. I had put a lot of pressure on myself for that match, and when I had a problem it all came out. I had to eat some crow and apologize to everyone for the scene I caused and for making everyone uncomfortable.

How you react to problems affects everything, including your performance. If you are so agitated after messing up on a previous stage then it could cause you to blow a few more later on. A single screw up generally isn't going to be that expensive, but a string could seriously hurt you in the standings.

I would love to give you a piece of advice which explains how you can calm yourself down after messing up in any sport, but it's not that easy. Depending on how competitive you are that surge of anger is hard to deal with. I'm not going to tell you to take up meditation or anything. I can say though that when you're out there on an important stage and you hear the range officer call out "Alpha, Mike, Alpha Mike, No-Shoot," and the pit of your stomach starts to turn, just think of the larger picture. In fact have someone videotape your reaction. Then watch that tape later with your friends and family, and let everyone see how you behaved. It'll clear you up in no time.

PRACTICAL PISTOL COMPETITION WORLD

If you're thinking about entering competition for the first time, just take things easy to start with. Get some cheapo equipment and let everyone else guide you. Don't try to outfit yourself with everything before you even are sure if you like the sport. You'll eventually find what you prefer and will develop your own style. Don't obsess over how "competitive" your equipment will make you. A skilled shooter can beat lots of people with stuff straight from the factory. Tuned gear will only give you a little bit of an extra edge. I've even seen Revolver shooters post up better scores than some Open division guys!

USPSA/IPSC

USPSA (United States Practical Shooting Association) is the American version of IPSC (International Practical Shooting Confederation- founded in 1976). The rules are identical in a lot of respects with a few peculiarities. This is the quintessential "practical pistol" sport. Competitors shoot with a variety of equipment from out of the box firearms to heavily modified race guns. We usually start with our guns in our holsters, then draw and engage multiple targets across a variety of positions while shooting and reloading on the move. The course of fire can include anything from a box to a sophisticated obstacle course. All courses of fire except classifiers are unique and are usually never seen again once shot. They are designed to be figured out by the competitor, and there are usually no guidelines on how to shoot a stage beyond the start position. Competitors must determine the best way to shoot the stage as quickly as possible. The IPSC motto is DVC- Diligentia, Vis, Celeritas which stands for Accuracy, Power, Speed.

The basics of scoring are the best two hits on each paper target, while each steel target (plate, pepper popper) must fall to score. All shooting is timed using audible timers that record each shot fired. Your last shot is your time. Each hit on the target is worth a certain number of points based on the accuracy. You can receive a maximum of 5 points per hit (paper targets take two hits and are therefore worth a possible 10 points), and a minimum of 1. Misses/No shoots are a 10 point penalty. At the end of the stage your score equals your number of points divided by the amount of time it took you to complete the course. 100 points in a 20 second stage would equal a score (hit factor) of 5.

Competitors are ranked according to their performance on classifier courses of fire or based on their results at a large match. There are over 80 classifiers currently available. The top hit factor for a classifier becomes the 100%, and all the others are scored as a percentage of that. For example, if the top hit factor on a stage was 5, and you scored a 4, then you would receive an 80%. Based on an average of the top 6 of your most recent 8 classifiers you will receive a rank. (You can't go down in rank once you have it.) The classifier percentages are as follows:

Grandmaster: 95% -100%

Master: 85%- 94.99%

A Class: 75%- 84.99%

B Class: 60%- 74.99%

C Class: 40%- 59.99%

D Class: Below 40%

Divisions are based on the modifications allowed to the gun. Ammunition is subject to a power factor test (bullet weight in grains x bullet velocity / 1000.) So a 180 grain bullet going 1000fps would be a 180 power factor. Major power factor is 165 and above (varies for IPSC). Minor is above 125. The theory of the scoring is that a lighter recoiling load (usually a 9mm) is easier to shoot, and therefore you should be more accurate.

Hits on the USPSA paper target that are from a major power factor bullet are scored:

Alpha: 5pts, Bravo/Charlie: 4pts, Delta: 2pts.

Hits on the USPSA paper target that are from a minor power factor bullet are scored:

Alpha: 5pts, Bravo/Charlie: 3pts, Delta: 1pts.

In USPSA, you'll need a belt (preferably a combination inner/outer belt like the kind made by CR Speed), a holster, magazine pouches, and cleats. The variations of these will change depending on division.

USPSA Production Division

Production division is by far the easiest division to get involved with as a new shooter. You can compete with a semi-automatic pistol with about 5 or 6 magazines, a basic holster and a couple of dual mag pouches. If you have these along with a sturdy belt, come on out! Specialty equipment doesn't mean a great deal in Production division, and will only save you a little bit of time here and there. Also holsters suitable for everyday wear (non race) are required, while magazine pouches must be behind your hip. You can literally take your street gun and be competitive in Production. Some of the top shooters do very little to their handguns to change them from factory condition.

A good sturdy inner/outer competition rig

Production division was created in order to prevent an "equipment race." This division is heavily restrictive in terms of how much you can modify your handgun. USPSA allows no external modifications to the gun except sights and grip tape, but you can do a trigger job provided that it doesn't disable any safeties. You can also use replacement parts that are about equivalent with factory specs.

USPSA requires the use of a maximum of 10 rounds in the magazine. This rule was created to appeal to shooters in states more restricted by firearms law. Since the division was created with the 9mm cartridge in mind, there is no major power factor. Everything is scored minor so there's no advantage in shooting hot bullets.

The most popular gun in the US for Production division is the Glock 34 without question. However, other guns that you'll find shot by champions are Smith and Wesson M&Ps, along with CZ SP01s. You will also find Sigs and Berettas sporadically around (Ben Stoeger has won a lot of matches with his Beretta Elite II). Popular holsters include various Safariland models, and the Bladetech DOH (Drop Offset Holster). Popular magazine pouches include the CR Speed single universal mag holders. However, if you're getting started, you can buy some plastic gear for about $60 total from Uncle Mike's or just use your carry rig.

Production division is very technical due to the magazine capacity limit and the power factor. In order to succeed, you need to be a very accurate shooter, and need to be able to read a stage so that you can plan your reloads.

Differences with IPSC:

- IPSC allows a maximum of 15 rounds in the magazine.

- IPSC allows no changes to the gun from factory settings except sights and grip tape at all- the trigger must be stock, not even polished.

USPSA Single Stack Division

Single stack division shares some similarities with Production in that the guns and magazine capacities are restricted and that it's a good entry class. To shoot this division, you have to use a 1911 which is based around the original design of the gun by John Browning. As such if you have one of these guns, then you can simply jump into competition with few barriers preventing you from getting started. Holsters also must be suitable for everyday use. If you have a 1911, try it out and see how well you do. As mentioned earlier, a top shooter with an out of the box Kimber will still win many regional matches.

1911s in 9mm, .40 S&W, and .45 ACP are all used in this division, with the most popular being the latter two calibers. If you're shooting minor (such as a 9mm or light loaded .40) then you can have 10 rounds in the magazine. If you're shooting major then you only get eight rounds. Almost everyone shoots major.

Modifications are somewhat regulated in Single Stack, but are mostly pertaining to the design, size, and weight of the gun. Usually you'll see at least see trigger work and aftermarket sights. However, unlike Production, at the higher end, you'll see completely custom built guns which are built to conform to a certain weight and include a wide swath of aftermarket parts (match barrels, competition hammers, ergonomic safeties, extended magazine releases/magazine basepads/magazine wells) and other accessories. Most of these guns are built off a frame by a specialty gunsmith.

USPSA Limited Division

This division is by far the most popular in USPSA. It attracts the most shooters due to the fast paced nature of the game along with iron sighted guns. Essentially the rules are that you need to buy a gun and magazines that are each under a certain length. Other than that you can do anything you want to it except adding a compensator or an optic (iron sights only). Holsters and magazine pouches can be of any type and mounted anywhere.

Most shooters use the 2011 double stack which incorporates large capacity magazines, usually in .40 S&W. However, the Glock 35 has been quite successful in skilled hands. Magazine capacity usually is in the 19-22 round range to reduce the number of reloads on a stage. Pretty much everyone shoots major ammunition. As opposed to production, speed is emphasized here more than accuracy.

A division exists called Limited 10 as well. This allows all of the modifications of Limited but with 10 round magazines. It was created in the US due to the Assault Weapons Ban.

IPSC:

Standard division is pretty close to Limited- except the entire gun with the magazine inserted must fit into a box and the Major power factor is 170 with a .40 caliber or larger bullet.

USPSA Open Division

The race gun division. Competitors only use specially designed guns which were built off the frame. This is the hardest division to enter from a cost standpoint. Essentially anything that you can possibly do to a gun is allowed here, provided that it fits in a certain size box. Most are built off a 2011 frame as well. C-More red dot optics are the standard, along with aggressive looking compensators which keep the gun steady under recoil. Thumb rests are used to control recoil even more. Big stick magazines in 9mm or .38 major (cases literally packed to the brim with powder) drive these guns.

Speed is paramount in Open. Competitors in this division will have some ridiculously fast times through a stage and will rarely stop moving.

IPSC:

Open division here is pretty much the same but a 9mm bullet must be used at a minimum. There is also a Modified division where the gun is unrestricted but must fit within a box and be over .40 caliber to make major.

USPSA Revolver Division

Revolver division is also very open when it comes to modifications. Essentially the rules are that the gun has to be a revolver, and it can't have optics or a compensator on it. You can use any other equipment you like, but the gun is limited to a six round capacity. The Smith and Wesson 625 is a dominating force in this division with major power factor ammunition.

IPSC:

Standard Revolver has slightly more specific rules, but uses more or less the same guns.

IDPA

The International Defensive Pistol Association was created in 1996 by a number of people including some of the founders of IPSC. Their belief was that IPSC was becoming too heavily dependent on equipment modifications and too far away from "real world" scenarios that you might encounter while carrying a gun on the street. While both sports are run on a clock, always have unique stages, and involve shooting two shots on paper and knocking down steel targets, IDPA's rules have many more requirements about where you can move and what you can do. Some rule examples:

- A concealment garment must be worn which covers your pistol and your magazines.

- Kneepads and cleats are not allowed.

- Holsters and magazine pouches must be suitable for concealed carry.

- Unless specified otherwise, all shots must be taken from behind cover where only 50% of your body can be exposed to targets.

- You can only carry two spare magazines on you, and all magazines are limited to either an 8 or 10 round maximum.

- Reloads must be performed from behind cover.

- Unless the slide locks back on an empty chamber, if you reload, you must retain the magazine.

- Targets must be engaged in tactical priority- such as near to far if viewed through a window, or by order of appearance if slicing the pie around a corner. If two targets are at the same distance and are exposed to you at the same time, one shot must be taken on each target before you can engage them with a second round. (A three target array would be one in the left, one in the center, two on the right, one in the center, one in the left.)

- All stages must have some kind of a basis in the real world as well as an accompanying stage description to match.

IDPA is also much more accuracy based than IPSC and involves a time based scoring system. Your time to complete each stage is added to by the accuracy of your shots. The IDPA target has a 0 seconds down "A zone", a 0.5 seconds down "C zone" and a 1.5 seconds down "D zone" and 5 seconds down for a miss.

The IDPA classifications are based on your performance in a single classifier course of fire. There are certain performance standards set by the organization to rank you as a Master, Expert, Sharpshooter, Marksman, or Novice.

IDPA also explicitly does not allow prizes by order of finish- just by random draw if at all. It's officially trophy only. (USPSA/IPSC matches always have a prize table.)

Stock Service Pistol

This is one of the most popular divisions, and essentially has USPSA Production rules. However for Glock shooters using aftermarket recoil springs/guide rods, you'll have to use a plastic guide rod to compete. (Vanek makes one.) The holster must be at belt level as well.

Enhanced Service Pistol

ESP is comparable to Limited 10, but there are a few more modification restrictions including those on barrels and dust covers, plus a requirement to fit in a smaller box. 1911/2011 pistols are popular in this division, but pretty much any SSP gun with a few more modifications will do. One of the restrictions is that no slide lightening can be performed. Guns also are only required to make minor power factor, so 9mms are common. No safeties can be disabled.

Custom Defense Pistol

Pretty close to Limited 10 also, but requires the use of 165 power factor ammunition and a .45 caliber bullet. You can only carry magazines with eight rounds loaded in them. No safeties can be disabled.

Stock Service Revolver/Enhanced Service Revolver

Very similar to USPSA revolver, except that the barrel length must be under 4.2". Stock service revolvers must be reloaded using a speed loader with rimmed ammunition and must be a maximum of 42 oz unloaded. Enhanced service revolvers can use moon clips to reload and can be 50 oz unloaded.

SCSA

The Steel Challenge Shooting Association is an organization that usually involves shooting an array of five steel plates (rarely it's six) as fast as humanly possible. There are 12 possible courses of fire, all of which are completely standardized. In the world championships, you'll typically find the eight most popular shot every year. 10 out of the 12 stages are shot from a single box. The two exceptions are shot from two boxes. There's no shooting on the move involved whatsoever, but on one stage (Outer Limits) you must run from one box to another on the clock. The starting position is always wrists above respective shoulders. Scoring is based on how quickly you can hit all of the steel plates, then the stop plate for the best four out of five runs (3 out of 4 for Outer Limits). Your time is your score.

This type of competition is similar to many other shooting sports in that you're doing the same thing every time. It's based on muscle memory and constant repetition. Some incredible times have been recorded by the top shooters that push the limits of human ability. There's a lot of pressure involved as well because just a couple of bad runs can destroy your match.

Equipment divisions include both IDPA and USPSA categories. There is no power factor.

NRA SHOOTING SPORTS

The National Rifle Association offers a wide variety of handgun shooting sports. These include Police Pistol Combat, Bullseye, Silhouette, Air Pistol and their version of Action Pistol. NRA matches are typically single position events with little movement (where the shooter may kneel, go prone, or shoot around a narrow barricade but not leave his/her shooting spot on the ground) with a high amount of emphasis on accuracy.

Courses of fire within these various disciplines are usually standardized according to the rule book. While most employ a static target, some such as the famous Bianchi Cup (National Championship Action Pistol Match) require moving targets across a rail. Equipment for NRA events varies drastically based on the particular sport. PPC for example actively discourages modifications to the handgun while Silhouette might have a high powered scope mounted on the pistol! Start positions also differ drastically. Bullseye begins strings of fire with the gun held one handed, pointed at a 45 degree angle towards the ground while others start in a holster.

As with other standards based sports, such as the aforementioned Steel Challenge, there have been some absolutely incredible scores posted by NRA shooters who specialize in a particular discipline. These matches are quite popular with Bullseye for example having over 40,000 classified shooters and the National matches at Camp Perry attracting hundreds upon hundreds of competitors every year.

IMPROVING YOUR TIMES

Lots of shooters on the competition circuit will eventually experience a plateau. They will hit a wall where they will not improve. Some people simply enjoy being out on the range and shooting off a few rounds. While it's fun to compete, they don't take it that seriously. This is perfectly fine- the sport is all about what you personally get out of it. However, others are quite driven and get frustrated when they do not see themselves climb in the standings. Here are some tips for improving your times on the range:

- Establish a set practice schedule and work on your weaknesses! You can't get any better by just going out and blasting away occasionally. You need to focus your training. At the beginning a little practice goes a long way and you'll get better really quickly. However, at the higher levels, it takes a lot more time to even see gradual gains. There's more on this in the next section.

- Work on your movement skills. Getting to point A from point B quickly will save you a lot of time. You should be sprinting when you can and getting in and out of position as fast as possible. Anyone can just stand there and shoot. Figure out how to incorporate as much movement as possible including shooting while you're moving into and out of positions. This includes setting your feet properly at the start position.

- With respect to the above, sometimes it's better to shoot from a stable position quickly and leave than try to hit targets while moving slowly. My general rule of thumb is that if there are a bunch of wide open targets up close and a lot of ground to cover, then I'll hit them on the move. If those shots are tougher and there's not a lot of ground to be gained, then I'll probably stand and shoot. You don't want to shoot half as fast while walking at 1mph towards the next array.

- Don't shuffle your feet. If you can take one big slide-step, then do it. Work on keeping your center of gravity low, and eliminating excess motion, particularly on your transitions.

- Smooth is fast. This is an old racecar analogy. Often people will allow their bodies to get ahead of their minds. They'll already be up on an array and will have shot it before they knew what happened. Their accuracy would have probably been highly questionable as well. Don't rush movements- they can be fast and deliberate at the same time. Try setting up a practice stage then shooting it as blazingly fast as possible, then do a run where you can call about 90% of your hits. Run the scores and see which one is better.

- Be consistent. Running one blazing stage is not indicative of your ability. It's what you can repeat that counts.

- Improve your stage approach. Chances are that you're shooting a stage with an inefficient plan. In USPSA Production, think about how you can minimize your number of reloads while doing them all on the move. Also, think about picking static positions that you can shoot a lot of targets from. (The most amount of targets from the least amount of positions.) There are risks associated with certain stage plans including missing targets and/or going to slide lock. You should know your capabilities and not be afraid of pushing the envelope. If you have to use an activator or shoot a swinger, how many targets can you hit before the swinger activates?

- Take your time getting prepared for the match. Have your equipment ready in advance (including your sights dialed in) and give yourself lots of leeway to look at the stages the day or morning before. Rushing never works out for you.

- -For USPSA, figure out the likely hit factor for the stage. It will help you determine your pace. If it's a 10 hit factor stage, that means one second is worth 10 points. If you're shooting Production for example, then shooting a Delta costs you 4 points. This is the equivalent of 4/10 or 2/5 of a second in time. In other words if you think it will save you that time to just blast away and get risk a delta then do it. Otherwise aim more.

STAGE BREAKDOWN- ACTIVATOR EXAMPLE

For example, let's say that you have to shoot an array from the draw with (from the left) two full targets, a steel popper activator that activates a clamshell with a no-shoot and a swinger all at about 10 yards. The clamshell target is fully exposed for a second before the no-shoot comes over it. How would you shoot it?

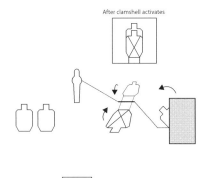

After clamshell activates

Shooting Box

1. In the IPSC game, timing is crucial. Usually you don't want to shoot a piece of steel then wait for the target to activate. It's too time-consuming.

2. I'll probably shoot the steel first, then look for something else to shoot while the swinger comes out. The two open targets on the left might be a possibility if the steel falls slowly.

3. If the steel falls fast and the swinger comes out really fast then if I shoot the clamshell first, I might miss the swinger on its first pass. Unless I time the swing really well, then I might end up standing there waiting on it to come back from behind the barricade on pass #2. However, if I shoot the swinger first then now I'll have a difficult shot on the head of the clamshell which will take some time.

4. If that swinger comes out slowly, then I'll probably try to hose the clamshell first before engaging it.

In this situation, it's better to be able to predict the position of the target that could cost you the most time with the highest degree of certainty. However, there are no hard and fast rules for stage breakdown since each one is unique. You'll pick up this skill mostly by watching better shooters. When you're first starting out, think about dividing the stage into shooting positions. Run from position to position to shoot. As you get better, add movement. So now you're entering and exiting those same positions while shooting. Next, add in more movement for the easy shots so that you don't have to pause your feet to hit them. And so on.

STAGE VISUALIZATION

It's important that you visualize every single shot and every single position that you take in competitive shooting. As I'm walking through a stage, I track every single step and motion that I will make when I'm on the clock. I remember the exact positions of the targets, the degrees of the transitions, and how fast I intend to shoot everything. As I'm waiting in line for my turn on the stage, I walk through the entire stage in my head and picture myself shooting each of the targets. Then just before that buzzer goes off, as I'm making myself ready, I'll do it one last time. There is 100% certainty of exactly how I'm going to do everything, no less.

I don't view visualization in the meditative sense as do other shooters. There's nothing spiritual at all about it. I'm just driving the course of fire into my short term memory- kind of like last minute cramming for an exam. When you're under the clock, your mind is working at maximum capacity. Your shooting and your stage plan become subconscious. You don't want to have to think about where to go and what to do next. If you can't close your eyes and know exactly where everything is then you need to take another look. I'll shoot the entire stage in my head about 20 times before doing it for real.

Try to find points of reference on the course of fire and simplify your instructions to yourself. Don't think in terms of "it's 7 yards to the next shooting position." Instead, for example, if during your walkthough you notice that if your left foot is on a certain notch in the fault line then you know that you're properly lined up to hit an entire array without moving your feet. In this case as you're running you're thinking "left foot on fault line notch." Or, if there's nothing on the ground, when you're running to a position you can be thinking "as soon as that target appears around the barricade on the left, stop, engage it, then pivot to engage the two others on the right."

I also like to think in terms of audio cues. A stage plan in my mind will sound something like this:

Draw to targets on left. BAM BAM, BAM BAM. Wide pivot to target on right with no-shoot. BAM.....BAM (slower because I know that I will have to aim more to avoid the no-shoot). Big sidestep to clear barricade. BAM BAM, BAM BAM. Reload. Look for steel popper on left while running. Slow down. Bing! (hit the steel popper). BAM BAM....BAM......BAM (one static target and one activated swinger). Sprint to put right foot on fault line stake. BAMBAMBAMBAM (two close range targets around a barricade).

Try to do what works for you, but have a plan that you can easily remember in both visual and audio terms. Don't try to remember a number sequence or precise distance. Try to use the same sensory input that you'll experience on a live stage.

SPECIALTY TARGETS

Here are a few specialty targets that you'll encounter in USPSA/IDPA:

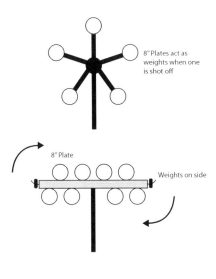

- **Texas Star.** These guys like to spin around a bushing. When plates are knocked down the weight on one side cause it to rotate. Shoot the steel at the top if it's perfectly level first, then hit the plate on the upper right. Then simply wait for the prop to spin right into your field of view.

- **Rotating Plate Rack.** The rotating plate rack involves four plates on top, four on the bottom, and weights on each side. If the prop is unbalanced and one of those weights drops off the side, it will spin really fast. There are a bunch of ways to shoot this, all depending on your level of confidence. I like to simply just mow down the top plates left to right, then the bottom plates right to left. However, you can also shoot out the middle plates first, then the two top and two bottom.

- **Swinger.** These are activated either by a prop on the stage or by shooting down a target. They usually take some time to appear so you can probably engage some other targets before coming back to them. In fact, this is usually what most people do. These are easiest to shoot at the bottom of the swing since that's where they move the least. If it's really fast (such as right off the activation or if there's a no shoot/barricade at the bottom of the swing) I'll put one in the center on the way down, and one on the way back up. Leads don't have to be considerable, and I'll usually move my gun a little to track the target as it moves within my field of view.

- **Clamshell.** These are more tactical decisions, as the shoot target is only available for a split second. You might be able to drill it and get away with it when the full target is exposed, or you might have to simply shoot the head. It depends on the stage specifics.

CHAPTER 15

PRACTICE, PRACTICE, PRACTICE

If you want to become a better shooter, you have to practice! Everybody knows this, but few actually put any significant effort into the type of training that they're doing. I hear people say to me "but I practice every weekend, I'm just not getting any better!" After awhile they get discouraged and lose motivation since they aren't seeing any results. My answer to this is that it's all about both quality and quantity. Inefficient practice won't get you anywhere.

You must learn to identify and train with a focus on your weaknesses. I cannot stress this point enough. Everyone is weak in some area of their shooting. Some people aren't accurate. Some people can't shoot on the move. Some people can't shoot weak handed. Some people are great all-around shooters, but repeatedly fold under match pressure. I know that it's really fun to go out to the range and just blast away to reinforce your strong suits, and that it can be tedious and boring to

How you structure your training is vitally important to success:

- *Train away your weaknesses*

- *Dynamically change your routine as you develop as a shooter*

- *Put in some work as often as you can*

build regimented drills on a schedule. Too bad. Success involves work; you don't win major matches with skills gained through osmosis.

You need to decide how serious you want to be about your practice time spent. As I've said before, if you just like to occasionally compete but aren't that dedicated, that's fine! You don't have to be. But you will eventually encounter a performance ceiling. It just depends what you want to get out of the sport.

The performance curve is logarithmic. In other words, depending on your natural ability you will get better at something at a certain rate given a certain amount of practice. However much like weightlifting, at the beginning it's really easy to see a lot of gains. Yet when you approach expert level, you'll have to really be focused and dedicated to squeeze those extra little bits of improvement out of yourself. It might only take you a year of periodic training to double your bench press. However, the next year you might have to lift twice as often to only get a 20% return. The following year you might have to be incredibly devoted to diet and a precisely engineered routine to only get 7.5% more strength. It always gets harder as you push the limits of your potential. Some things come easier to some people, but you can still beat them depending on how intelligently you organize your time to concentrate on your goal.

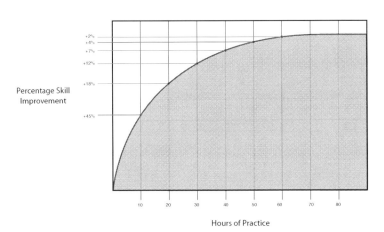

DEVELOPING AN
EFFECTIVE TRAINING ROUTINE
IDENTIFYING/TRAINING AWAY WEAKNESSES

Take some video of yourself and compare your performance to others. Have other people watch you shoot. Determine where you're losing time on standards drills, or where you think that you're uncomfortable. Where are your confidence limits in a match or in the real world? You need to find out these things. The reason you're not the best is because you're weaker than others in some capacity (you're probably stronger than others in some as well). You need to find out what these weaknesses are so that you can eliminate them.

A good buddy of mine constantly trained with airsoft equipment because he couldn't find the time between work and family to get out to do live fire. While his movement was excellent and his transitions were solid, he didn't have enough experience with recoil control. As a result, sometimes his accuracy suffered when he would start to shoot quickly. He couldn't call his second shot as well during rapid fire. So while he and I might arrive at the same first position on a stage at the same time, I'd be able to shoot the array more quickly than he would. So then he'd check his scores against mine and determine that he shot the same amount of points (or perhaps a few more) than me, but was considerably slower. So on the next stage he'd try to speed up his shooting to catch up to me. However, then he would start pushing beyond his recoil control limits and would shoot a time that's close to mine but throw a lot of penalties which would kill his score.

If I were to develop a training routine for this person, I wouldn't bother having him do any draw, transitions, or accuracy drills. Those would be a waste of time because as long as his recoil control is the biggest element holding him back then those other skills won't help him win. I would have him go out to the range with some super high powered ammunition and do bill drills all day with a factory recoil spring. I would have him do the same kind of routine for a few weeks while getting used to handling hot ammo and keeping the gun on target. After awhile, when he goes out and trains with his regular competition equipment not only will he be used to shooting a hard recoiling gun, but his grip will be much more solid. His normal competition equipment will feel like butter and he will have improved confidence to shoot fast. (I sometimes even have students remove their holsters before a class and start everything gun in hand so that they don't worry about doing a quick draw and instead attend to implementing what I'm teaching with a good grip.)

A few summers ago, I knew that my movement skills were lacking. I had to stand still to shoot targets, and was too afraid of lighting off a round while my feet were moving. So what did I do? I went out to the range and did nothing but movement drills for three months. Every time I was there I was shooting on the move. Consequently I got really good at it and became proud of these abilities. There's a famous Arnold Schwarzenegger story about his bodybuilding days. At one point, like many people in the gym at the time, he was only training his upper body. He was strong and he was good at it. He could impress people. However, he was ashamed of having chicken legs which he never worked on. So what did he do? He cut off the legs on all his pants so he would force himself to overcome his weakness. It's a lesson we should all be able to learn from.

Point of note: Train for harder shots/scenarios than you'll ever find in a match. This way everything looks easy to you.

STRUCTURING A TRAINING PROGRAM

In spite of the comparisons above, training for shooting has to be focused in a different way than other forms of athletic training such as weightlifting or distance running. What they have in common is that they're both very perishable skills. If you don't run or lift for a month or so, you won't feel that great when you arrive back at the gym. The same goes with shooting. They also all require a considerable amount of effort to become elite at. However, as far as structuring a training routine goes, that's where the likenesses end.

Shooting requires a lot of dynamic training. I've seen people static programs such as:

Monday- 50 draws, 50 reloads, draw to shoot two shots on two targets.

Wednesday- 50 draws, 50 reloads, draw to shoot one target at 20 yards strong hand only

Friday- 50 draws, 50 reloads, bill drills at 15 yards.

This doesn't work so well because the program is too stagnant. Why has this person decided to do 50 draws/reloads before every session? Are his gunhandling skills lacking? He might be spending 20 minutes at the beginning of every training session on something that's only going to save him one tenth of a second on a stage. Furthermore, if this person plans out a training schedule like that for the next couple of months, then he might be resigning himself to put effort in the future into something that might not be so useful.

However, you can also be too unfocused in your training. Lots of people will go out to the range and put together a practice stage and just shoot it a bunch of times. If you're shooting a 26 round stage over and over again, what are you really practicing? There are a hundred skills required to shoot that stage quickly. How do you know where you're slow and where you're fast? When you practice too many skills at once, you're not going to be able to put enough effort into each one to build it substantially.

Matches and practice stages should serve as diagnostic tools. Once you use them to discover where you're weak/slow/unconfident, then you need to build a short term training program to counteract those problems. For the shooter I mentioned in the previous section with the recoil control problem I would have built a two week training program with simple drills which only develop that skill. Remove superfluous elements from your training and focus on what needs to be done. After a few weeks of training that one skill, go shoot another match and re-evaluate yourself. Maybe that skill needs more refinement. Perhaps there's now a different deficiency that stands out.

The only thing that you should pre-plan well in advance is making time to get out to the range as often as you can. However, let your abilities decide what you do there on a bi-weekly basis. If you can't make it out very often then seek out other training options.

Point of note: Try to train as often as possible. If you can't shoot, shoot airsoft. If you can't shoot airsoft, dry fire. If you can't dry fire, practice your motions and movement without a gun. Do some form of practice whenever you can.

Another point of note: A shooting coach or experienced mentor is very useful in immediately being able to pick up on what you need to train and to suggest drills to help you out. If you're a novice then it might be difficult to interpret what you're doing wrong. This is where other shooters can give you some valuable advice. Don't be afraid to try new things.

AIRSOFT EQUIPMENT

Airsoft is a great tool for any competition or defensive shooter for when you can't make it to (or can't afford) live fire all the time. While you obviously won't be able to work on recoil control, you can easily put time into your transitions and movement. I prefer it to dry fire because let's be honest, dry fire is boring! I love plinking away in my garage even if it's just for a few minutes. It's even fun and safe for kids to try if they're properly supervised.

There are many realistic pistols out there which you can buy, as well as some pretty cool target systems. I would recommend getting yourself a gas blowback pistol (with a reciprocating slide) and some paper/steel to shoot at. All you need is a painter's cloth as a backdrop to stop the BBs from going in unintended directions and some eye protection. Various shot timer applications are available for the iPhone, or you can buy specially designed timers to record your shots with surprising accuracy.

For targets, I recommend BAM Airsoft for their steel poppers, texas stars, and resettable plate racks, all of which are reduced for size and scale to simulate what you would find on a real range. They have a pretty accurate Steel Challenge simulation as well. Also, Competitive Edge Dynamics sells reduced sized USPSA paper targets which are handy.

GRIP STRENGTH BUILDING

Your grip strength is vitally important to your shooting. Lots of the best handgun guys/gals have incredible grips. This allows them to hold the gun firmly while being able to dexterously operate the trigger. If my maximum crush grip is 250lbs, then that means I can hold the gun with only 50% force (relatively little) and still exert 125lbs of pressure on it. If your maximum grip is 125lbs, then you will tire yourself out and will be muscling the gun all over the place trying to match my grip. As a result I'll have better recoil control than you will, and as a result faster and more accurate shots.

If your recoil control is suffering, then it may not be a technique issue at all! You might just not have big enough forearms! Go check out the Captains of Crush® grippers and some of the other products available from IronMind. Try taking some wall/rock climbing classes. Start a grip strength training program. You'll quickly recognize the difference.

FIXING PROBLEMS

Guns are machines, and like all machines they sometimes have problems. In this section, I'll detail some of the common malfunctions that you will one day experience and what to look for to correct them. Although I've tried to identify multiple causes, keep in mind that they're not always the only cause. A myriad of factors might be at work causing your gun to jam.

Ultimately the key to fixing issues with your gun is the same as with every other machine. You have to figure out how it works first. As you'll see below, there are many possible explanations for a given error. However, it's impossible to be completely comprehensive. Usually these issues are pretty simple to fix but occasionally you'll run into a situation when it simply won't run. I've encountered some absolutely dumbfounding problems with guns before. If your gun is unreliable either due to bad design or poor maintenance then it should be a major concern. Some are just finicky or worn out in which case you might need a better gun.

Jams are a fact of life. You will eventually encounter one:

- *While clearing a jam, keep your finger off the trigger! You don't want the gun to accidentally discharge.*

- *Many causes are avoided by routine maintenance and testing ammo*

- *Practice clearing jams in case you have one when it's least convenient.*

COMMON PROBLEMS (MALFUNCTIONS)

- **Off-Center Light Primer Strikes.** These are commonly found on semi-autos. You pull the trigger and the hammer falls. However there's no boom. You take the unfired cartridge out of the gun and look for the telltale dimple in the primer. However the dimple is not in the center of it. This means that the gun was not fully into battery (slide completely forward) when the hammer or striker fell on it and the primer was struck at an angle. To solve this, you must determine why the gun was not in battery:

    - When loading the gun, instead of pulling the slide all the way back and letting it fall on the next round in the magazine you followed it with your hand. Pulling back the slide is one motion- pull back then release. Pulling it back then pushing it forward results in the slide moving forward with less force and a possible out of battery strike.

    - The recoil spring is too light. If this is the case, then the recoil spring isn't pushing the slide forward with enough force to propel the slide into battery. This is often caused by the spring being worn out. Replace it.

    - The magazine spring is too stiff. If you are using new magazines, or especially new reduced capacity magazines (such as 10 rounders required for certain states) then the magazine spring is pushing the first round up against the feed lips of the magazine with a LOT of force. This additional pressure could be slowing down the slide as it picks up the next round. The solution is to load the magazines and keep them loaded to wear out the spring a little, replace the spring with a lighter one, or cut a coil or two off it.

    - If you're using an aftermarket guide rod there could be friction between the guide rod and the slide, causing it to slow down. This is a potential issue when you're using heavier materials such as tungsten in the guide rod. Look for wear points on it.

    - Some external force is slowing the slide down, such as your support thumb exerting a lot of pressure on the slide, or part of the port or barricade you're shooting through/around is touching the slide or catching the sights.

    - The ammo you're using might be improperly sized or deformed. This can easily be determined through inspection with a case gauge- a standard device you drop rounds into to make sure they'll fit in your chamber (or you can use your barrel). This can be caused by reloaded ammunition with a bulge at the bottom of the case from a past firing.

Standard case gauge

    - Your chamber can have foreign material in it, or your gun can be really dirty, preventing the next round from chambering correctly.

– The revolver cylinder is not rotating correctly either due to short stroking the trigger (not allowing it to completely reset while shooting double action) or due to the cylinder not indexing properly (likely due to debris/dirt).

– The extractor is too tight and is not allowing the rounds to chamber properly. (Found most often in 1911s.)

– The loaded round is too long and doesn't fit in the gun properly.

- **Centered Light Primer Strikes.** In this case your firing pin is hitting the primer where it should, which means that the gun is in battery fine, there's just not enough force to detonate the primer. These are caused by:

  – An overly aggressive trigger job. This is either due to a lightened mainspring or striker spring, but can also be caused by a lightened hammer. When certain modifications are performed to reduce the amount of force needed to pull the trigger they can also reduce the amount of force the gun hits the primer with. This is not a factor in all trigger jobs, it just depends what you change.

  – A dirty gun. When the gun is fired a lot crud builds up. Sometimes this crud gets stuck in the channel that the firing pin goes through. So when the firing pin is activated it gets slowed down by all of the crud and therefore hits the primer with less force than necessary.

  – Cylinder Carbon. This occurs on revolvers when a bunch of crud builds up on the cylinder. When a fresh moon-clip is thrown into the revolver this crud pads the incoming rounds against the steel of the cylinder. When the hammer comes down then the crud absorbs the impact as the rounds are cushioned against it instead of being held in place by a solid base.

  – Hard primers. Some ammunition manufacturers produce harder primers than others, and there are certain tolerances in the manufacturing process. You might get a harder lot than another by chance. CCI tends to make harder primers, while Winchester/Federal tend to make lighter primers.

  – Poorly seated primers. Some ammo might have primers that are seated too high or way too deep (far less common). As a result when they're stuck, they just absorb some of the force of the strike and seat deeper. This can be tested by just looking at the primers. Correct depth usually is just a very tiny bit below flush with the case rim.

  – Damaged Firing Pin. This is by far the least common, as firing pins are usually made out of very hard metal and do not wear very easily. However, aftermarket lightened pins can have less durability.

- **Stovepipe Jam.** This is when the fired shell case in a semi-auto gets stuck in the slide without properly ejecting. It's called a stovepipe because it looks like an exhaust smokepipe coming out of the gun! (The expression probably dates back quite awhile.) The usual culprits are:

    - Improper recoil spring/load combo. If you use really light target ammo with a heavy recoil spring, the spent shell case won't have enough force to pop out of the gun when it hits the ejector because the slide is moving too slowly.

    - Excess tension in the magazine. This is similar to the off center light primer strike problem. If you are using new magazines, or especially new reduced capacity magazines (such as 10 rounders required for certain states) then the magazine spring is pushing the first round up against the feed lips of the magazine with a LOT of force. When the slide moves back, it rubs against the first round at the top of the magazine which could slow it down enough to cause a jam. This type becomes especially evident when shooting from a prone position with the base of the magazine jammed into the ground.

    - The gun is dirty or requires lubrication (or too much sticky grease). Excessive friction will slow the slide down, preventing it from properly ejecting rounds. Alternatively you could have put a ton of grease inside the slide and caused it to slow down.

    - The extractor is too loose. In this case it isn't properly gripping the rims of the rounds causing them to eject erratically. This is found most often in 1911s (requires mechanical tensioning of the extractor), but can occur if the extractor spring wears out on other guns such as the Glock (this is an incredibly rare condition).

    - Squib load. The round you've just fired had little or no powder. It will have made a *poof* sound and there would have been very little felt recoil. Do not fire the gun again in this condition. It can be extremely dangerous because there might not have been enough force to propel the bullet out of the barrel, in which case it would still be stuck in there. Take the gun apart and inspect the barrel. Use a rod and hammer to knock out the stuck projectile (in the direction it was fired).

    - Broken ejector. In this case the ejector has worn down and needs to be replaced. Less material on it means it hits the shell casing with less force than intended.

    - Some external factor is slowing down the slide, causing it to short stroke.

- **Failure to Eject.** This is when the spent shell case in a semi-auto remains in the chamber after firing.

    - Squib load. This is the most likely condition and is possibly very dangerous. See above.

– Broken or way too loose extractor. In this case you could have the notorious "double feed" jam where the spent shell casing is still in the chamber but the slide cycles and tries to push another round into the back of the old casing. It's a hassle to clear on the fly.

– Recoil spring way too heavy or ammo way too light. In this case, the slide doesn't move.

– Some external factor preventing the slide from cycling.

- **Failure to Feed.** This malfunction occurs in semi-autos when the next round in the magazine fails to properly go up the feed ramp and into the chamber, allowing it to close and the gun to fire. Many of these problems are due to user error, ammunition selection, or magazine problems. Generally the causes are:

  – Limp Wristing. This is a common problem with new shooters. In this case, the shooter has taken a very weak, low grip on the gun. Instead of the slide moving back in a normal direction, instead it moves like a parabola. Whiplash causes the slide to move way too quickly, and the next round in the magazine nosedives (instead of pointing up in the normal direction) under the force. This causes the next round to get stuck before feeding properly. To correct this, improve your grip, and get higher up on the gun.

  – The magazine is not properly seated in the gun.

  – Magazine spring cannot keep up with the cyclic rate of the gun. In this case the slide moves so fast that the magazine cannot feed rounds quickly enough. This can be caused either by weak magazine springs or too tight of a recoil spring. This becomes more evident the fewer bullets you have remaining in the magazine (less tension on them).

  – Magazine springs are too stiff. In this case, again especially evident with reduced capacity magazines, the first round at the top of a loaded magazine is in there so tight that the slide doesn't have enough force to successfully pull it out of the magazine. In some cases, the slide will literally stick on the top of the magazine.

  – The gun is dirty. In this case, either the feed ramp to the chamber has a ton of crud on it that the rounds going in are getting stuck on, or there's either way too little or way too much lubrication in the gun. As mentioned above, the former causes a lot of friction while the latter's viscosity slows the slide down.

  – Feed Lips Damaged. If the feed lips of the magazine are damaged then either the round is held in too tightly, or too loosely. In the former case, the slide might get stuck trying to feed the magazine. In the latter case, the round might come up at a strange angle and not enter the chamber properly. If the round is getting stuck at a weird angle (such as vertical) this is a common cause. If this is the case, buy new magazines.

– Magazine followers are old/worn out. The follower is the plastic/metal piece at the top of the magazine that uses spring tension to push the bullets in the magazine upwards. If these are badly designed or misshapen then they could cause the bullets to sit at the wrong angle in the magazine, thereby not allowing them to feed properly. This can be corrected either by buying new magazines or different followers.

– The ammunition you're using is either too long, or the face of the bullet is at too sharp of an angle. For example, some guns don't like truncated cone ammo, but will feed JHP round noses very easily. In this situation, there's nothing wrong with the ammo per se, but it doesn't work well with your gun. Ammo can also be produced poorly, such as having a badly sized or bulged case. Here it's the manufacturer's fault. A case gauge (mentioned above) will help isolate the problem.

– The recoil spring is worn out. In this case you've shot way too many rounds through the gun, and the recoil spring doesn't have enough force to load another round out of the magazine. (It would have to get pretty worn out by this point, as usually just the force of the slide bouncing off the frame under recoil would be sufficient to allow the gun to feed.)

– Extractor is too tight. In this situation, the excessive extractor tension is not allowing the rim of the next cartridge in the magazine to properly seat under the extractor. So when the slide moves forward, the next round literally gets stuck on the extractor, thereby stopping the slide.

– Magazine does not work when pushed against the ground while shooting from the prone position (could be from over-insertion). This can possibly cause jams if there's no magazine stop on the frame, and the only thing positioning the magazine is the mag catch.

– Accessory interference. In some cases, installing something heavy on the front of the pistol such as a bulky flashlight can cause a weight imbalance. Test your accessories extensively to see if they have this effect.

- **Failure to Drop Magazines.** In semi-autos, sometimes when you hit the release button, the magazine will stick in the gun (usually will fall a tiny bit, then stop). In this case there's no mechanical action holding the magazine in place, just friction.

  – Grip/magazine design. In some guns there is a lot of tight clearance in the magazine well. Some magazines are thicker than others by slight margins, and others are not designed to drop free when empty. My recommendation here is to buy/borrow a bunch of magazines and test them on an empty gun. Slam an empty magazine in there with the slide locked back then try to drop it free. If you're sure it's a design problem, then you can look for different magazine or components which are either heavier (usually through an aftermarket basepad, which is a cheap & easy way) or thinner (possibly from a different manufacturer). Secondly, you can take a file and remove a little material from the inside of the magwell. This option is easier than it sounds, and you don't need to remove that much. If you don't feel comfortable doing this kind of work, take your gun to a gunsmith. These types of problems may sometimes only exist with reduced capacity magazines (required by law in certain places). These usually have a ridge down both sides of the center of the magazine to force the rounds to single stack instead of stagger. This might cause it to be thicker or more rigid.

– Dirty gun. If your gun or magazines are dirty and there's a bunch of crud in the magwell, then you're going to get friction here as well. This could be a buildup on the magazine catch itself, or just within the magwell. Make sure you wipe off your magazines and keep them clean if you drop them. Also, when you're cleaning your gun, wipe down the inside of the grip with some shop towels.

– Magazine brake. Some guns such as the CZ SP01 have a magazine brake in the grip. This is a strip of metal designed to wedge the magazine securely in the gun when it's loaded and falls between the magwell and the mainspring housing. This might have to be modified. To check it, remove the grips from the gun and look at its position against the magazine to check for possible friction points.

– Internal components/ammunition. Sometimes your ammunition can get wedged against internal components such as the slide release. Put in a magazine with the ammunition you're going to use, then check for places where friction could be created.

- **Failure to Seat Magazines.** This can occur if your magazine is loaded all the way up to capacity. You give it a push into the magwell, but it doesn't go in far enough to cycle the next round. This usually occurs because the round at the top is in there really tight and doesn't give against the slide when the mag is inserted.

    – Load your magazines for awhile to compress the springs if they're new. This fixes most problems.

    – If you're living in a state where you're limited to 10 rounds, then firearm companies make magazines in strict compliance so that 10th round is very very tight. To prevent that tension from building up and preventing the magazine from seating, first try cutting a coil or two off the bottom of the magazine spring. This could be enough to get a little extra room. If that doesn't work, disassemble the magazine to see where the tension is coming from. Sometimes you might have to trim the follower or the baseplate to get another millimeter to two so the 10th round goes in easier.

– This could also be caused if your magazines don't have long enough basepads to be seated properly.

Even though the above list seems daunting, it's because I've tried to keep things somewhat comprehensive. These jams can happen, but in a decent pistol, they shouldn't happen at all. Usually the source of a jam can be isolated and corrected quickly. If you have a handgun that's experiencing multiple types of jams seemingly at random, then you should take it to your gunsmith, or return it to the factory. Semi-autos can have lots of different types of jams because there are a lot of moving parts operating in synch. However, even a semi-auto that's known for being only moderately reliable should go many thousands of rounds without a jam. When a gun is heavily customized it will tend to have more issues though because it works under tighter conditions than tested by the factory.

CLEARING JAMS

If you shoot enough, you're bound to get some of these pesky jams every now and then. There's a simple and basic way to clear each one of them on the fly, and it would behoove you to practice doing so swiftly and fluidly. You want to develop the appropriate muscle memory so that if a jam occurs at the wrong time, you will know exactly what to do.

When I tell you to "pull back on the slide" there are two ways you can do this:

- Keep the gun relatively close to eye level and use your thumb, index finger, and middle fingers to pull back on the rear slide serrations. This approach assists you in getting the gun back on target faster once the jam has been cleared because the gun is already up and ready to be aimed and your hands are in close proximity to their shooting positions. (Best for competition)

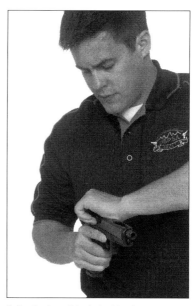

- Drop the gun down to chest level and grip the rear slide serrations with your entire hand. (You don't have to go down as low as in the photo if your slide isn't difficult to pull back, it's wherever you're comfortable) This approach guarantees that you'll get the best possible grip on the slide and will be able to overcome the force of the recoil spring to pull it back all the way. It won't be as fast as the first style in getting follow up shots on target, but the slide will have the least chance of slipping from your hand under stress. (Best for defense)

Pulling back on slide at chest level

Here are some tips by type of jam:

- **Stovepipe Jam.** Rotate the gun towards the ejection port side (pretty much always the right side) and then pull back sharply on the slide. The shell should fall out and also sometimes extract the next live round that was headed into the chamber. This is because at the point at which stovepipes occur, the extractor might have already latched onto the next round coming in. (If this happens, it is possible to pull back the slide just enough to clear the stovepipe but keep the next round in the chamber, but the motion is very precise and will drastically increase the time it takes to fix the jam.) It's important to get them both out of the gun fast. If they don't immediately fall out, turn the gun more and shake them out. Once the shell has dropped out of the gun and is clear, release the slide and let it go forward entirely on its own power. Trying to push the slide forward manually might cause another jam.

- **Failure to Feed.** Tap the magazine to ensure that it's seated, then simply pull back all the way on the slide and release. If it doesn't work, try again. If it still doesn't work, replace the magazine and try a third time. Sometimes you'll get a failure to feed in which the next round will deflect off the feed ramp of the barrel, and will get caught in the top of the slide like a stovepipe. In this case, you have to clear it like a stovepipe. Make sure the rounds don't get jumbled up in your chamber. It's probably a failure to feed if you perform a reload and one round fires, but the gun goes *click* on the next shot. In this case the magazine was only partially in the gun.

- **Double Feed.** This is where the spent shell casing fails to eject but the slide cycles and attempts to push a new round into the rear of the old casing (or when you mess up clearing a failure to feed). It's a detestable jam, and difficult to quickly clear because now you have spring tension holding the case in place. First, try the same procedure as the stovepipe jam to try and get the bunched up rounds to fall out. If that doesn't work, drop the current magazine out of the gun and pull the slide back to drop the unfired round out of the gun. Rack the slide all the way forwards and backwards rapidly by hand to try and eject the spent shell casing. Once it's out, reinsert the magazine, rack the slide and start shooting. (If it still doesn't come out, grab a knife or screwdriver and wedge it out from the extractor rim. Be careful you don't cut yourself while doing this.)

- **Light Primer Strike.** Simply rack the slide to eject the unfired round and seat a new one in the chamber.

- **Revolver Failure to Rotate the Cylinder.** Chances are this is happening because you're not completely letting the trigger out while shooting in double action. It's called "short stroking." Make sure you correct your technique. Alternatively the gun could be dirty, or there could be a mechanical problem, the only way to take care of this on the range is to unlock and relock the cylinder back in place.

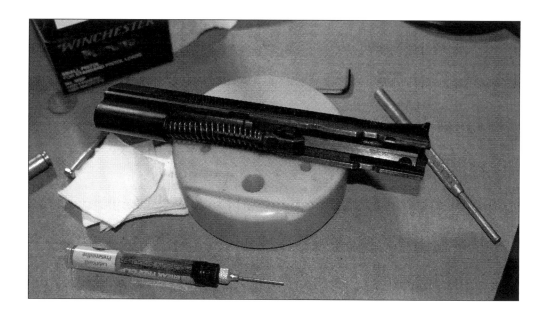

CHAPTER 17

WORKING WITH THE HANDGUN

CLEANING AND MAINTENANCE

When I bought my first handgun (or rather my father did for me) I cared for it with intense dedication. This included an elaborate cleaning routine which took well over an hour that resulted in a spotless well oiled gun that could be mistaken for something on a collector's shelf. However, after doing this for a few years I realized how much I hated it. Some people enjoy cleaning, just as some people enjoy reloading. I view them as a necessary evil, an annoyance to be dealt with between shooting sessions so as to facilitate future shooting sessions.

Here's a secret: You don't have to clean your gun that much. Seriously. Older guns used black powder, which is notoriously dirty and corrosive. However, modern guns pretty much exclusively use smokeless powder which tends to burn a lot cleaner. Furthermore thanks to the wonders of modern engineering, most decent

As a gun owner, you should know your equipment:

- *Regular maintenance is important, but don't overdo it*

- *Don't begin modifying your equipment when you first start out*

- *Modifications cannot compensate for lack of experience*

handguns are designed to last a whole bunch of rounds without malfunction between cleaning sessions. (One major advance is a melonite/tennifer coating to the handgun which prevents rust and fouling. Another is simply development of better mechanics.) As a matter of fact I rarely clean my competition/practice guns. I usually go about at least 1,000 or more rounds between cleanings, and just remember to drop a few drops of oil on the gun every couple hundred rounds. This has become common for me because I typically go to the range to practice multiple times a week and have other things to do with my life than pick away at crud in my frame.

Now certain guns are more fickle than others. This depends on both the level of modification performed on the pistol as well as the overall quality from the factory. I'm not suggesting that you clean your guns so rarely, but your gun will tell you when it needs a wash- usually by jamming. If you're practicing frequently then don't worry about cleaning your gun all the time because a little dirt won't hurt the firearm. Obviously if you're hanging out in the Louisiana bayou all the time and your gun gets wet, you might want to clean it a little more often to prevent surface rust from forming. Also if you're planning on storing the gun for a long period of time you might want to give it a brief wipe down too.

Now, when I do clean my handguns I do so thoroughly. For my Glock I tend to completely detail strip it (take every part out of the gun) for cleaning. For some guns that's too difficult and time-consuming, but if you can do it quickly I recommend it- especially on moving parts of the trigger. Some people take FOREVER to clean guns, and when they're done, there's still debris left inside. With some tips and tricks I'm about to tell you, even a complete detail strip clean and lubrication can take less time than someone doing a standard cleaning incorrectly. Remember the old mechanic's adage: "If it's too difficult, you're probably doing it wrong!"

I recommend:

- **Flannel Cotton Bulk Patches.** Buy a ton of these in your caliber. If you can get the more abrasive twill kind from Brownells, then do it, but it's not a big deal.

- **Cleaning Rod.** Available wherever guns are sold. Don't get one too long.

- **Patch Jag.** This is a brass device that fits to the end of your cleaning rod that pushes a tightly fit patch down the barrel. Don't use those patch holders (the black plastic ones with the slot in the middle) they suck, and won't get anything out of your barrel.

Patch jag

- **Brass Brush.** Buy one of these for your caliber. Don't get nylon.

- **Shop Towels.** Go to your local auto parts store and buy a whole bunch of those thick blue shop towels.

- **Break Free or Equivalent CLP Oil.** This stands for cleaning/lubrication/protection.

- **Shooters Choice Bore Cleaner.** The best bore cleaner on the market, bar none.

- **A big paperclip or dental pick.**

- **A cleaning brush.**

- **Hoppes 9 Oil.** This is your lubricant

- **Slide Glide.** Also a good lubricant.

- **A Cleaning Mat.** Rolled up newspaper will do, but we don't want these stinking up the kitchen trashbin, now do we?

- **Latex Gloves.**

So here's what you do:

1. Put the gloves on, lay out the mat, and follow the instructions for your gun to strip it down for cleaning. Again, for my Glock I like to take apart the whole gun to get in the nooks and crannies.

2. First since your hands are currently oil free and you don't want to get oil all over the grip (this causes slipperyness), start by cleaning the grip. Pretty much just rub the blue shop towel everywhere. Do not oil the shop towel first! This is meant to be done dry, as it involves less mess. Dig in those hard to reach places, and make sure you clean out the magwell. If there are any spots that are too big for your fingers, that's what the paperclip is for. Make sure you get under the frame rails.

3. If there's any really really badly built up spot of crud, put a drop of CLP on the blue towel and scrub. Make sure you dry immediately. When finished wiping all oil and dirt off the frame set it aside.

4. Pick up the slide and do the same thing. Make sure you scrub behind the extractor and the breech (where the firing pin comes out). Try to use as little oil as possible. If you see a big buildup of crud, try to scrape it away either with your paperclip or a dental pick, then mop up the rest with a drop of CLP. Try to avoid getting oil down the firing pin hole. Oil attracts crud and you don't want any crud in your firing pin channel. Make sure you get inside the slide rails.

5. Finally pick up the barrel. Most people have trouble cleaning these. First, make sure you scrape all the crud off the feed ramp/face of the barrel using the paperclip (or a dental pick). Take your cleaning jag, put it on the end of your cleaning rod, and push a CLP soaked patch onto the end. Insert it into the barrel, swab out the chamber, and scrub up

and down the barrel with it for awhile. Keep the patch inside the barrel and move it back and forth. When you're done, push all the way through and remove the patch.

6. Replace the jag with your brass brush. Dip the brush in Shooters Choice and get a good deal of solvent on it. Immediately put into the barrel. Pointing the barrel away from you (solvent will splash out the other end off the brush) push the brush through all the way through. Then pull it back all the way through. Repeat about 15-20 times.

7. Replace the brush with the jag and a clean patch. Put the clean patch down and scrub a lot more against the walls of the barrel. When done do a CLP soaked patch and scrub, then three clean patches and scrub. This should remove any excess solvent. To check the barrel look through it with a white surface in the background. There should be no black stuff inside and it should just be smooth shiny metal. Wipe down outside of the barrel with a blue shop towel.

8. Take out your lube. For 1911/2011s I recommend Slide Glide. It will slow down your slide a little bit due to the viscosity of the grease. For all others, use the Hoppes 9. Add a couple drops to the frame rails on both the slide and the frame, and add a little bit to a patch to wipe friction surfaces with (such as the end of the barrel). If the manufacturer recommends it, like Glock does, put a drop on the trigger mechanism as well (for Glock, it's where the trigger bar contacts the connector in the rear of the gun).

9. Reassemble. Rack the slide a bunch of times to distribute the lube and dry fire a bunch. Check to make sure the trigger resets properly and you're good to go. Wipe down the exterior one more time with a shop towel. Don't use those silicon cloths. They're good for adding a protective coat for storage, but will otherwise make the frame slippery, which is bad for shooting.

Maintenance tips: Check your springs! These will likely be the first part on the gun to fail. Make sure that you replace the recoil spring frequently (about every 3,000-5,000 rounds). Some guns can go many more rounds without a replacement, but it's better to avoid frame damage and keep this part in check. If the recoil spring is sold as part of an assembly with the guide rod, just replace the whole thing. Also, every 25,000 thousand rounds, take the gun to your gunsmith and have him replace all the springs. It will improve reliability and function.

A good way to test the recoil spring is to load a round (do this with a dummy round or snap cap for safety) into the chamber of the gun, tilt the gun so that the muzzle points towards the sky, and pull the slide back about a quarter inch. Then release the slide as slowly as possible. If the gun fails to go into battery, then it's too light/worn out.

You should also perform a detail clean of the gun about every 10,000 rounds as well. Taking apart a gun completely isn't very hard, and you'll find that not only will you learn more about the gun but you will also keep the action running smoothly. If you're uncomfortable doing this, your gunsmith should be able to help you out at a relatively low cost.

GUN MODIFICATIONS

My philosophy to gun modifications is simply that you should have a reason to need them. You should say, I'm having XYZ problems, and my equipment is holding me back. To put this in perspective, let me tell you about my buddy who used to work in a performance cycling store. They sold everything, from entry level equipment to carbon fiber frame precision engineered stuff that looked like it came from NASA. Evidently there were two types of people that bought those space age bikes: either sponsored riders that competed on a national level or newbies with large checkbooks.

If you're an inexperienced shooter that's unfamiliar with firearms, there's no reason why you should shell out large quantities of cash to heavily customize your handgun (or rifle for that matter). There are multiple reasons for this. First off, you should develop the fundamental skills on a functional basic piece of equipment. That way you won't cheat yourself by just getting used to really good stuff which might compensate for your bad habits. Secondly, you don't want to spend a ton of money on something that you might get bored of or not use. Third, modifying a gun extensively could compromise some of its reliability. Fourth, buying something that looks cool only of that reason might even be counterproductive to performance (and will make you look silly to people in the know). A lot can be accomplished with factory equipment. Guys like Bob Vogel and Dave Sevigny (USPSA Production division champions) can smoke practically anyone in a shooting competition with a gun that's never been touched after the assembly line.

I don't intend to give you a comprehensive guide to gunsmithing. Instead here's some information about what can be done as well as some basics on work you can do yourself. That being said, I'll go into some detail about the types of modifications you can make as well as the reasons for doing them.

SIGHTS

Sights are generally the first changes anyone will make to a handgun. Obviously the first thing that you have to do in order to hit a target is to aim at it. Most factory sights come with some sort of white lined or dotted rear notch and a big front white dot to put in the middle. While these are okay for certain purposes, you need to decide what you're planning on using the gun for and why you'd want to change them out. Two main applications are:

- **Target Shooting Sights.** Typical target shooting sights come in two configurations, either all black sights, or a flat black rear with a fiber optic in the front. This is because the rear notch is not an important focal point. It's simply there in the peripheral vision while the focus remains on the front sight. This is true for both bullseye as well as practical pistol sports. It's very easy to shoot accurately at distance with a flat black front sight. Front fiber optic sights glow in the sunlight to enhance transition and target acquisition speed. (A channel to fit the fiber optic is drilled in the front sight at the factory.) Just put the dot on what you're trying to hit.

Fiber optic low mount competition sights

For target shooting, a thinner front blade is usually desirable because it lets a lot of light in and makes it easy to finely adjust your aim. Ideally the light channels between your front sight and rear notch should be about half as wide as the front blade on each side. (So out of the total 100% space in the rear notch when holding the gun at arms length, 50% is occupied by the front sight.) This is important also when trying to quickly pick up your sights. If you have a really fat front blade, then you will sometimes have trouble aligning it perfectly in the rear notch.

A good light bar distribution in your sight picture

- **Defensive Sights.** Defensive sights come in an assortment of possibilities. Most of the time the front sight is large (to draw your focus) and is filled with tritium which makes it glow in the dark. Sometimes the rear sights also have tritium dots in them. These are extremely useful for aiming when there's little ambient light around you. Other variations include a triangular front sight which forms the tip of the triangle such as the one SureSight offers. The idea is not for aiming very much or hitting distant targets. These designs are tailored towards high speed close quarters engagements. Due to the fact that the front sights are generally quite large, there is usually very little light that goes between the front sight and the rear notch, making precise aiming difficult.

  One thing to be aware of is that if you buy a set of night sights AND you use a flashlight, the night sights won't do you much good. The flashlight will drown out much of the luminance the tritium has, and you'll be looking at a black silhouette anyways.

If you're looking to swap out your sights, I recommend the following providers:

- Warren Tactical. These guys make excellent target shooting sights, and have tritium inserts in their carry versions. I believe that these sights have the optimal front sight to rear notch width ratio of any on the market.

- Trijicon. Makers of the famous ACOG (Advanced Combat Optical Gunsight) used extensive by the US Military. They specialize in low light applications and have developed a ton of night sights for various pistols.

- Dawson Precision. Makers of a number of different sight configurations for various pistols and makes some good adjustable versions.

As a point of note, I don't like having white dots on the rear at all. They're distracting when your focus should just be on the front sight. You should just be looking for that front dot. This works for both extreme accuracy shooting as well as defensive shooting. If you have a gun with them (and many are like this from the factory) don't worry about buying a new set of sights right away. Go buy a Sharpie and black out those dots. Trust me on this one.

If you do choose to buy new sights, a determination you'll want to make is whether you want to have adjustable or fixed sights. Adjustables tend to be more expensive and also do not have as many options available. They also tend to sit higher on the gun. However, they can be clicked into place according to your ammo type very easily thereby allowing you to dial your gun in quickly.

Fixed sights take a bit more work to get your point of aim/ point of impact down. In order to adjust them you're going to need a hammer, a bench block (big piece of non marring plastic) or vice, and a brass or nylon punch (you can get these from Brownells). For semi-autos, fixed sights are usually press fit into the sight channel and held in place by a little screw that adds pressure. However, your gunsmith might not install them exactly aligned or you might have occasional group changes depending on the ammo you use.

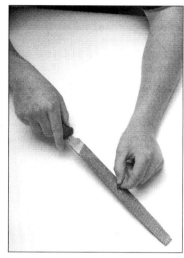

Filing front sight

If you want to install them yourself, you're going to need a metal file in order to remove some material from the bottom of the sight because they're usually slightly over tolerance from the factory. To install them, file a little off the bottom at a time, then push in by hand. Once you've taken off enough material and the sight goes about 1/2 of the way into the sight channel, then take out your hammer and punch, and whack it the rest of the way in. In order to adjust them, you're going to need to loosen the screw attached to the rear sight and whack the sight a little to either side using the punch and hammer. Just hit low on the sight blade to adjust it and don't worry about damaging it, it's made of hardened steel and your punch is of a softer material. This is called "drift or windage adjustment."

Adjustments for sighting in a handgun work as follows. Whack the rear sight in the direction you want your group to go. If you're aiming dead on and the group is to the left, then whack your rear sight to the right, and vice versa. If the group is too high or too low, then you'll need to change your front sight (unless you have both elevation and windage adjustable rears). If your group is too high, then get a taller front sight. If your group is too low, then get a shorter front sight.

One cool tool you might want to consider buying is called the Sight Mark. It's a little laser that attaches by magnet to the front of your barrel. Once you've dialed the gun in, go take the gun to a fixed distance and put on the laser. See where the laser points in relation to your sights. It should be dead on. Either way, make a note of it, and if you ever worry again about knocking around or replacing your sights or re-dialing in the gun, you can use the laser as a point of reference to know where they should be pointing.

GRIPS

As has been established earlier, ergonomics of a handgun are very important to both recoil control as well as manipulation of the trigger and controls. Some guns have interchangeable grips (such as the Gen4 Glocks), others don't and require actual frame modifications (such as the 3rd Generation Glocks). Depending on the amount of aftermarket support available, you can purchase these to accommodate smaller or larger hand sizes. Additionally, replacement grips can offer increased tack, allowing you to get a better handle on the gun under slippery conditions.

As far as materials are concerned, these typically come in plastic, rubber, wood, or metal. (Yes John Woo fans, you can get pearl as well) They also can have finger grooves embedded into them. I generally feel that grips aren't supposed to be comfortable, they're supposed to allow you to hold the gun better. Usually to accomplish this you'll need to seek out a rougher texture.

My recommendation for selecting the proper grip is to look at ergonomics first. For example, for my SP01, I've included thinner profile aluminum grips to help me reach the trigger better. The next consideration is tackiness. I think that grip tape is a useful addition to a pistol (the 3M stuff they put on ladders which you can buy at Home Depot). This will provide some good grit and can be stacked to improve palm contact with the gun. Beware however, that the more grippy the gun is, the more difficult it will be to rotate the gun in your hand to make grip adjustments on a draw or during a reload. This is one of the reasons that I don't like really thick finger groove rubber grips, as manipulating the gun under stress becomes much more difficult.

Like all other modifications, if you're planning on swapping grips, ask yourself why, and please don't tell me it's so your gun can look cooler!

TRIGGER JOBS

A trigger job is defined as anything that makes your trigger smoother, have a lighter break, or improves your pretravel, overtravel, or reset. The idea here is that the gun requires less pressure or manipulation from you trigger finger making it easier to shoot and preventing you from moving the gun off target during the trigger press. My advice is for you to get used to shooting a regular trigger first, then upgrade once you're ready. Don't mask technique problems with equipment fixes. However, also keep in mind that especially if you've purchased a used gun to run it by the gunsmith to make sure there's nothing wrong with the trigger too. (I shot a cop buddy's duty Sig, and was appalled by the condition of the trigger that was issued to him)

Trigger jobs typically involve smoothing out and/or removing material from the surfaces of the contact points. This allows the mechanism to glide more easily, and reduces the movement required for it to operate. It's a simple principle. Each manufacturer uses its own geometry to cause the gun to fire. It's often proprietary, except sometimes in guns built to a well known government spec such as a 1911. As a result, there are some guns that can be worked on by an amateur who will more or less get it right the first time, and others that should likely be taken to a gunsmith. I recommend that unless you're a gunsmith (and if you are, then you have little reason to read this section) you should limit your work to what you can easily swap out and not have to cut into.

Some people claim that a trigger job makes the gun less reliable. This ultimately depends on how light and finely tuned you're going to go. If you get the break down to about 1lb with no overtravel/reset then you've pretty much just created a situation where there's very little material and friction holding the trigger from firing. In some instances, by removing too much material the gun could accidentally go full-auto on you, which is a really bad situation, or sacrifice some safety features. Generally speaking, smoothing out a trigger to eliminate roughness is pretty safe for those who are less experienced. Once you start removing material you start to run into a little more detail oriented territory. A competent gunsmith can get you one that's really light but also functions perfectly. However, if an amateur does it then reliability can start to decrease.

Below, I'll give you some information on a common and very easy trigger job and how it works.

Glock Trigger Job.

The Glock has some of the simplest geometry available on the market. Just looking at the gun, it's pretty evident how everything works and how to change it for a great trigger. The Glock trigger functions as follows:

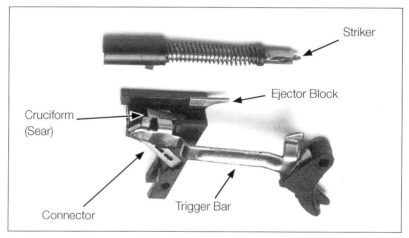

Glock trigger assembly

1. The gun starts out with the bottom part of the striker sitting on the cruciform at the back of the trigger bar. The striker is connected to its own spring which holds it under tension. The striker spring is stretched out and wants to compress and propel the striker forward. However the striker is prevented from moving forward by the trigger bar. When the trigger is pulled, the trigger bar moves down and out of the way of the striker, causing the striker to rapidly move forward and strike the primer, allowing the gun to fire.

2. The trigger bar also makes contact with three other things:

    a. **The Connector.** The downward diagonal angle at the top of this is what directs the trigger bar down and to the rear when the trigger is pulled. It operates somewhat like a spring when the trigger resets.

    b. **The Ejector Block.** The slot in the ejector block guides the back and forth movement of the trigger bar and keeps it in a certain range.

c. **The Trigger Spring.** Connecting from a hole in the bottom of the trigger bar to a hole in the ejector block, this spring causes the trigger bar to move back upwards once the gun fires. (You'll see how this works)

3. Once the trigger is pulled and the the gun fires, the slide moves backwards, and a little ledge on the slide runs into the top of the connector. This pushes the connector inwards, towards the center of the gun and away from the trigger bar which breaks (disconnects) contact with the downward diagonal ledge.

4. Once this happens, the trigger spring pulls the trigger bar upwards so now the trigger bar sits on the outside of the connector.

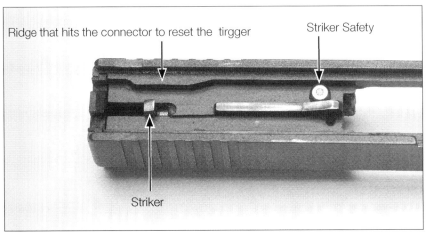

Underside of slide

5. As the slide comes back, the striker now makes contact again with the cruciform on the rear of the trigger bar. As you let the trigger out with your finger after the gun fires, you'll feel a little click. This click is the trigger bar moving forwards and allowing the spring-like connector to snap back into place behind it. Now when the trigger is pulled again, the angled ledge of the connector will be able to push the trigger bar down and out of the way again to fire the gun a second time.

Striker safety

These are the following parts needed to be swapped/altered:

- **Connector.** There are many aftermarket connector options, including Ghost Rocket and even Glock itself. Changing the angle on this piece allows the trigger to be pulled more easily with a crisper reset, and polishing the surface smoothes out the trigger pull.

- **Ejector Block.** The slot in the ejector block serves as a guide to the trigger bar, which moves back and forth a lot with the factory settings. Inserting a set screw at the front and back of this changes the pretravel, overtravel and reset. Pretty much all you do here is drill a hole on each side and put in a small set screw (usually one with a 1/16" allen wrench) to limit the motion of the trigger. Just screw the set screw in more and more until the gun doesn't fire anymore, then back it out a little bit to eliminate the overtravel.

- **Trigger Bar.** A little polish on the contact surfaces with the connector and the firing pin safety goes a long way here.

- **Trigger safety.** If you decide to put in the pre-travel screw then you'll have to file down the back of the trigger safety so it doesn't contact the frame of the pistol at rest (I usually don't adjust pre-travel).

- **Striker Spring.** In order to further reduce the pull, change out the factory striker spring to a reduced power one. Make sure your ammo works with it as it will strike the primer with slightly less force.

- **Striker (Firing Pin) Safety.** You can either replace this with a rounded edge aftermarket version, or you can round it off and polish it yourself with a Dremel tool.

As mentioned above, what you're doing with this trigger job is to smooth out rough edges in order to make the trigger break more crisply and with less force. The above steps will result in a trigger that's about 2.5 to 3lbs with a good reset and overtravel. In my experience this trigger will still be very reliable. All of the above can be accomplished even with a drop in trigger kit from a manufacturer such as Vanek that takes about 5 min to install.

Keep in mind that you don't have to do all of the above to produce a clean breaking, smooth trigger. For example, you can disregard the steps about the striker spring, the ejector block, and the trigger safety so that the factory travel will remain intact, but you'll just have something that eliminates roughness. Many USPSA competitors literally spend about 5 minutes adding a little polish to get something that works for them. Trigger jobs are about purpose and preferred feel. I generally like a crisp 3.5lb trigger.

Other Trigger Jobs
There is some debate as to how effective drop in parts can be in a trigger. Although all guns of a given model come from the same assembly process, one can detect slight variations in the parts of the gun. Also, the wear and tear on a pistol will cause the dynamics to change somewhat. For example, if you've shot a gun for awhile, you might find that the tolerances between the frame and the slide have become somewhat looser due to friction and heat. Drop in parts are made generically, and sometimes have to be fit in order to be effective.

That being said, there are numerous drop in kits ranging from complete assemblies (such as a 1911 complete hammer, sear, disconnect, and spring kit) down to individual parts (such as a drop in sear for the S&W M&P which is available from the factory.) In spite of this, unless the modifications are pretty straightforward (such as the above Glock) I recommend that you find a capable gunsmith to perform the work on your own parts, because not everything is going to fit perfectly the first time. Trigger jobs, like much else in the firearm world, comes down to testing and evaluation. The objectives of are simple, but sometimes the execution requires careful precision.

One main point of note: Yes, having a lighter spring that either activates the hammer or the striker (mainspring/striker spring) will produce a lighter trigger. However, be cautious as this will cause the firing pin to hit the primer with less force, possibly resulting in light primer strikes.

FLASHLIGHTS/LASERS

Flashlights are a popular addition which are usually either held in your hand or mounted to the accessory rail of the firearm. Typically they require a specialized holster as well if you're carrying them on your gun. These are tremendous for helping you quickly identify and illuminate possible threats. In a home defense situation you're going to want to know if that sound in the next room is an armed burglar or just your teenage daughter's boyfriend sneaking in (maybe the burglar would get more leniency). One advantage to a gun mounted flashlight is that at close range the center of the flashlight is going to be where your shot goes. Also, looking into the light you will be able to see a black outline of your sights which will help you aim. There are many different brands of these; Surefire, Fenix, Blackhawk, and Streamlight are some of the most popular.

In spite of their low light advantages, guns with flashlights carry some issues as well. First off, they can occasionally cause jams on some firearms because of the additional mass. (If you install something on your accessory rail, then test it first with a few hundred rounds.) Second, if you're in a dangerous situation and trying to clear a room by yourself (this should be your last resort) remember that if you can see the light, they can see the light. All someone has to do is crouch down behind a piece of furniture and aim at the light source while you try to find them with a 25 degree cone of vision, you'll never see it coming.

I'm sure plenty of people have seen the movies where the SWAT team enters the building, throws in a flashbang, and you can see the cool lasers glowing red in the smoke. The bad guy sees all of the dots on his chest and immediately surrenders. This undoubtedly has been the reason why many people have purchased laser accessories for their firearms. Lasers generally come mounted in three different configurations:

- **Accessory Rail Lasers.** These can be combined with a flashlight.

- **Grip Lasers.** Integrated into the grip of the pistol so that the laser turns on when you grab the gun.

- **Guide Rod Lasers.** These are integrated into aftermarket guide rods and come right out from underneath the barrel.

Lasers have advantages and drawbacks. Using a laser as a substitute for your sights is bad technique and often people will try to look at the target and shoot from low ready. Lasers should be a backup sight, not a primary. It may take some effort to dial a laser exactly straight to your point of impact, tight shots might be more difficult. Also, if you're just looking at the laser to aim, then you pull the trigger, the laser will dance all over the place making follow up shots quite difficult. However, companies like Crimson Trace make some very good laser systems which can be effective at close range or in dark environments where seeing your sights might be difficult. Sometimes that flash of the laser on the target is what you need.

Flashlights and lasers are expensive, but can be incredibly valuable in the right hands of professionals. A flashlight aimed at a person's eyes, especially in a dark environment will have a dazzling effect and your adversary will not be able to see much of anything- which can give you the upper hand. A strobe function will dramatically amplify this effect. However, if you're planning on getting one for concealed-carry, it's probably not the best idea. (They're bulky which limits their CCW use.) While a flashlight is tremendous for helping you see in a dark environment, a civilian that's just been to the range a few times shouldn't go room clearing with it on unless he/she absolutely must go help a family member in possible danger. That person would be better off just playing it defensively by finding a big piece of cover, scanning the area for threats, and calling the police. A grip mounted laser on the other hand does not have the bulk problem and can have many benefits in a CCW or close range application. But train to use your sights first!

Blinding effect of a flashlight

I generally prefer lasers to be combined with a flashlight if possible. The advantage to a combo light is that the center laser will give you a pretty good idea where the bullet is going if you need to make a quick reactive shot. (The models have allow you to activate them with your trigger finger via a lever are a good choice.) If you're in a dark environment, and get a quick glimpse of a threat with your flashlight, seeing that laser through your sights will be a good aid to have.

SPRINGS

All guns have springs of some sort in them. For the purposes of this section however, there are two different types that you'll most likely be replacing outside of a trigger job on a handgun:

- **Recoil Springs.** This is what holds a semi-auto locked into battery and also absorbs the forces of recoil when the gun fires. Guns that have very stiff recoil springs such as the Sig P226 tend to have heavier recoil. Why is this? Because the spring acts as a shock buffer. The stiffer it is, the more force that gets transferred to your frame, and therefore your hands.

If you want to reduce the amount of recoil you're feeling with the gun then you just have to lower the poundage of the spring. The easiest way to do this is to order a replacement from a provider such as Wolff. They sell aftermarket guide rods as well that fit in with your selection. (Steel is usually a good material for a guide rod even if your gun came with a factory plastic rod, but don't think about adding a heavier metal such as tungsten. They don't give any performance advantages and can drag on the slide in some models.)

Recoil springs also are also essential to tune your gun to fire certain loads. If you're using lighter ammunition, then sometimes there's not enough force to cycle the slide with the amount of resistance your recoil spring is putting up. In this case lighten the spring. If you're using heavier loads such as +P+ then you're going to want to put in a heavier spring. Be careful that you don't use too light of a spring because then the slide is just going to bounce off the frame. This not only causes more amounts of recoil, but could also damage your gun over time. Also in striker fired handguns you don't want to go too light because it might make your gun unreliable as the striker spring power might overwhelm the recoil spring.

You ideally want to make sure that when you're firing your brass goes a few feet away from you. If it's barely coming out when you're shooting then that likely means that you need a lighter recoil spring. If brass is being flung really far away from you, then it means that the slide is being propelled back really fast and the brass is whacking against the ejector. In this case you probably want to add a pound or two to the spring. It could also be a case of your recoil spring wearing out.

Under normal use, you should replace your recoil spring every 3,000-5,000 rounds.

- **Magazine Springs.** It's important to have a magazine that's feeding properly into the gun in a semi-auto. Your gun will only be as reliable as the magazine inserted into it. Just as part of normal maintenance it's a good idea to swap these out maybe once every couple years, possibly more often if you shoot frequently or keep them always loaded. Magazine springs can also be changed to accommodate different modifications you've made to your gun. For example, if you have a slide that cycles quickly (either by having it lightened, or by shooting really hot ammo with a light recoil spring) then sometimes the slide will cycle too fast to properly pick up the next round and put it into the chamber. In this case you might need stiffer magazine springs.

  Another modification I've found useful is for 10 round reduced capacity magazines (due to state law). Sometimes these fail to seat properly during a quick reload. This is because the 10th round is under a tremendous amount of tension and it pushes hard against the bottom of the slide. In this case, installing lighter springs , trimming the followers, or cutting a few coils off the magazine spring will allow it to seat in the gun easier during reloads.

.22LR CONVERSIONS

Ammo can be expensive! This is especially true when you shoot as much as I do. However, if you own a popular gun frame design such as a 1911 or Glock, then you're in luck. Aftermarket sources (such as Tactical Solutions and Advantage Arms) are probably offering a .22LR conversion for your gun. Essentially what it does is replace your magazine and your slide to allow you to shoot this smaller, less expensive projectile. Furthermore, slides aren't registered with the DOJ in any state, so you can just order these without having to go through the hassle of dealing with an FFL. .22LR conversions are a great way to practice using the gun you already own at a fraction of the price. They typically run in the $200-$300 range, and can be swapped in seconds.

There are a few drawbacks that you should be aware of however. First, reliability of these conversion kits can be a factor. Typically there are only a few higher velocity cartridges that can be used in these (they need to be powerful enough to cycle the slide) and you can expect some jams, mostly in the failure to feed/extract to come your way. Second, you have to consider how much you'll be shooting during the year. A box of 9mm costs about 4x as much as the equivalent of .22s. Make sure that the conversion is worth your money in ammo. Third, sometimes if you have a trigger job done on your gun, these uppers might not work (more of an issue with striker fired handguns). Fourth, there are other practice options such as airsoft to consider, which offer similar recoil and you don't have to be at a shooting range.

.22LR uppers are definitely worth checking out, but be aware of all the factors before making a purchase.

CALIBER CONVERSIONS

Some guns come with an easy ability to switch calibers. This involves shooting a larger or smaller diameter bullet, and is not to be confused with a revolver capable of firing both a .38 Special and a .357 Magnum (same diameter but different case length). In this situation, you could prefer to practice with 9mm ammunition due to lighter recoil and cheaper ammo, but want to carry a defensive handgun in .40 S&W due to the higher power of the cartridge. In order to do this some parts on the gun have to be changed, always involving the barrel, the ejector, and the magazine (other parts can be needed). Different guns have different options on this, and there is no standard. Glocks tend to allow quick caliber conversions with aftermarket barrels, and Sigs even market that ability as a primary feature on some of their guns.

AMMUNITION SELECTION

There are an incredible number of ammunition choices that you can make. Each is intended for a specific purpose and I'll cover some of the basics here. One thing to keep in mind is that a given bullet category might have characteristics of other bullets. One example is the fact that an FMJ simply refers to the type of jacket the bullet has. That bullet can then be made into different shapes depending on the manufacturer. Below I'll explain some of the more common characteristics and abbreviations you will encounter when buying ammo:

- **Bullet Type.** Bullets come in a wide swath of materials and designs. Some are intended for defense, others for target shooting, and even more simply for cost.

- **FMJ. Full Metal Jacket.** An FMJ bullet usually has a lead core which is surrounded by copper plating making it gold colored. This "jacket" can extend either entirely around the core (sometimes referred to as a Complete Metal Jacket) or expose the base, and allows for a more durable bullet (lead is malleable) in addition to preventing leading of the bore when firing. These tend to be round nose bullets which facilitate easy feeding into the chamber of a handgun and will have more penetration of a target due to their streamlined design.

FMJ, TC, JHP

- **TMJ. Total Metal Jacket.** These are a less expensive version of the FMJ due to electroplating the bullet with copper instead of mechanically casting it. These bullets never have an exposed lead core but the jacket is usually thinner than FMJ.

- **JHP. Jacketed Hollow Point.** The notable characteristic of these is the fact that they have a huge divot cut into the face of the bullet. They also usually have a lead core with a complete copper jacket except the exposed lead at the tip. The purpose of these is to expand and stop upon impact with a target, and you will often find expansion grooves (a fractured face) in the tip to encourage the bullet to mushroom. These by far the most common type of defense ammunition. It has also been argued that hollow-points are more accurate in handguns than FMJs (as noted from their enhanced accuracy in rifles) with no clear determination.

- **TC. Truncated Cone.** This type of bullet can come in either jacketed (most I've seen have been TMJ) or lead. Instead of a round nose front, it simply plateaus at a flat surface. These tend to be cheaper and somewhat less accurate than the others (but still pretty accurate overall). There are versions of this shape called JSP (Jacketed Soft Point) which involve a partial jacket and a flat lead tip.

- **Lead.** This is obviously the oldest/cheapest type of bullet, as it's just a bunch of lead rolled into a shape. This shape can be pretty much anything you want (even wadcutter, which is just a flat tip nearly flush with the top rim of the case), but the most common is the round nose. These are not jacketed at all.

- **Moly Coated**. These bullets are relatively new, and involve a lead bullet coated with Molybdenum Sulfide. The idea is to prevent leading of the bore and improve accuracy. They are also on the cheap side.

- **Frangible.** Products such as the Glazer Safety Slug are good examples of this bullet that doesn't have a solid core. The design is to encourage fragmentation upon impact, minimizing ricochets and danger to bystanders while simultaneously delivering the full force of the bullet to soft targets.

- **Load Strength.** The amount of powder put into the bullet is a major consideration for how much force the bullet is propelled with as well as how consequent recoil the explosion will produce. The easiest way to find this out is through the velocity of the cartridge, which is usually listed on the manufacturer's website. There are many different types of loads that can be conjured up by either the individual loader or by ammunition companies. These range from target shooting loads (light on recoil and slower) all the way up to super high velocity defense loads. Higher velocity rounds commonly are demarked with the "+P+" designation. When selecting load strength, figure out what you need it for and compare different loads between companies. Also, make sure that your gun can handle the load strength. Putting too hot of a load in a gun that's not designed for it could be very dangerous. Read your gun's manual for acceptable load parameters.

- **Case Material.** Cases are regularly made out of brass. However, certain manufacturers load with other materials such as nickel, steel and aluminum Nickel was supposedly released to prevent "tarnishing" of rounds stored in magazines exposed to the elements and doesn't expand as much under pressure as brass. Aluminum and steel (milder steel that's not as hard as other parts on the gun) are just cheaper.

- **Reloads or Factory?** A "reloaded" cartridge designates something that uses a piece of already fired brass. In other words, someone has already shot a round out of the brass case, it was picked up and cleaned, and a new bullet/powder/primer combo has been seated in it. Reloads are less expensive than factory ammo, and are almost always just as reliable. Some issues can exist such as improperly sized cases or cases that have been weakened due to multiple firings. However, these are quite rare if the reloads are done by a reputable person or organization. Factory ammo simply means that it's new brass and the cartridge comes from a large scale provider.

Ammunition selection, like selection of anything else in the world of firearms, involves looking for something that suits your needs. Here are some tips for finding the right ammo for you:

- If you're just going to be shooting targets all day, then buy some cheap bulk FMJ ammo that doesn't have a lot of recoil. There's no reason to otherwise hurt your hand or spend more money.

- Leaded ammo tends to cause a lead buildup in barrels and more smoke when firing. Lead isn't recommended for guns with polygonal rifling such as Glocks due to a possible danger of increased pressure due to this buildup over many rounds (though you'd have to shoot a lot). Also, if you're shooting in an indoor range, there will be more lead in the air for you to breathe in. However, even though you might have to clean the gun a bit more, lead ammo is pretty cheap.

- Don't worry too much about different case materials if you're not reloading or shooting for extreme accuracy. Brass will be easier to reload than nickel, and you won't be able to reload aluminum or steel at all. Brass also tends to have better expansion characteristics (when the gun fires, the brass expands under pressure and creates a "seal" in the chamber) than the others. However, for most shooting purposes it won't make much of a difference. Per nickel, it was originally created to allow for more longevity in the outdoor elements. However, my opinion is that if you're a cop and are storing your ammo on your belt long enough to worry about tarnishing it then you should be replacing your ammo more often.

- Some "defense ammo" is really expensive but is known to expand better than standard hollow points. While trying to avoid the "stopping power" debate, the idea is that a faster moving bullet that can expand quickly in a target will lose kinetic energy faster thereby causing more damage. This effect is called the "temporary cavity" where the tissue impact area is in proportion to the loss of kinetic energy of the projectile through contact with the surface. To give you a visual of this, imagine the difference between a golf ball hitting a window and penetrating it (leaving a small golf ball shaped hole) versus hitting a car door and leaving a huge dent.

   However, as I've said time and time again, you don't want to put your life in the hands of an untrusted load. If you want to use defensive ammo, make sure it feeds properly into your gun and works under rapid fire. (Sometimes the super aggressive exposed lead hollow point can catch on the barrel feed ramp and cause a jam.) To test this, buy at least 100 defense loads and shoot them as fast out of your gun as possible. If you get one jam, then pick another type of ammo that doesn't jam during the test or you might have that reliability issue at the absolute wrong time.

- Go with reloads if you can for practice. They'll save you a bunch of money and are plenty reliable. I reload all my own ammo, and am very careful about it. Guess how many ammo related jams I've had out of 30,000 rounds so far this year? Zero. Now some reloaders (such as those found at commercial shooting ranges) can vary in quality. I've seen some really good ammo, and some really awful ammo. Just be discriminating.

- Some guns don't like certain ammunition types. It doesn't mean that the gun or the ammo is bad, it just means that you need to find another load that works with your gun.

- Buy yourself a MagLula (upLula for handguns). It's a cool little speed loader tool that will help you load magazines faster without hurting your fingers.

CHAPTER 18

TIPS FOR HANDGUN OWNERS

STORING A HANDGUN

Owning a handgun is a responsibility. There are various laws, procedures, and safety requirements that you should get acquainted with. Some of these are simply common sense. Below I'll give you a few tips and tricks for storage, travel, and shipping. If you have kids, pay special close attention to educating them about firearms and preventing them from accessing your guns when you're not around.

When storing a handgun, it's important that you prevent unauthorized people from getting access to it. You should be concerned about keeping your kids away from it when you're not there, preventing it from getting stolen, and also allowing easy access to it in case of emergency. Depending on your circumstances, each one of these will have varying degrees of importance. Obviously if you live by yourself in a dangerous neighborhood you're not going to worry too much about keeping your gun locked up at night.

Be safe and know the rules:

- *Know where you're storing the gun and how difficult it is to access*

- *Be mindful of children in your house!*

- *Understand airline and shipper policies*

There are a number of products available from different manufacturers that facilitate safe storage of a handgun. These include:

- **Cable Locks.** These are long steel cables that are designed to feed through the action of a handgun and lock on the other side, either preventing the slide or the cylinder from closing. These are pretty cheap and easy to use, and are mandated in some states with a purchase.

- **Trigger Guard Locks.** These are either key or combination locks that bolt onto a trigger guard of a handgun. They allow the gun to be loaded and stored, but not fired unless the lock is removed.

- **Locked Case.** Sometimes a purchased gun comes with an easy to lock case, sometimes it doesn't.   You can always purchase either a little pouch (ensure that the trigger cannot be pulled inside the pouch, or that the gun isn't kept loaded) or a hard sided case with a simple three digit combination lock. A loaded gun in here will be easy to get to for you, and difficult for children to access. Just remember to keep the hammer down.

- **Gun Safe.** These range in size from small to large and can be quite effective in storing both handguns and long guns. Many of them are fire resistant and pretty darn hard to break into. You guns will be safe in here.

FLYING WITH A HANDGUN

With current TSA procedures, travelling with a handgun can be a bit of a pain. Also, there is a wide variation of airport policies that you must contend with. Having to fly out of San Francisco or New York City will produce a vastly different experience than say Phoenix. Here are some tips for getting through security with no problem:

- Know your airport. Possessing a handgun in NYC for example requires a special city permit, so carrying your bag through the airport if you don't have one of these could land you in hot water, even if you're driving to Pennsylvania from there. Make sure you check local laws prior to flying, even if it's just a layover. There is some protection from the Firearm Owners Protection Act's "Safe Passage" clause where transporting a firearm through states that have more legal restrictions on ownership is exempt. However, you should exercise caution lest your guns be confiscated. Also, certain types of bullets are illegal in certain states under certain conditions, like carrying hollow points in New Jersey.

- Buy yourself a hard case such as a Pelican case or StormCase for your handgun. Then go to Home Depot and buy some three digit TSA approved combination locks. This way you'll never lose the key and your box can be opened if inspected. Make sure it's unloaded and magazines are elsewhere in your bag.

- If you're travelling with ammo, make sure that it's in standard labeled manufacturer boxes secured closed by tape. While good security personnel actually have read the law indicating that ammunition must be stored "in fiber (such as cardboard), wood or metal boxes or other packaging that is specifically designed to carry small amounts of ammunition" others will just delay you even though they're technically wrong. For example, I reload my ammunition and at one time tried to bring it with me in blue case-separated aftermarket containers (Dillon Precision) which complied with the law and were designed explicitly for that purpose. The gate agent (SFO) told me that my ammunition had to be in manufacturer packaging (meaning a brand name). I replied that I was the manufacturer, and I was stuck there for 20 minutes. If you reload and want to travel, buy some ammo from the store, dump it out of the box, and put yours in.

- Only bring 10lbs of ammo or less per person. This is usually airline specific. This is about 300 rounds of .40 S&W or 350 rounds of 9mm.

- Don't travel with large quantities of solvents or gun oil. Gun oil isn't flammable, whereas certain solvents are. Flammable liquids are prohibited on airplanes.

- If you need to bring large quantities of ammo or solvents somewhere (for example you're visiting someone for a long period of time and want to have all your stuff) make sure that you ship it to your destination instead. It's not that expensive and will save you the hassle.

- Ask questions in advance of arriving at the airport, not during the security check. Doing it then will only delay you further. Also, know the law, because you will often encounter people who don't.

- Arrive at least 90 minutes prior to your flight to account for additional processing time.

- Be friendly, polite, and patient. If you disagree with something, then ask nicely for a supervisor. Everyone is just trying to do their job.

SHIPPING HANDGUNS

Sometimes you have to ship guns and ammo places. Typically you'll ship the former to a gunsmith or buyer that's out of state, and you'll tend to ship the latter to yourself if you don't want to fly with it. Here are some tips (these are only to the best of my knowledge and should not constitute legal advice!!!):

- Handguns must be shipped overnight air and declared to the shipper. UPS and FedEx both offer this service for non-FFLs (such as you and me), but I've found UPS easier to work with. USPS only ships FFL to FFL for handguns and is the cheapest method. Firearms must be shipped from a main distribution point (UPS' is called a Customer Center) or from a customer account pickup and cannot be dropped off at local stores such as FedEx Kinkos or The UPS Store. Also, you can only ship to a non-FFL if the receiver is in your state. All out of state shipments must go to an FFL.

- Don't mark "firearm" on the outside of your box. It's prohibited by carriers as well.

- The legal definition of a handgun is its receiver. That means its grip. The slide, barrel, magazine, miscellaneous parts, and pretty much everything else that can be removed from the grip is not legally considered a handgun, and can thus be shipped ground. When I'm shipping anything but the receiver and have to declare the contents I usually like to call these "machine parts" because that's what they essentially are.

- Ammunition can be shipped ground, and must be marked with ORM-D on the outside of the box. Package it securely, and declare it to the shipper.

- Shipper employees will have varying degrees of familiarity with their company procedures. For example, I was trying to ship ammo from UPS to a hotel I was going to be staying at out of state for a big match. I walked up to the counter at the Customer Center and declared that I was shipping ammo. The lady at the counter replied "Sorry, but we don't ship ammunition." I pointed out that the box that I was using had already been used by an ammo company to ship ammo to me, and STILL HAD THE UPS STICKER ON IT (along with about a dozen "Contains Small Arms Ammunition" signs printed on the side). She chuckled, said "Oops, I guess we do!" and helped me along my way.

- Be patient, and if helpful, bring a copy of the company's policies with you. The shipping company employee isn't trying to inconvenience you, they just might not ship those items very often.

SAVING MONEY

If you plan on practicing a lot of shooting your wallet probably won't thank you very much (unless your government agency gives you lots of free ammo). You might eventually think about investing in a reloader. Dillon is a fantastic company that produces a lot of high quality machines that can reload anywhere from 350 rounds an hour (Dillon 550) to 800-1000 rounds an hour (Dillon 1050). Just find a good source of brass either through a dealer or picked up off your local range (make sure you tumble and inspect it first) and buy the rest. Instead of paying $18 plus shipping for a 50 round box of .40 S&W cartridges, you can load your own for $6 (prices may vary depending on the quality of components). Investigate reloading and decide if it's right for you.

Point of note: Lots of brass fired from Glocks bulges at the bottom, so if you're picking you'll need a full length sizing die (sometimes called undersized) to get the proper case dimensions. Enjoy!

POSTSCRIPT

I sincerely hope this book has helped you improve your shooting mechanics and learn more about handguns! I have striven to be as detailed as possible so that even the novice shooter can see a clear path to becoming an expert. I remember the countless hours I've spent on the range to learn even some of the most remedial things. If this book can help you save even a little time and money by sending you off in the right direction from the beginning then I'll feel like I've accomplished my mission.

Remember to question everything you learn and understand why something is the way it is. There's always room for improvement. Good luck, and I'll see you on the range sometime!

Made in the USA
Middletown, DE
10 September 2024

60673388R00148